FORUM BOOKS
General Editor Martin E. Marty

Old Testament Issues

edited by

Samuel Sandmel

SCM PRESS LTD

LONDON

SBN 334 01166 3

© Samuel Sandmel 1968

First British edition 1969
published by SCM Press Ltd
56 Bloomsbury Street London WC1

Typeset in the United States of America
and printed in Great Britain by
Fletcher & Son Ltd
Norwich

To

Dr. Jacob R. Marcus

In Deep Affection

CONTENTS

ACKNOWLEDGEMENTS

The following is a grateful acknowledgement to the publishers for permission to reproduce the copyrighted contents of this book and, at the same time, a listing of their sources.

ERNEST G. WRIGHT, "Theology as Recital" in *God Who Acts*, SBT 8, SCM Press, 1952, pp. 33–58.

FRANK M. CROSS, JR., "The Priestly Tabernacle" in *The Biblical Archaeologist Reader*, ed. by G. Ernest Wright and David Noel Freedman, Doubleday & Company, Inc., Garden City, 1961, pp. 201–228.

EDUARD NIELSEN, "The Role of Oral Tradition in the Old Testament" in *Oral Tradition*, SBT 11, SCM Press, 1954, pp. 39–62.

SAMUEL SANDMEL, "The Haggada Within Scripture" in *Journal of Biblical Literature*, Vol. LXXX, Part II, Philadelphia, 1961, pp. 105–122.

MARTIN NOTH, "The Homes of the Tribes in Palestine" in *The History of Israel*, A. & C. Black Ltd., 1960², pp. 53–84.

JOHN BRIGHT, "The School of Alt and Noth: A Critical Evaluation" in *Early Israel in Recent History Writing*, SBT 19, SCM Press, 1956, pp. 79–110.

MITCHELL DAHOOD, "Introduction to Psalms" in *Psalms I, 1–50*, Doubleday & Company, Inc., Garden City, 1966, pp. xv–xxx.

ROBERT GORDIS, "Wisdom and Job" in *The Book of God and Man; A Study of Job*, University of Chicago Press, Chicago, 1965, pp. 31–52.

SAMUEL SANDMEL, ALBERT SUNDBERG, JR., and ROLAND E. MURPHY, O. Carm., "A Symposium on the Canon of Scripture" in *Catholic Biblical Quarterly*, Vol. 28, No. 2, April 1966, pp. 189–207.

ABBREVIATIONS

AASOR	Annual of the American Schools of Oriental Research
AfO	Archiv für Orientforschung
AJSL	American Journal of Semitic Languages and Literatures
ANET	Ancient Near Eastern Texts
ARI	William F. Albright, Archaeology and the Religion of Israel
BA	The Biblical Archaeologist
BASOR	Bulletin of the American Schools of Oriental Research
BDB	F. Brown, S. R. Driver, and C. A. Briggs, eds., A Hebrew and English Lexicon of the Old Testament
BJRL	Bulletin of the John Rylands Library
BZAW	Beihefte zur Zeitschrift für die alttestamentliche Wissenschaft
EB	Enchiridion Biblicum
FuF	Forschungen und Fortschritte
GVI	Rudolf Kittel, Geschichte des Volkes Israel
HUCA	Hebrew Union College Annual
JAOS	Journal of the American Oriental Society
JBL	Journal of Biblical Literature
JNES	Journal of Near Eastern Studies
JPOS	Journal of the Palestine Oriental Society
JSS	Journal of Semitic Studies
JTS	Journal of Theological Studies

KS	Kleine Schriften zur Geschichte des Volkes Israel
MVAG	Mitteilungen ver Vorderasiatisch (-Ägyptischen) Gesellschaft
PJB	Palästinajahrbuch
RA	Revue d'Assyriologie et d'Archéologie orientale
RB	Revue biblique
RHR	Revue de l'histoire des religions
TCL	Textes cunéformes du Louvre
VT	Vetus Testamentum
WAT	Die Welt des Alten Testaments (^{2}1953)
WO	Die Welt des Orients
ZATW	Zeitschrift für die alttestamentliche Wissenschaft
ZDPV	Zeitschrift des deutschen Palästina-vereins

THE READER will notice that the authors represented in this volume vary in their spelling of biblical names and terms and do the same respecting some English words as, for example, archeology versus archaeology, and the Hebrew deity appears as Yahweh, Jahveh and Yahve. There are similar inconsistencies. No effort has been made to superimpose a consistency which could conceivably be distasteful to an individual author.

FORUM BOOKS

The editors of this series recognize the need for books of a convenient size on religion and related topics. Laymen and clergymen, students and the interested general reader can use *Forum Books* for personal study, or as a basis for group discussion. At a time when religious institutions are experiencing dramatic change, when religious ideas are being debated with new intensity, and when religious elements in culture are being called into question, the books in the series gather together examples of important writings which reproduce both historical and contemporary reflections on these subjects. Each editor has taken pains to provide helpful background comment as a context for the readings, but for the most part the selections speak for themselves with clarity and force.

MARTIN E. MARTY, *General Editor*
Divinity School
University of Chicago

I

INTRODUCTION

THE TITLE, *Old Testament Issues*, is the clue to the contents of this book, a series of examples illustrating many of the debated and debatable stands in present-day biblical scholarship. In general, the debates array mid-twentieth-century interpreters against nineteenth- and early-twentieth-century scholars. In part the debates arise from the ever-increasing knowledge gained through biblical archaeology, Semitic linguistics, and the ever-growing scientific scholarship, and represent the correction, as it were, by the present of the past. Yet to a greater extent, and going far beyond mere correction, there exists a rejection today of some of the theorems and corollaries of the past, and this drastic revision of views amounts to almost an upheaval. The essays which have been chosen illustrate these changes in many of the relevant details, and it is needless here to anticipate and to list them. A generalized statement, however, is in order.

The older scholarship, as typified in the Graf-Wellhausen hypothesis, was singularly free of both humility and modesty, and as a result was certain that the major problems of Scripture had all been solved. That scholarship was able to supply a completely confident answer to the question about the way in which the Pentateuch, surely not written by Moses, had come into existence, this through the progressive blending together of layers of writing; these were principally J, E, D, and P. The acute analysis which yielded these sources was, however, only the prelude to the significant step of utilizing the results so as to be enabled to fashion a credible account of the history of the religion of Israel, in place of the incredible elements which Scripture itself presents. To take a single example, Scripture ascribes the origin of priesthood, priestly functions, and the priestly paraphernalia to the Wilderness period and to the time of Moses; the nineteenth-century scholarship was persuaded that this was all fabrication, the result of ascribing to the ancient Wilderness period the developments which really occurred about a thousand years later, in the early postexilic period. The leitmotiv in the older scholarship, as must be emphasized, was not so much that this detail or that was historically untenable, but rather that virtually the totality was untenable. And once one set aside what the Bible said, one was under the obligation so to understand the materials as to recognize in them legend and myth and theological tendentiousness, and to handle the relevant factors in such a way that some unassailable true history could be written. Accordingly, the Pentateuch was compiled by priests who concocted a basic document, P, around 450 B.C., and who inserted into this document quotations from older sources, D, E, and J. J, the oldest source, was composed in Judea to the south about 850 B.C., E in Ephraim to the north about 750 B.C., and the two blended together by an editor or redactor RJE about 650; D arose about 621, in connection with the reformation in the time of Josiah, usually called the Deuteronomic reformation. These older sources themselves, however, were scarcely tenable historically. At the same time, the traditional ascriptions of authorship of biblical books, as of the Psalms to David, Proverbs to Solomon, and the Book of Isaiah to the eighth-century prophet by that name, were challenged directly or indirectly. The acute inner analysis of such books, so the older scholars believed, could yield their date, or dates, of composition, and could even suggest the possible true authorship, and supplant the traditional. Thus, the Psalms were deemed to be Maccabean, and not by David or from the age of David, for surely there did not exist an adequate literacy in that age to have produced these magnificent poems. Proverbs was not by Solomon, but was an anthology compiled in very late times. With Chapter 40 of Isaiah, we find ourselves in the sixth century, not the eighth, and the latter part of Isaiah has to be ascribed to a number of men who can be cited as Second, Third, Fourth, and even Fifth Isaiah. Short books, such as Obadiah, one single chapter, reflected at least three authors; Amos represented eight and a half chapters of relative authenticity, and a half chapter was added long after Amos' time to soften the stern character of the preceding eight and a half chapters; indeed, there were throughout Amos, and the Minor Prophets, late additions of consolatory verses, or doxologies, or the application of prophecies against the Northern kingdom, destroyed in 721, to the Southern kingdom, this by judiciously added phrases. In short, the problems were all solved.

In this light, the patriarchal period was largely myth, not history; the conquest by Joshua was theology, not history; the creative age was the pre-exilic period, marked by the eminent literary prophets; the age of institutional religion was the exilic and post-exilic periods, when the praiseworthy, older, Hebrew religion of a Micah and Jeremiah declined into the sacerdotalism of Ezra, Nehemiah, and the Chronicles.

By the beginning of the twentieth century, this series of inter-related views, however much a single scholar here or there might dissent on a detail, gained the ascendancy in most of the universities throughout Europe and the United States, and even in most of the great Protestant seminaries.

To be sure, all along there existed an opposition on the part of religious conservatives, Protestant and Jewish, and Roman Catholics, to the extent that the latter then participated in this stream of scholarship.

What has arisen in the past fifty or sixty years is pre-eminently a challenge to the certainties of the nineteenth-century scholars by modern scholars who work in the same general frames of reference and similar assumptions. To clarify this latter, the chief present-day issues are not between religious conservatives or supporters of tradition against "modernists," for this is a continuing and unresolvable issue, and not a new one. It is true that between the recent scientific scholarship and the old there lies a related and hence confusing issue, namely, that the nineteenth-century scholarship was prone to doubt all the history in Scripture, and the new is prone to accept very much of it. Yet there is still a gulf between the traditional conservative religionist and the modern scholar, even when they chance to agree, for the former affirms the history largely by antecedent commitment, and the latter, by the accumulated learning which has moved him away from the nineteenth-century skepticism.

Two major considerations have forced the reconsideration whereby the issues have arisen. By and large the science of biblical archaeology flowered only in the twentieth century; as a consequence, the nineteenth-century scholars had worked almost entirely on the basis of literary analysis. One can point this up by reference again to the Psalms and the theory of illiteracy in the age of David. That view was quite consistent with the then prevailing opinion that the bulk of literary activity, such as the creation of the Pentateuch, was postexilic. In 1929 discoveries at Ugarit yielded Psalmlike poems, some verses indeed being almost identical with verses in the Psalms, and written in a language remarkably kindred to biblical Hebrew; these Ugaritic poems are authentically datable in the thirteenth and twelfth centuries, and they disclose a literary ability that well predates David. In short, archaeology has verified as historically tenable many biblical statements which nineteenth-century scholars regarded as completely untenable. Archaeology, both in the artifacts and in the remarkable recovery of linguistic data, has been one factor in necessitating the reconsideration.

A second factor might be termed philosophical, in the sense that it has involved a particular stance. For one thing, the nineteenth-century scholars, excited by evolution, tended to make the biblical literature conform to an evolutionary pattern; first come the free and intuitive religious person or persons who are themselves within a tradition and reshape it, or else might stand athwart a particular tradition, but create some new impulse. Next, the immediate followers of these highly gifted persons fashion an ever-increasing focus on the leaders, as faithful disciples will do. Third, the next generations proceed to fashion institutional forms which usually manage to blunt or debase the religious clarity of the original, intuitive persons. Accordingly, the religion of Israel in the pre-exilic period was that of the "charismatic" literary prophets, but then the men themselves were regarded as the norms, and finally, in the postexilic period, a debasing priestly institutionalism took place. Consistent with the evolutionary view, one felt the need to set the prophet over and against the priest, and the ethical demand over and against the cult. In brief, the nineteenth-century scholars devised a remarkably patterned view, buttressed by Hegelian philosophy, and all was beautifully arrangeable. To the demand which arose out of archaeology that the older views be challenged, there was added the growing reservations about the neatness, the patness, of the reconstruction of the religion of Israel which resulted from the general philosophical attitude of the nineteenth-century scholars.

In a different dimension, another type of reservation arose, this after World War I. Up to that point the nub of scholarship was historical, not only in the sense of asking whether or not the data in the Bible were tenable, but especially in the sense that the answers given by the scholars were by implication of no special relevance to modern man. The ancient ideas could be explored and clarified, but as products of a bygone age, and applicable only there, modern man had no stake at all in the ideas or in the doctrines. There arose, then, after World War I a challenge to what was described as "mere historicism," and the shortcomings of the merely historical were to be made good by the discipline of "biblical theology." One consequence of the emergence of the determination to go beyond mere historicism was the recognition that biblical themes about man's loneliness, helplessness, and evil, which seemed inapplicable to nineteenth-century man, seemed all too applicable after the carnage of World War I. Whereas the nineteenth century had discarded such views of man, or relegated them to the past and inapplicable to the present, newer scholars saw these views in a new perspective, and considered them true to human experience. This newer view is usually called Neo-Orthodoxy, from the circumstance that it re-espouses views which had once been orthodox but had been discarded. It differs from orthodoxy in its premises, usually in this way: orthodoxy affirms the biblical "doctrines" as products of the ancient supernatural revelation; Neo-Orthodoxy, however, affirms them as true to man's real situation, that is, true "existentially" respecting man. There is, then, a sense in which biblical theology constitutes not only an issue, but a relatively new one, even though by now it has passed through about four decades. Though biblical theology as an entity still meets with some resistance, that resistance seems to me to be continually declining. One could conclude that biblical theology is here to stay, at least for the present; within this framework of its broad acceptance there are some divergencies on record.

Respecting the Dead Sea Scrolls, and the so-called "battle of the Scrolls," for the scholarly disputes were at times quite heated, the issues belong more to the area of New Testament than Old. The quarrels have arisen primarily around that portion of the Scrolls which reflect the Qumran community, and its alleged relationship to early Christianity; that portion of the Scrolls which are total, or partial, on fragmentary copies of Old Testament books has been outside the arena of dispute. There has arisen from the battle of the scrolls, however, something of a challenge to all biblical archaeology, as if to imply that its claims have been exaggerated and its confirmation of biblical data overextended, and an array of fresh problems bypassed. On the one hand, one eminent biblical archaeologist, Father North, has asserted that biblical archaeology has raised as many problems as it has solved; on the other hand, the only essay I have discovered which discusses this issue on a broad base is largely an attack on a single book by a single archaeologist, so that the real issue is there somewhat obscured. I had wanted to include an essay reflecting the challenge to biblical archaeology, but I have found none that has seemed suitable for inclusion. To my textbook, *The Hebrew Scriptures: An Introduction to their Literature and Religious Ideas,* I added an appendix (pp.507–516) which surveys the admirable record of biblical archaeology, and which ends in these words:

What does archaeology confirm in the Bible? It never confirms the faith in the Bible, nor that distillation of convictions which in the aggregate represents to *biblical authors* the truth of the Bible. Their contention that God is disclosed in the events of history is beyond confirmation or denial either by archaeologists or by literary critics.

The archaeologist has not yet found proof of the enslavement of the Hebrews in Egypt. Suppose he were to find confirming inscriptions. Would these prove, as the Bible contends, that it was God Who brought the Hebrews out of Egypt? Archaeology can recover civilizations; it can find the traces of natural events, such as the Exodus, or the Conquest, or the establishment of the Temple, or the Babylonian exile. It can confirm or contradict historical statements in the Bible, but it scarcely touches on that which is most important in the Bible, that is, the faith in God possessed by the biblical writers.

It must suffice here to indicate that, respecting the external events in the Bible, it is normally the uninformed popularizer, or the newspaper columnist, whose overstatements call forth sharp rejoinders, not alone from those who have reservations about biblical archaeology, but also from its exponents themselves.

The selections chosen have appealed to me as representing very basic matters. No end exists of minor issues, of disputes over details, as, for example, the date of the fall of Jericho; or the dates of Ezra; and indeed, the denial that there ever was an Ezra or an Ezekiel. The dividing line between what is basic and what is only a detail is admittedly difficult at some points to distinguish. The clue to my procedure, however, may be exemplified in the matter of the apocalyptic literature, about which Professor H. H. Rowley, a truly great scholar, has written in eloquent praise of its continued relevance, and I have not agreed with his estimate; to my mind, however, the issue here is in detail and not basic, and hence I have not felt the need to include the matter. So, too, with innumerable other matters.

One dilemma has been difficult to deal with. It is the question of whether certain of the essays may or may not be very difficult for students who are university undergraduates and who could conceivably not have the total background out of which some of the essays will be readily comprehensible. I searched very diligently for more popular materials which were adequately faithful to the issues involved, but I did not succeed in finding what I was looking for. It seemed to me, accordingly, preferable to confront the student with essays which are somewhat difficult but authoritative and true to the scholarship, rather than to select inferior materials which might be more readily comprehensible. In my own teaching I think I have discovered that if students are aware that some of the material is difficult, they do not shrink from it; indeed, the majority seem to me to prefer the authentic but difficult to the easy but less authentic. Moreover, the supposition in this book is that there will be a teacher as mentor who will be able to help students over some of the possibly difficult paragraphs or sections.

I had wished to include a rounded essay on the prophets in the newer scholarship, but could find none that seemed suitable. I especially wished to indicate the newer thinking which no longer sets the prophet so sharply over and against the cult, and some stirring questions, only briefly touched on in the essay by Professor Nielsen, respecting the transmission of the prophetic texts. Early in the task of preparing this anthology came the recognition that some things which I wanted to include necessarily had to be omitted.

I have inserted meanings of Hebrew and German and some technical terms, and transliterated Hebrew words. I have not altered the spelling of transliterated Hebrew, but have retained the transliteration used by each author. The same word, accordingly, appears in diverse English spellings.

SAMUEL SANDMEL

2

THEOLOGY AS RECITAL

Ernest G. Wright

Professor Wright, an eminent archaeologist, is also a foremost figure in the field of biblical theology. Himself a highly disciplined historian, he is concerned with the possible meaning of the Bible beyond the data of the history of biblical men or people. He sees the profound historical element not in what biblical man has done, but in what God has done.

This fine essay not only provides an exposition of Professor Wright's concern with biblical theology; it also provides the important context and the background information by which the issue of biblical theology takes its place in the array of modern biblical concerns.

I

Biblical theology has long been dominated by the interests of dogmatic or systematic theology. Indeed, throughout the first three centuries of Protestantism the two disciplines were scarcely distinguished, at least among conservative churchmen. All theology was Biblical theology in the sense that it was a system of doctrine drawn from the Bible and supported by collections of proof-texts. While the fact of the Reformation is illustrative of the perennial tension which has always existed between the Bible and theology, nevertheless the separation of Biblical theology as an independent subject of study occurred in a new form within pietism and eighteenth-century rationalism, when the Bible was used to criticize orthodox dogma. Johann Philipp Gabler in 1787 seems to have been the first in modern times formally to advocate a distinction between the two disciplines. To him Biblical theology is an objective, historical discipline which attempts to describe what the Biblical writers thought about divine matters. Dogmatic theology, on the other hand, is didactic in character and sets forth what a theologian philosophically and rationally decides about divine matters in accordance with his time and situation.[1] Nevertheless, in organizing the data of Biblical faith the rubrics of systematic theology continued in use, the chief of these being the doctrine of God, the doctrine of man, and the doctrine of salvation.

During the nineteenth century, however, the historical nature of the Bible was more clearly seen than ever before. As a result, men came to believe that Biblical theology must concern itself primarily with the development of religious ideas. This point of view made the task of the Biblical theologian so difficult that few scholars attempted anything other than a history of religion in the Old and New Testaments. Perhaps the greatest work in Old Testament theology produced during the last century was that by the German scholar Hermann Schultz.[2] He tried to solve the problem by presenting first a historical account of the development of Israel's religion and then by giving a topical treatment in which theological concepts were traced through the various historical periods. In other words, no attempt was made to present a systematic theology of the Old Testament as a whole. The growth of religious concepts through the history was thought to be too great to permit a systematic survey. A different type of treatment is illustrated by the work of the French pastor, Ch. Piepenbring, first published in 1886.[3] He presented three cross sections through Israel's history, the first being the pre-prophetic period beginning with Moses, the second the age of prophecy, and the third the Exilic and post-Exilic age. In each period he systematically treated the doctrines of God, man, worship and salvation under a variety of chapter headings.

It will be noted that these works are based upon two presuppositions. The first is that the evolution of religious concepts in the

Bible is so great that there are virtually different theologies in different periods. The second is that the procedure of dogmatic theology is normative for all theology, including the Bible. If both these presuppositions are correct, then the task of Biblical theology is quite clear. It is either to trace the evolving history of religious concepts through the various Biblical periods, as did Schultz, or else it is to take a cross section through the Bible at one period and treat that as systematically as possible.

With regard to the first presupposition there is an increasingly widespread belief today that while historical development is indeed a very important factor in the Bible yet it is one which has been overemphasized. A living organism is not a blank tablet on which all writing is done by environmental, geographic and historical conditioning. If it were, then a description of a historical process might be sufficient to enable us to comprehend its inner significance. But in every organism there is something given which determines what it is and what it will become. Environment and geography can explain many things in ancient Israel, but they cannot explain why Israel did not undergo the same type of evolution as did her pagan neighbors, nor why the early Church did not become another Jewish purist sect or Hellenistic mystery religion. One explanation for this difference in evolution which positivist scholars have been wont to give is the presence in Biblical history of a remarkable series of religious geniuses: Moses, the prophets, Jesus, Paul. Yet every genius is in part a product of his historical situation in a given social context. He cannot be explained apart from certain inner, spiritual factors which are a vital part of the cultural situation in which he arose. In other words, there is in the Bible something far more basic than the conceptions of environment, growth and genius are able to depict. It is this "given" which provided the Bible's basic unity in the midst of its variety and which sets Biblical faith apart as something radically different from all other faiths of mankind.[4]

The realization of this fact leads most Biblical scholars today to believe that far more unity exists in the Bible than was conceived fifty years ago. They are thus confident that a Biblical theology is possible which is something other than the history of the Bible's religious evolution. Yet, for the most part, the second presupposition mentioned above is still accepted. That is to the effect that theology is propositional dogmatics, the systematic presentation of abstract propositions or beliefs about God, man and salvation. The churches retain and encourage this conception in their liturgy and creeds. For example, every elder, deacon, commissioned church worker and minister in the Presbyterian Church of the U.S.A. is required to affirm when he or she is ordained that the confession of faith of that church contains "the system of doctrine taught in the Holy Scriptures." But does the Bible contain a *system* of doctrine? Certainly none of its writers was primarily concerned with the presentation of such a scheme. Consequently, we must say that static, propositional systems are those which the Church itself erects by inference from the Biblical writings. The systems are very good and very important, but we cannot define the Bible by means of them. No system of propositions can deal adequately with the inner dynamics of Biblical faith.

Yet most of the recent attempts to describe the theology of the Old and New Testaments proceed along the old lines by adopting the rubrics of dogmatic theology and by attempting to force Biblical faith into this mould.[5] Indeed, one of the most serious and careful discussions of the history and nature of Old Testament theology, that of Robert C. Dentan published in 1950, concludes that the discipline is to be defined as:

That Christian theological discipline which treats of the religious ideas of the Old Testament *systematically*, i.e., not from the point of view of the historical development, but from that of the structural unity of Old Testament religion, and which gives due regard to the historical and ideological relationship of that religion to the religion of the New Testament.[6]

Since any arrangement of the material will be one which we impose from the outside, he believes it best to adopt one which is simple and meaningful to us:

For this purpose it seems difficult to think of a better outline than that which is used by systematic theology, since this outline arose from an attempt to answer the basic questions concerning human life: What is the nature of God in His perfection? (theology); what is the nature of man in his weakness (anthropology); what is the nature of that dynamic process by which man's weakness becomes reconciled with God's perfection? (soteriology).[7]

Simple and persuasive though this point of view appears to be, it fails to take into account the fact that the Biblical writers were uninterested in ideas in the sense that we are. They were not primarily systematic teachers of religious ideas. Are we to assume, then, that Biblical theology is solely a modern discipline which we seek to impose on a literature that is devoid of any *primary* interest in it? I should rather say that we must first ascertain the central interest and methodology of the Biblical writers and define Biblical theology accordingly. Otherwise how can it be the serious, historical discipline that we insist it must be? The rubrics of systematic theology are too abstract and universalized to fit the Biblical point of view. The exclusive use of them must of necessity compel us to do violence to that standpoint, to omit large sections of materials or at least to arrange them in such a way that their proper interrelation is obscured. Can another way be found which is more in keeping with the Biblical material itself? Unless there is, then we should abandon the whole conception of Biblical theology to those who insist that it must be nothing more than the popularization and preaching of the faith to the modern day.[8]

Such is our present dilemma. Is Biblical theology a history of Biblical ideas? Is it a systematic cross section of those ideas, treated under the rubrics of a dogmatic theology which the Bible does not possess? Or is it merely the packaging of the foods of Biblical research for the consumer in the Christian Church? Most of our current thinking seems to be wavering among these three procedures.

II

In considering Biblical faith, it seems to me that the point at which we must begin is not with the history of its evolving ideas but with history in another sense. It is history as the arena of God's activity. Biblical theology is first and foremost a theology of recital, in which Biblical man confesses his faith by reciting the formative events of his history as the redemptive handiwork of God. The realism of the Bible consists in its close attention to the facts of history and of tradition because these facts are the facts of God.

A comparison of the Bible with the religious literatures of other people points up this fact as its chief distinguishing characteristic. Why is the Bible in contradistinction to all other "bibles" centered in the story of the life and historical traditions of one people? To ask this question is virtually to ask why the Bible is what it is. The national literature of other people at the time exhibits no such interest in history. To be sure, the ancient kings and nobles of Egypt, Canaan and Mesopotania had many historical inscriptions and records inscribed on stelae, and on temple, tomb and palace walls. Such annals, however, were concerned almost solely with the personal glorification of those for whom they were prepared. The Egyptians produced a number of excellent short stories, while the Babylonians composed the remarkable Babylonian Chronicle. Yet these are scarcely serious attempts to write history, even though historical events are recorded; they had another purpose altogether. The specifically religious literature of the ancient polytheist contained numerous tales of demi-gods and heroes, but it was not actually interested at all in history as such since the primary focus of its attention was upon nature. A great deal has been written to compare the literature of Israel with that of its environment, but one will note that the only worthwhile comparisons are in the areas of law, poetry, didactic or proverbial sayings and creation myths. In aesthetic, imaginative and affective faculties Israelite literature, it is affirmed, is by no means inferior to the products of the great civilizations of the ancient Near East; indeed in most respects it is superior to them. In fact, says Professor W. F. Albright, "a very large section of modern religion, literature and art actually represents a pronounced retrogression when compared with the Old Testament."[9] Yet when all has been said about the comparison of the literature of Israel with the other literatures of the Near East, the most obvious difference is the one most rarely touched on: that is, the peculiar Israelite attention to historical traditions. The Biblical point of view is concentrated, not merely on the individual exploits of heroes and kings, not merely on court annals like the Babylonian Chronicle which were especially important for the calendar and the royal archives, but rather on the unity and meaningfulness of universal history from the beginning of time until the end of time. It is in the framework of this universal history that the chronicles of individual events are set and ultimately receive their meaning.

It was impossible for the ancient polytheist to have a primary interest in history as such, because the concentration of his attention was upon *nature,* not history. Nature was the indigenous realm of the superhuman, and the forces of nature were the gods he worshipped. Man experienced in nature a plurality of these powers. Yet world order had been established through a delicate process of integration of divine wills and through the establishment of a hierarchy of authority. Man's security was found in the way he fitted himself into this divine harmony. His religious literature was inevitably centered in nature myths which depicted the action and interaction of the powers that produced this harmony. Man's greatest good was to be caught up within this cosmic rhythm of nature. Consequently his life moved in a cycle corresponding to the cycle of nature. The miracle of renewal and birth in the spring, followed by the decline and death of summer, by revival in the fall and again by the miracle of spring —such was the movement of nature. Such also was the movement of human life, for man was born along with the rise and fall of nature's life. This rythmic movement was the greatest good which natural religion had to bestow upon human existence. Consequently, such religion could never have any real concern with history, unless one is to define history as this rhythmic natural cycle, repeated anew each year. The religious literature of the polytheist, therefore, was concerned with the mythological stories of the gods, together with the great variety of hymns, prayers, incantations, sacrificial regulations and the like, by means of which the natural powers were worshipped.

B

In India, China and Persia religion developed from this polytheistic base into higher and more sophisticated forms. Indeed, in Persia especially, Zoroastrianism represents, at least in its original form, a radical departure from typical polytheism. Yet the type of religious literature produced in all these countries is very different from the Bible. The Veda of Hinduism, the Pali literature of Buddhism, the Confucian Classics and the Avesta of Zoroastrianism are all composed for the most part of liturgical material and especially of *teachings* on a great variety of subjects. None of them has any particular historical interest. Even the Koran of Islam, a religious heresy of Biblical faith, is chiefly a series of teachings from the auditions and visions of the prophet Mohammed. There are numerous stories in all this literature, but the interest is not as a rule in the story, but in the teaching which it is meant to convey.

In Greece, on the other hand, there was indeed an interest in history and historical traditions. It is with Herodotus and Thucydides of the fifth century B.C. that the modern historian of history first feels himself at home.[10] The achievements of these men and of those who preceded and followed them, are indeed amazing in that ancient world, for it was the Greeks who liberated the mind from shackles of what has been called the mythopoeic apprehension of reality which characterizes polytheism.[11] Yet they never achieved that view of human history as a meaningful process *en route* to a goal which is the chief characteristic of Biblical writers. History was not primarily a theological production with a theological purpose. This is true of the philosophers as well as of the historians. History remained for them all a cyclical process. The circle of events was never broken and straightened out into a line. One writer has said about Aristotle, for example, that he

appears to leave no place for historical development in the animated kingdom. He admits, indeed, that the human race has at different times and in different places grown out of barbarism into civilization, and by the progressive cultivation of art, science, and philosophy has repeatedly attained perfection. Whenever this has taken place, he thinks that deluges or other convulsions of nature must have swept away the entire race, all but a few individuals left on the mountain tops, or otherwise preserved for the repopulation of the earth, left, however, as under such circumstances would necessarily have been the case, destitute of all the apparatus of the arts, and having to begin again *de novo* the development of civilization. With the strange conception of a cyclical rise and fall in the civil history of mankind, Aristotle combined the view that Nature as a whole is eternal, and must for ever have been in all essential particulars just as it is now.[12]

For Herodotus the war between the Greeks and Persians was an inevitable conflict of opposites. The equilibrium of the world had been destroyed by the accumulation of vast human and material resources in the hands of the Persian king. The nemesis which overwhelmed Xerxes restored the harmony or equilibrium of affairs. History is thus like the oscillation of a pendulum; matter or substance in this world is in continuous motion, the elements of which ceaselessly group and regroup themselves in a monotonous upward and downward curve. Such a view excludes completely any prospect of progress or movement toward an earthly millenium, whether the latter is to be achieved through the gradual evolution envisaged by modern liberal idealism, or through the revolution conceived by Marxist communism. History is in movement, but it is going nowhere. It is filled with forces which move on an upward or downward path or else in a circle as though around a wheel. Consequently, when Christianity entered the classical world, it encountered great difficulty in making itself understood over against the pagan conception of history. Origen, for example, in protesting against the theory of cycles, derides the idea that in another Athens sometime in the future there will be another Socrates married to another Xanthippe. And Augustine cannot conceive of another Plato teaching his pupils in another Academy in a succession of ages endlessly repeated. "God forbid," he says, "that we should swallow such nonsense! Christ died once and for all, for our sins." Human history, on the contrary, far from consisting of a series of repetitive patterns, is in sure movement, even though unsteady, to an ultimate goal.[13]

Israel broke with the ancient conceptions in the first instance because of a radically different view of God. As the philosopher

Hegel pointed out over a century ago, when we enter the Old Testament we find that: "Nature—which in the East is the primary and fundamental existence—is now depressed to the condition of a mere creature. . . . God is known as the creator of all men, as he is of all nature, and as absolute causality generally." It is true, he observes, that in India, there existed the "pure conception of 'Brahm'; but only as the universal being of Nature; and with this limitation, that Brahm is not himself an object of consciousness. Among the Persians we saw this abstract being become an object of consciousness, but it was that of sensuous intuition—as Light. But the idea of Light has at this stage in Judea advanced to that of 'Jehovah'—the *purely One*."[14]

Biblical man conceived of himself as existing in a particular, unique history which possessed significance because God through it was revealed as in process of redeeming all history. Thus while the Israelite existed in nature, he was lord of nature, using and subduing it for his own purposes, and his focus of attention was not on nature but on history. Nature was not an independent object nor the kingdom of powers to be worshipped; it was instead a handmaiden, a servant of history.

How had Israel, in the first instance, arrived at such a view? It was certainly not because there existed in the nation a series of great metaphysical philosophers. On the contrary, the religious leaders were uninterested in anything which might be considered abstract philosophy. We can never be sure of the true reason for this particular Israelite view of nature and history. It is the one primary, irreducible datum of Biblical theology, without antecedents in the environment whence it might have evolved. The earliest forms of literature which Israel produced are filled with it. This is evidently true, not only of the oldest preserved poetry and prose, but of works which are quoted though not preserved: e.g., "the Book of the Wars of Yahweh" (Num. 21:14) and "the Book of Yashar (or, of the Upright)" (Josh. 10:13; II Sam. 1:18). It is likewise true of the traditions as they were circulated in their pre-literary forms.

The most probable supposition regarding the origin of Israel's preoccupation with history is that it arose in the earliest days of the nation's history as the only possible explanation available to the people of the manner in which God had made himself known to them. As Walther Eichrodt has written:

The roots of this peculiar viewpoint, by which Israel clearly is to be differentiated from all other Near Eastern peoples, doubtless lie in those happenings of the early time, which gave the impulse to the genesis of the Israelite people, in the events of the time of Moses. The deliverance from Egypt and the uniting of kin and families of wandering cattle-breeders in a sacral tribal covenant during the wilderness period were those events which have impressed the national Israelite consciousness as the basis and determining acts for all time of the Divine self-disclosure. If one observes the completely unique importance which these events have gained in the total religious praxis and tradition, in the cultic hymns no less than in the prophetic admonitions, in the liturgy and cultic instruction of the priests as well as in the parental teaching to the children, in the explanation of the pastoral and agricultural festivals no less than in the establishment of all law-giving at the time of Moses, then no doubt can exist that this first experience of a Divine encounter was decisive for the fundamental conception of the Divine revelation in Israel. Here one learned to understand the being of God from history and to exhibit his works in the forms of history.[15]

At the center of Israelite faith lay the great proclamation that the God of the fathers had heard the cry of a weak, oppressed people in Egypt. They had been slaves, but then freed by mighty acts which demonstrated God's power to the Egyptians and to the world. As slaves for whom the justice of the world made no provision, they were delivered by a most extraordinary exhibition of Divine grace. This was a sign, a wonder, not to be explained by fortune or irrational chance, but solely by the assumption of a personal Power greater than all the powers of this world. This was a God who could make the forces of nature serve him as well as the recalcitrance of the heart of Pharaoh. He was one who for some reason had set his love on a defenceless people and had chosen them for his own.

Israel's doctrine of God, therefore, was not derived from systematic or speculative thought, but rather in the first instance from the attempt to explain the events which led to the establishment of the nation. While living in the world of natural religion, they focussed their attention not on nature and the gods of nature, but on the God who had revealed himself in an extraordinary series of historical events. The knowledge of God was an inference from what actually had happened in human history. The Israelite eye was thus trained to take human events seriously, because in them was to be learned more clearly than anywhere else what God willed and what he was about. Consequently, in all that happened subsequently the Israelites simply interpreted the meaning of events by recognizing and acknowledging in them the God who had formed the nation by the remarkable events at the Exodus and in the wilderness. The half-hearted, fearful and defeated attempt to break into Canaan from Kadesh-barnea in the south was attributed to rebellion against God and lack of faith in his leadership (Num. 14; Deut. 2:26–46). The long stay in the wilderness thus was seen to be God's judgment upon the people for their sin. Yet subsequently the successes of the conquest of Canaan were occasioned solely by the powerful leadership of Yahweh. The initial defeat at Ai in the tradition found ready explanation in Achan's violation of the Divine command that all booty was to be "devoted" to God and none was to be taken for personal gain. The ideology of Holy War depicted in the books of Deuteronomy, Joshua and Judges was more than a mere rationalization for the nation's wars. It was based on the recognition that God who had saved Israel at the Exodus had a historical purpose and program. The battles of Joshua and the Judges, therefore, were more than the mere fightings of men; they were holy because they were God's war. According to an old fragment of the law of this Holy War, a priest was required to explain to the army whenever it was ready to go into battle: "Hear, O Israel, ye approach this day unto battle against your enemies: let not your hearts faint, fear not, and do not tremble, neither be ye terrified because of them; for Yahweh your God is he that goeth with you, to fight for you against your enemies, to save you" (Duet. 20:3–4).[16]

When Israel settled in Canaan and attempted to make their

living from the soil, it was easy for many of them simply to interpret the agricultural pursuits in the same manner as their Canaanite neighbors and teachers. Thus, we are told, they "did evil in the sight of Yahweh, and served Baalim. And they forsook Yahweh, God of their fathers, who brought them out of the land of Egypt, and followed other gods, of the gods of the people that were round about them, and bowed themselves unto them, and provoked Yahweh to anger" (Judg. 2:11–12). It was thus possible to interpret the wars of the period of the Judges in this light. The judgment and the grace of God were seen in the oppressions and deliverances, and correlated with the idolatry, repentance and faith of the people.

When Israel was caught up within the struggles of the world powers during the first great empire-building epoch of history, Yahweh was not lost within the events, nor did he perish with the state he had founded. On the contrary, he rescued a remnant as a brand from the burning. For with what must have seemed to pagans as infinite presumption, Israel proclaimed that it was Yahweh himself who was directing these wars to his own ends, even though the conquering armies did not know or acknowledge it. The Assyrian was the "rod of his anger" (Isa. 10:5); Nebuchadnezzar was his "servant" (Jer. 27:6); and Cyrus was his "anointed" (Isa. 45:1). Let all the nations be gathered together, said Second Isaiah; let them take counsel and see if they can interpret either past or present (Isa. 43:8–9). Let them haste in the confusion of preparing their idols. Let these gods "bring forth and show us what shall happen; let them show the former things, what they are, that we may consider them and know the latter end of them, or declare us things to come. Show us the things that are to come hereafter, that we may know that ye are gods. . . . Behold, ye are as nothing and your work is of nought. An abomination is he that chooseth you" (Isa. 41:7, 22–24).[17] Yahweh alone is in charge of history. As one who had met Israel in historical event, he thus was recognized as the Lord of all events who was directing the whole course of history to his own ends, for nothing happened in which his power was not acknowledged.

III

This meant that nature could not be left to the prerogatives of the pagan Baal. The epithets and functions of this Canaanite god of the storm were taken over for Yahweh. Lightning was his arrow and thunder his voice (e.g. Ps. 18:8, 14). Theophany was depicted in terms derived from a violent storm. At Mount Horeb in the time of Moses and again in Elijah's day the appearance of God was accompanied with the dark cloud or smoke, thunder or trumpet blast, lightning and the shaking of earth that accompanies great thunder (Exod. 19:16 ff.; I Kings 19:11–12).[18] No one could penetrate the mystery of his presence. His being was envisaged as surrounded and hidden by a cloud of smoke, or a brilliance which had the appearance of fire. Such phenomena which surrounded and hid him from view were called his "glory." It was thus the "glory" of God which descended upon the completed tabernacle and again on the temple of Solomon; it led the people through the wilderness as a pillar of cloud by day and, as it were, fire by night (Exod. 40:34–38; Num. 9:15–23; I Kings 8:10–11). Isaiah saw it in his vision (Isa. 6:4), and at the destruction of Jerusalem its departure from temple and city was the sign to Ezekiel of Yahweh's abandonment of both to defilement and destruction. Psalm 29, dominated by this nature imagery, is thought to have been originally a hymn to Baal, but borrowed and used of Yahweh.[19] It is Yahweh, not Baal, who "maketh the hinds to calve" (Ps. 29:9), and gives the blessings of heaven (rain), of the deep (springs and rivers), of breast and womb (Gen. 49:25; Deut. 33:13 ff.). Indeed, Hebrew psalmody is filled with nature images, most of them borrowed from Canaanite religion.[20]

One of the most vivid evidences of this assertion of Yahweh's complete control over nature was Israel's poetic use of the Canaanite creation myth, in which the monster dragon of chaos, Leviathan (Lotan), was slain by Baal. This unruly force was connected with the uncontrollable power of the deep and the sea. And in Israelite poetry, it is Yahweh, not Baal, who has either slain the dragon or made him a faithful servant, and who controls the sea for his own purpose.[21] God's answer to Job is cast in the form of a demonstration of his power over nature, and the most spectacular evidence of that power is that God alone can control Leviathan, the symbol of the mighty destructive forces of nature (Job 41). Job, then, cannot use his own individual predicament to deny the universal evidence of the providence of God.[22]

In spite of this application to Yahweh of the natural functions of the Canaanite storm-god Baal, images and metaphors drawn from nature were not the primary language by which he was known. The vocabulary of the nature myths of Canaan was used extensively but it was set in a historical context. Psalm 74 affirms that God who has performed such wonders in nature will surely come to the aid of his people in their distress. Yahweh's control over the sea and its monster was a language which could be historicized and used to describe the deliverance at the Egyptian Exodus; and this in turn was the ground for the hope of the new exodus in Second Isaiah (Isa. 51:9–11). Leviathan became the symbol of the historical enemies of God, who at the inception of the new age will be defeated (Isa. 27:1); and to the author of Revelation, the dragon is Satan, the personification of *historical* evil, not of the destructive power of nature. In the New Jerusalem "there shall be no more sea." (Rev. 21:1); in the light of the long history behind that word there could be few more graphic symbols for the abolition of evil in this world.[23]

Furthermore, the very anthropomorphism of the Biblical vocabulary concerning God is witness to his primary relation to history and human society. In polytheism the central and original metaphors and symbols for depicting the gods were drawn for the most part from the natural world. With the growth of social complexity the gods increasingly took on social functions, and such terms as king, lord, father, mother, judge, craftsman, warrior and the like were used. Yet Baal of Canaan and Enlil of Mesopotamia never shook off their primary relation to the storm which typifies nature's force. Anu, the head of the pantheon in Babylon, originated as the numinous feeling for the majesty of the sky.

He was thus given form as heaven, though subsidiary forms were the king, and the bull of heaven. The mother of the gods was Ninkhursag, who arose from the feeling for the fertility of the earth and was thus given form as the earth, with subsidiary forms ascribed as mother, queen and craftsman. Ea was the sweet waters, who could be given form in the ram and the bison, but more especially as the knowing-one, the craftsman, the pundit and the wizard. Shamash was the sun who took over the function of divine judge as "Lord Order." *Sin* was the moon, who became also lord of the times, seasons, signs and portents. Ishtar was the planet Venus who typified a young maiden, somewhat spoiled and headstrong, a leader of war, a lover and wife of the vegetation-god for whom she mourned at his yearly death.

Thus the catalogue of pagan gods might continue. In the Bible, on the contrary, God is known and addressed primarily in the terms which relate him to society and to history. The language of nature is distinctly secondary. God is Lord, king, judge, shepherd, father, husband and the like, but these appellatives are not superimposed upon a central image in nature. Nature as God's creation contains no forms on which one can focus a religious attention. The first two commandments of the decalogue make this perfectly elear. No other powers are to be associated with Yahweh as objects of worship, and a primary reason given is historical. It is because no other power was with him when he accomplished his great saving acts. He alone can and is directing the course of history (e.g. Exod. 15:11–13; Deut. 32:12, 39; Isa. 43:10–13). No images are to be made of him, or of anything else in heaven or earth, for, it is affirmed, while the people heard the voice of God at Horeb, they "saw no manner of form" on that day (Deut. 4:15). Nothing in heaven and earth may be used to picture God, but the nature of his revelation indicates his primary concern for, and relation to, man, society and history. Consequently, the only image of him possible is the mental image of a person, and the only language by which he may be addressed is drawn from the institutions of human society, as Lord, King, Father, Judge, etc. Anthropomorphism thus indicates God's personal relation to history, and to assume that we can dispense with it as belonging to a primitive stage of our religious development is to separate ourselves not only from the Bible, but from the Biblical conception of the true meaning of history.

IV

If the primary and irreducible assumption of Biblical theology is that history is the revelation of God, then we must affirm that the first inference to be drawn from this view was not concerned solely with the power and attributes of God, but rather with the explanation of what God had done at the Exodus. That is, the initial and fundamental theological inference was the doctrine of the chosen people. The use of the term "inference" here does not mean that Israel was consciously employing a method of reasoning by logical deduction in the philosophical or Greek sense. The inference was an interpretation of an event, which to Israel became an integral part of the event and which thus could be used for the comprehension of subsequent events. How else could Israel explain what had happened except by a conception of election? The God who had rescued a depressed people must have had a reason for doing so. It is unrealistic to assume that Israel's belief in herself as the especially chosen recipient of Divine favor was simply the projection of the nation's egoism or the over-compensation for an inferiority complex. How else was Israel to account for her existence, except that God had set his love upon her? No explanations of special spiritual or moral merit were sufficient to explain God's actions. The Divine election was not based on merit because the leaders of the faith, at least, constantly pointed to the faithlessness and rebellion of the nation, which began with the murmurings in the wilderness. Israel's greatness lay in what to the nation was a simple fact, that God had chosen her; and God's choice rested in his own mysterious grace. That grace was not and would not be explained; it could only be inferred and accepted in faith and in gratitude. Evidently, God was at work with some purpose of his own in history, and for some reason he had chosen Israel as his special agent in accomplishing that purpose—the weak of the earth to confound the strong.

Once such an inference was made, it was inevitable that those who collected and edited the earliest traditions of Israel should portray all history in this light. The knowledge of the Divine election was the only means by which the Patriarchal saga could be interpreted. Thus in Genesis Abraham was the recipient of wonderful promises, repeated to each of the fathers, and his righteousness lay in his acceptance and belief in them (Gen. 15:6). The subsequent history from Moses to David marked the stages in God's fulfillment of the promises. Consequently, when the people "sighed by reason of their bondage . . . , God heard their groaning, and God remembered his covenant with Abraham, with Isaac, and Jacob" (Exod. 2:23–24).[24]

The faith in a special election was one which always pointed forward to a future in which the full purpose of God would be manifest. The controversy of God with his chosen agent is perhaps the central theme of the Deuteronomic and prophetic writings. Yet the purpose of that controversy was not for Israel's sake alone; the agency of Israel in God's earthly program is the deeper issue. Consequently, the prophetic eschatology is not a new invention of religious genius. It had its roots in the presuppositions of the older histories and in the attempt to interpret the work of God in the current crises of history. God's dealings with Israel were of profound significance for universal history because his revelation to Israel was the light which must some day through Israel illumine all nations,[25] and those who refused it were the enemies of God who would be destroyed before the new and final age dawned.

The doctrine of election was an inference from historical events which thus gave a peculiar meaning to nationality in Israel. Nationality was more than a collocation of people, determined by a common blood and a common soil. It was an entity which God had brought into being, so that Israel was *his* people, "a congregation of Yahweh," "a holy nation" to whom he had imparted a measure of his own holiness by separating them to himself in the events of the Exodus (Exod. 19:6; Lev. 11:45, etc.). This special relationship to God, which was the basis of Israel's nationality, was given concrete expression more widely in the language of a legal covenant than in any other. Israel was a community held together by a solemn compact with God. Form criticism and comparative study have shown that the type of organization which distinguished Israel from the other nations in the first period of the nation's history in Palestine, before the establishment of the monarchy, was that of a tribal amphictyony, an organization of tribes held together around a central shrine by a religious compact or covenant. The conception held within it the framework for political organization. God was conceived as the direct and actual ruler of the nation, so that the law, which is at the basis of all social life, was believed to be his own gift to the nation. Yahweh was thus the Lord, the King, the Judge and the Lawgiver of his people, who were his subjects or servants. He exercised his rulership by mediate means; that is, by leaders like Moses, Joshua, Gideon, Deborah, whom he called for specific purposes and to whom he gave the power and ability to fulfill their calls.[26]

Covenant thus involved a political anthropomorphism which was believed to be literally relevant for Israelite life. Under the impact of the Philistine oppression the attempt to live within it failed and a permanent form of human leadership was demanded by the people. Centralized government, however, while a political necessity was nevertheless a theological problem, for it had to be fitted into the framework of the theocratic covenant. And there were always those in pre-Exilic Israel who looked with suspicion upon the kings. To them, kingship was simply God's accommodation to the needs of a sinful people who had refused to keep the covenant (e.g. I Sam. 8). The covenant theology was thus kept alive, even though as an ideal rather than as a political reality. As such it furnished a language which could be used to explain subsequent events. The crises of the nation were due to Israel's breach of their pledged vows; sin was rebellion, a violation of the relationship of nation to God. Therefore, God's controversy against his people, his *ribh* or legal case with the resultant sentence, judgment or penalty was the conceptual language used by the Deuteronomists (in Deut.–II Kings) and the prophets to explain the meaning of the people's tragedies. A large proportion of the religious vocabulary of Israel was drawn from jurisprudence, and its source lay in the sense of the covenant between God and nation.

Yet behind it was the knowledge of the extraordinary grace and purpose of God, so vividly shown apart from legal merit in the Exodus and in the wilderness of Sinai. Consequently, the conception of legal penalty as an explanation of the destruction and captivity of Israel and Judah could not be envisaged as exhausting the work of God. The Exodus salvation together with the repeated triumphs through the periods of the Conquest and the Judges gave that knowledge of God which created hope, a hope that burned the most brightly in hopeless times. It was a hope which lay in history and projected a future in history, that is in human society on this earth. The relationships in the world of nature may be radically revised in the age to come, but the Bible envisages no abolition of nature as the locus for a redeemed society. The Biblical sense of the meaningfulness of history possessed a hope which could look far beyond the current history, but the final age to which God was directing events was one which had concrete substance. It was no ethereal, impersonal, substanceless existence beyond history; it was the fulfillment of history, beside which the hopes of other religions appear either as completely illusory or as quite hopeless. Consequently, while the breach of the covenant was from the standpoint of law and justice irreparable, yet because of the known grace of God, the future hope could portray a "new covenant," an "everlasting covenant," a "covenant of peace" (e.g. Jer. 31:31 ff.; Ezek. 16:60; 37:26–27). Before the Exile the prophets seemed to believe that the punishment and judgment of God in the current historical events would in themselves bring about the inner purification of a remnant which was the necessary requisite of the new age. To Ezekiel, however, the actual situation among the captives in Babylon evidently seemed the proof that destruction and captivity does not necessarily bring about the reformation of the inner man. Consequently, God himself, he believed, would miraculously give unto the remnant of Israel a new heart and a new spirit, put his Spirit within them and cause them to walk in his statutes. Then indeed would they dwell in the land which he gave to their fathers; they would be his people and he their God (Ezek. 36:24–31). Then and only then would the fulfillment of God's purposes in the covenant be achieved.

Now to us the interpretation of the meaning of election for Israel's life in terms of a covenant is a projection of faith by means of analogical or metaphorical language. Israel inferred from the Exodus event that God had chosen her and, therefore, had established a special relationship between himself and her. This relationship, we are inclined to say, was made clear by means of the covenant ideology drawn from Patriarchal society and given an extended meaning.[27] Not so Israel, however. For her the covenant was an actual event which took place at a certain historical time and place, namely at Sinai. There God actually had demonstrated his presence to Israel (Exod. 19), so that the Deuteronomist could say that the people heard his voice though they could not see his being (Deut. 4:15; 5:22). And this, he further asserts, was a unique event which no other people had experienced (5:26). At Sinai Moses ascended into God's presence and brought down the tablets of the decalogue. There, too, God revealed to Moses the Book of the Covenant (Exod. 20:22–23, 33), indeed the whole law governing the cultic and the common life (*cf.* Lev. and Deut.). After the law had been received, there was a formal ceremony in which the Book of the Covenant was publicly read, the people formally assented to its conditions, and their bond with God was sealed with "the blood of the covenant, which Yahweh hath made with you" (Exod. 24:3–8). Thus, for Israel the covenant, by which the meaning and implications of election were concretely stated, was not faith projected on history, but a real event of history which illumined the meaning of subsequent history and for the priestly editor of Genesis the meaning also of pre-Mosaic ages.[28]

V

From the above survey we are now in possession of the chief clues to the theological understanding of the whole Bible. There is, first, the peculiar attention to history and to historical traditions as the primary sphere in which God reveals himself. To be sure, God also reveals himself and his will in various ways to the inner consciousness of man, as in other religions. Yet the nature and content of this inner revelation is determined by the outward, objective happenings of history in which individuals are called to participate. It is, therefore, the objectivity of God's historical acts which are the focus of attention, not the subjectivity of inner, emotional, diffuse and mystical experience. Inner revelation is thus concrete and definite, since it is always correlated with a historical act of God which is the primary locus of concentration. Mysticism in its typical forms, on the other hand, subtly turns this concentration around, so that the focus of attention is on the inner revelation, while the objectivity of God's historical acts is either denied altogether or left on the periphery of one's vision. Important as Christian pietism has been in the Church, it has not escaped this subtle inversion with the result that the central Biblical perspective has been lost.

Secondly, the chief inference from this view of history as revelation was the mediate nature of God's action in history: that is, his election of a special people through whom he would accomplish his purposes. This was a proper inference from the Exodus deliverance; and the migration of Abraham to Canaan was believed to have been occasioned by a Divine call which involved election. In Genesis the election is portrayed as the goal of history and the divine answer to the human problem. After the Exodus, it formed the background for the interpretation of Israel's life in Palestine and a central element in prophetic eschatology and in the apocalyptic presentation of the Book of Daniel.

Thirdly, the election and its implications were confirmed and clarified in the event of the covenant ceremony at Sinai. Israel's sin was the breach of this covenant, which, therefore, enabled the faithful to see that election was not unalterable. It could be annulled by Israel herself. Consequently, covenant was something that had to be periodically renewed by ceremonies of re-dedication.[29] It involved the interpretation of the whole life of the people, in the social, economic, political and cultic spheres. The law of the society was the law of the covenant, given by God with the promise of justice and security within the promised land. Consequently the central problem of Israel was envisaged as the problem of true security in the midst of covenant violation and international upheaval. This security was seen by the prophets as only to be found beyond the suffering and judgment of the Day of Yahweh. There would be a revival of the community, but only after the elect people had become scattered and dry bones (Ezek. 37).

These three elements are together the core of Israelite faith and the unifying factor within it.[30] They have little abstract or propositional theology within them. They are based on historical events and the inferences drawn from them. They cannot be grasped by the abstract rubrics of dogmatic theology. And these very same elements are the center and core of the faith of the early Church. For this reason the advent of Jesus Christ could not be understood solely or chiefly as the coming of a teacher of moral and spiritual truths. His coming was a historical event which was the climax of God's working since the creation. All former history had its goal in him because God had so directed it. All subsequent history will be directed by him because God has exalted him as Lord. In doing so he will fulfill the promises of God in the government of Israel, assuming the royal office of David at the right hand of God and providing the security which the sin of Israel made impossible of achievement. The election of Israel as the agent of God in universal redemption is reaffirmed in the New Israel (e.g. I Peter 2:9–10), the Body of Christ, which is the partaker of the New Covenant in Christ's blood. In Christ God has inaugurated the new age, foreseen of old; entrance into it is by faith and by the sharing of Christ's cross, for in him our sins are forgiven and our alienation from God done away with. Thus God in Christ has completed the history of Israel; he has reversed the work of Adam, fulfilled the promises to Abraham, repeated the deliverance from bondage, not indeed from Pharaoh but from sin and Satan, and inaugurated the new age and the new covenant. To be sure, the world is unredeemed and the final consummation is yet to appear. Yet Christ is the sign and seal of its coming. Hence he is the climactic event in a unique series of events, to be comprehended only by what has happened before him, but at the same time the new event which marks a fresh beginning in human history.

This, then, is the basic substance of Biblical theology. It is true that we simply cannot communicate it without dealing with the *ideas* of which it is composed. Yet to conceive of it primarily as a series of ideas which we must arrange either systematically or according to their historical development is to miss the point of it all. It is fundamentally an interpretation of history, a confessional recital of historical events as the acts of God, events which lead backward to the beginning of history and forward to its end. Inferences are constantly made from the acts and are interpreted as integral parts of the acts themselves which furnish the clue to understanding not only of contemporary happenings but of those which subsequently occurred. The being and attributes of God are nowhere systematically presented but are inferences from events. Biblical man did not possess a philosophical notion of deity whence he could argue in safety and "objectivity" as to whether this or that was of God. This ubiquitous modern habit of mind which reasons from axioms and principles or universals to the concrete would have been considered as faithless rebellion against the Lord of history who used history to reveal his will and purpose. Hence the nearest approach to atheism which the Old Testament possesses is the fool who says in his heart there is no God (Pss. 14:1; 53:1). Yet the Psalmist means by this, not a theoretical atheism, but rather the practical atheism of a sinner who calls God's works, not his being, into question.[31] Jeremiah clarifies the point when he speaks of people in his day who refuse to believe that the great events which then are happening are the work of God. They thus "have denied Yahweh and said: 'It is not he; neither shall evil come upon us; neither shall we see sword or famine' " (5:12). To refuse to take history seriously as the revelation of the will, purpose and nature of God is the simplest escape from the Biblical God and one which leaves us with an idol of our own imagining.

Consequently, not even the nature of God can be portrayed abstractly. He can only be described *in relation to* the historical process, to his chosen agents and to his enemies. Biblical theology must begin, therefore, with the primary question as to why the Bible possesses the historical nature that it does. It thus must point in the first instance to this confessional recital of traditional and historical events, and proceed to the inferences which accompanied those events, became an integral part of them and served as the guides to the comprehension of both past and future. Biblical theology, then, is primarily a confessional recital in which history is seen as a problem of faith, and faith a problem of history.[32]

NOTES

1. So Robert C. Dentan, *Preface to Old Testament Theology* (New Haven, 1950), p. 8.

2. See his *Old Testament Theology*, trans. from the 4th German ed. by J. A. Paterson, 2 vols. (Edinburgh, 1892).

3. *Theology of the Old Testament*, trans. from the French by H. G. Mitchell (Boston, 1893).

4. See further the monograph by the writer, *The Old Testament Against Its Environment*, and that by Floyd V. Filson, *The New Testament Against Its Environment* (London and Chicago, 1950).

5. Thus, for example, Ludwig Köhler, *Theologie das Alten Testaments*, Zweite Auflage (Tübingen, 1947), attempts to organize the data under the basic headings of God, man and salvation. So also with elaboration does Paul Heinisch, *Theology of the Old Testament*, trans. from the German by William Heidt (Collegeville, Minn., 1950). Otto J. Baab, *Theology of the Old Testament* (New York and Nashville, 1949), follows the same pattern, with the insertion of chapters on sin, the Kingdom, death and evil. Millar Burrows. *An Outline of Biblical Theology* (Philadelphia 1946), is a very useful, descriptive work which attempts to treat the whole Bible together. Introductory considerations on authority and revelation are followed by three chapters on the conceptions of God, Christ and the universe. These are followed by Chaps. VI-IX which deal with anthropology, Chaps. X-XII on soteriology and Chaps. XIII-XVIII with the worship and service of God. Perhaps the greatest work on Old Testament theology ever produced is the three volume treatment of Walther Eichrodt, *Theologie des Alten Testaments* (Leipzig, 1933–1939). He attempts to organize the material under three headings: God and People,

God and the World, God and Man. This arrangement has been criticized because it leads to repetition and overlapping. The chief unifying element he takes to be the covenant. This too has been criticized as a serious weakness since it has been commonly held that "idea of the Covenant is far from omnipresent in the Old Testament, and only by a *tour de force* can it be made to appear so" (so Dentan, *op. cit.*, p. 38). This writer can only agree with the criticism in part, and for a different reason, that is that election is more primary in Israel than covenant. While the two go together, the latter is a conceptual language for expressing the meaning of the former and it makes considerable difference as to which receives the primary emphasis. Yet, whatever we may say, Eichrodt has seen more clearly than anyone else the danger of using the categories of dogmatic theology for Biblical theology. His work is an extremely significant pioneer effort which attempts to hew a new path.

6. *Op. cit.*, pp. 48 and 66.

7. *Ibid.*, p. 64.

8. *Cf.*, for example, Millar Burrows, *Journal of Bible and Religion,* Vol. XIV, No. 1 (Feb., 1946), p. 13: "The task of biblical theology is, as I see it, to bridge the yawning chasm between our basic critical studies . . . and the practical use of the Bible in preaching and religious education. . . . Biblical theology must package the foods for the consumer." *Cf.* also Otto Eissfeldt, *Zeitschrift für die alttestamentliche Wissenschaft,* Vol. XLIV (1926), pp. 1–12, who sees the distinction between the history of Biblical religion and Biblical theology as the distinction between the methods of reason and faith. The latter takes seriously only those elements which are regarded as the revelation of God in the Bible by the particular point of view, confession or church to which one adheres.

9. *Archaeology and the Religion of Israel* (Baltimore, 1942), p. 33. Chapter I of this book is a fresh treatment of this whole question. *Cf.* further T. Eric Peet, *A Comparative Study of the Literatures of Egypt, Palestine and Mesopotamia* (London, 1931).

10. *Cf.* James T. Shotwell, *The History of History* (New York, 1939), Vol. I, Part III; James W. Thomson and Bernard J. Holm, *A History of Historical Writing* (New York, 1942) Vol. I, Chap. II.

11. *Cf.* H. and H. A. Frankfort in *The Intellectual Adventure of Ancient Man* (Chicago, 1946), pp. 373 ff.

12. Quoted from a review of Grote's *Aristotle* which appeared in 1872, by Thomson and Holm, *op. cit.*, p. 37.

13. See C. N. Cochrane, *Christianity and Classical Culture* (London, New York and Toronto, 1944), pp. 245, 467 f., 483 f. *Cf.* also the brief treatment in Oscar Cullmann, *Christ and Time,* trans. from the German by Floyd V. Filson (Philadelphia, 1950; London, 1951), pp. 51–60.

14. Georg Wilhelm Friedrich Hegel, *The Philosophy of History,* trans, by J. Sibree, rev. ed. (New York, 1900), p. 195.

15. Walther Eichrodt, "Offenbarung und Geschichte im Alten Testament," *Theologische Zeitschrift*, 4. Jahrgang, Heft 5 (Sept./Okt. 1948), p. 322. See also Artur Weiser, *Glaube und Geschichte im Alten Testament* (Stuttgart, 1931), pp. 4 ff.

16. See further Gerhard von Rad, *Deuteronomium-Studien* (Göttingen, 1947), pp. 30–41; and *Der Heilige Kreig im alten Israel* (Zürich, 1951).

17. For discussion of these passages with references, see most recently C. R. North, "The 'Former Things' and the 'New Things' in Deutero-Isaiah," *Studies in Old Testament Prophecy: T. H. Robinson Volume*, ed. by H. H. Rowley (Edinburgh, 1950), pp. 111–126.

18. To historicize such images in such a way as to make one assume that Sinai was actively volcanic and, therefore, to be sought in Arabia (e.g. W. J. Pythian-Adams, *The Call of Israel* [London, 1934], pp. 129 ff.) seems too much like translating the image, the vividly pictorial and the poetic into bold literal prose. Note the remark concerning this by J. Pedersen in *Israel: Its Life and Culture*, III–IV (London, 1940), p. 662: "A search might with equal justice be instituted for the mountains that melted like wax when Yahweh passed over the hills of the earth. The author has done all that he could to convey the idea of the might of Yahweh." In Psalm 29:6 Lebanon and Sirion are said to dance like a wild bull, but this would scarcely be reason to conjure up volcanoes in their area or to move them to a volcanic area.

19. *Cf.* H. L. Ginsberg, *The Biblical Archaeologist*, Vol. VIII (1945), No. 2, pp. 53–54.

20. See John H. Patton, *Canaanite Parallels in the Book of Psalms* (Baltimore, 1944).

21. *Cf.* Psalms 74:12–15; 89:9–10; Job 3:8 (read *yam*, "sea," for *yom*, "day"); 7:12. 9:8 (*yam*, "sea"); 26:12–13; 38:8–11, 41; Amos 9:3; Habakkuk 3:8–15 (see W. F. Albright, "The Psalm of Habakkuk," *Studies in Old Testament Prophecy*, pp. 1–18).

22. Most of the older commentaries do not understand the significance of this mythological dragon and attempt to identify it with an Egyptian crocodile. The recovery of the Canaanite religious literature now enables us to grasp the deeper significance of Job 41.

23. *Cf.* Howard Wallace, "Leviathan and the Beast in Revelation," *The Biblical Archaeologist*, Vol. XI (1948), No. 3, pp. 61–68.

24. For an analysis of the two different emphases in the literature as to the origin of the election, whether at the Exodus or at the time of Abraham, see especially Kurt Galling, *Die Erwählungstraditionen Israels* (London, 1950), pp. 19 ff. (Giessen, 1928); and H. H. Rowley, *The Biblical Doctrine of Election*

25. For the evidence that this consciousness was at least as early as the tenth century, see the writer, *The Old Testament Against Its Environment*, Chap. II; Gerhard von Rad, *Das erste Buch Mose, Genesis Kapitel*

1–12 (Göttingen, 1949), pp. 14 ff., 132 ff. Contrast the very limited acceptance of this position by H. H. Rowley, *op. cit.*, pp. 65 ff., at least as regards Genesis 12:3. The popular conception of a Day of Yahweh, which is older than Amos 5:18, and the theology of kingship sponsored in the Davidic court are further factors which must be considered in this regard.

26. *Cf.* Martin Noth, *Das System der zwölf Stämme Israels* (Stuttgart, 1930); *Überlieferungsgeschichte des Pentateuch* (Stuttgart, 1948); *Geschichte Israels* (Göttingen, 1950), pp. 74 ff.; Albrecht Alt, *Die Staatenbildung der Israeliten in Palästina* (Leipzig, 1930).

27. So the writer, *op. cit.*

28. *Cf.* the priestly outline of events: The Divine command and promise to man in Genesis 1; the promissory covenant with Noah as universal man, the sign of which was the rainbow (Gen. 9); the promissory and everlasting covenant with Abraham as the representative of the chosen nation, the sign of which was the institution of circumcision (Gen. 17); and the covenant with all Israel at Sinai, the sign of which was the sabbath (Exod. 31:12–17).

29. For a brief review of these ceremonies, see the writer in *The Old Testament Against Its Environment*, Chap. II. Form criticism has led some scholars to the highly probable view that in early Israel, at least, the ceremony of covenant renewal was a yearly affair: see Gerhard von Rad, *Das formgeschichtliche Problem des Hexateuchs* (Giessen, 1938), and Martin Noth, *Überlieferungsgeschichte des Pentateuch* (Stuttgart, 1948), pp. 63 f.

30. For the problem of the wisdom literature in this connection, particularly Job, Proverbs and Ecclesiastes, see the treatment in [my *God Who Acts,*] Chap. IV.

31. *Cf.* Ludwig Köhler, *Theologie des Alten Testaments*, Zweite Auflage (Tübingen, 1947), p. 1.

32. An affirmation of Artur Weiser, *Glaube und Geschichte im Alten Testament*, p. 19, here used in a somewhat different context.

3

THE PRIESTLY TABERNACLE

Frank M. Cross, Jr.

As was stated in the general introduction, the Graf-Wellhausen school considered the P document to be relatively late, that is postexilic; it was held to reflect the postexilic times, but it read the postexilic situation back into the Wilderness period. Professor Cross accurately reflects the older judgment in citing the Wellhausenite term for this retrojection as "pious fraud." Professor Cross's essay rejects both the very late date which had been ascribed to P, and he rejects, as do many, the supposition that the material in P is devoid of accurate early history. In a sense, then, Professor Cross, though working still within the framework of JED and P. reassesses the materials in the drastically different way of seeking for solid older history in the document he believes is not quite as young as his predecessors held it to be.

Professor Cross provides great illumination on the Tabernacle, but quite beyond that, his essays show vividly the way in which the older source analysis and source dating have given way to conclusions quite at variance with the older skepticism. This essay, because of its technical nature, will be difficult for the student. Yet rather than reproducing here some general and abstract divergency of the recent scholarship from the older, it seems preferable to illustrate this divergency through the specific matter of the Tabernacle. Even if the beginning student finds the essay a little abstruse, he can nevertheless find it doubly informative, that is, both for its manner respecting P, and for its data on the Tabernacle.

1. Traditions about the tabernacle in the latter part of Exodus are no longer of interest to the casual student of the Bible. Scholars from time to time delve into the tedium of the tabernacle installations, but by and large theologians and preachers look elsewhere for biblical insights. In past generations this was not true. Few students of the Bible were without ideas as to how the tabernacle should be reconstructed from the biblical data. Its attendant theological concepts were heralded as setting forth the ideal age of Israel, the prototype of the Kingdom of God, and the typology of the New Covenant.

One of the causes for the eclipse of these traditions has been the general acceptance of the findings of the great biblical critics of the nineteenth century which cast grave doubts on their historicity. Perhaps the name of Julius Wellhausen more than any other has come to typify this line of scholars. His brilliant treatise, *Prolegomena zur Geschichte Israels* (1878) remains an important and constant companion of biblical scholarship, and his reconstruction of Israelite history continues to dominate much of the historical and critical study of the Bible. A rough sketch of his basic ideas will help to set the present study of tabernacle traditions in perspective.

2. Fundamental to the thinking of the Wellhausen school is the history of the cult. According to the older sources of Judges and the so-called JE materials of the Pentateuch, many altars and cultic establishments existed in early Israel. But with the promulgation of the Book of Deuteronomy in the Josianic Reform (622 B.C.), the dogma of a central sanctuary and one official altar for the whole of Israel was laid down. In the Priestly materials of the Pentateuch, however, the tabernacle is assumed to be the central sanctuary and the only official place of worship. Such a situation cannot be squared with the Mosaic era but presumes the conditions of the post-Exilic community.

The sacrificial system is said to follow a similar pattern of evolution. In the ancient sources, sacrifices were carried out simply. They consisted primarily of spontaneous "peace-offerings" (šĕlāmîm), accompanied by feasting and joy. The Deuteronomic materials provide a transition period from spontaneity to formal-ity. Beginning in the Exilic writings of Ezekiel, however, the sacrificial cult has become elaborate, stereotyped, overburdened with the consciousness of sin, and bent on expiation. The tabernacle traditions seem to reflect the culmination of this development. Incense, a cultic feature only of highly sophisticated peoples, according to Wellhausen, found its way into Israelite usage after the Exile. Yet it is to be found in the ritual of the tabernacle. Wellhausen in similar manner traces the history of the clerical orders, finding the concept of hereditary priesthood, the sharp dichotomy between priest and Levite, and the office of the high priest to be post-Exilic anachronisms in Priestly legislation.

Israelite political and ideological history followed the same line of evolution according to this school. In the time of Moses and the Judges, Israel as a nation did not exist. Individual tribes, free and autonomous, went their several ways, worshiped their various gods, and were finally banded together by Saul and David, only under the duress of Philistine oppression. In the time of the monarchy, Yahweh (in particular) became Israel's national God. In the days of Josiah, the doctrine of the covenant was promulgated in definitive form. With the centralization of cult came henotheism as a corollary. But only after Israel had been scattered in Exile were the historical conditions propitious for Israelite writers to rise to the concept of a single universal God. The tabernacle tradition, however, describes the formation of an Israelite amphictyony (a confederation of tribes about a central shrine) at the foot of Sinai. Under Moses, God chose Israel and established an everlasting covenant with her. According to the Wellhausen reconstruction of history, such monotheistic and theocratic motifs can reflect only the period of the post-Exilic Jewish Church. Thus the tabernacle legislation, rather than describing an actual political theocracy established by Moses, presents an unreal idealization of the golden past. The Priestly Code is a utopian constitution drawn up by a downtrodden religious community to serve as a substitute for a political state.

The Wellhausenist states unequivocally that the description of the Priestly tabernacle found in Exodus 25–31 and 35–40 is a pious fraud. On the basis of ancient passages such as Exodus

33:7–11, it may at most be conceded that there had been a primitive tent-shelter for the Ark in the desert. It was Wellhausen's conclusion, however, that the Priestly tabernacle (*miškān*) was demonstrably the fancy of the post-Exilic Priestly writers; or more precisely, a description of the Temple in flimsy desert disguise.

THE NEW OUTLOOK ON ISRAELITE HISTORY

3. In recent years the Wellhausen reconstruction of history has undergone sweeping revision. As long ago predicted by Rudolph Kittel, revolutionary progress in biblical research had to await the advance of biblical archaeology and philology. This is not to underestimate the contributions of such scholars as Kittel himself, Gunkel (the deviser of the technique of *Gattungsgeschichte)*, Driver, Gressmann, and others whose basic work was completed before the major phase of the archaeological revolution.

While the basic outlines of biblical criticism were drawn in the nineteenth century, archaeoligical research has established itself as a scientific tool in the hand of the Old Testament student only in the twentieth century. Only in our generation have archaeological data reached such proportions as to affect seriously the conclusions of literary and historical research.

Today the Old Testament lies in a new setting. The horizons of ancient Near Eastern history have been pushed back. Israelite history can no longer be made to climb the three-flight staircases of Wellhausen's Hegelian reconstruction. While the broad outlines of the Documentary Hypothesis (J, E, D, and P) remain intact, and in fact have been strongly supported by the implications of biblical archaeology, the history of Israel requires thorough reinterpretation.

4. Unfortunately only a few of the results of archaeological and philological research which are of particular importance for a revaluation of the Priestly source of the tabernacle traditions can be given in our limited space.[1] We begin with the Patriarchal Age.

Data dug up with spade, documentary and nondocumentary, in the period between the wars have transformed our knowledge of the second millennium in Near Eastern history. The milieu of the Patriarchs is no longer shadowy.[2] The Amorite or Proto-Aramaean connections of the Patriarchs in the region of Harran and Nahor (*Naḫur*) can no longer be doubted. The Cappadocian Tablets (nineteenth century), Babylonian documents from the First Dynasty of Babylon (The Age of Hammurabi, *ca.* 1830 to the fall of Babylon, *ca.* 1550), and especially the Nuzi Tablets (fifteenth century) and the archives of Mari (eighteenth century) have given remarkable parallels to the mores, the religious practices and background, and the names of the Patriarchs.

Of particular interest are the occurrences of the name Abram in contemporary Babylonian records, and the longer form of the name Jacob (Ya'qub-el) in the records of Chagar Bazar (eighteenth century).[3]

The religion of the Patriarchs has also been illuminated. The appellations of gods found in the narratives of Genesis indicate that they worshiped old Northwest Semitic deities: primarily El, the head of the pantheon, and Hadad, the mountain and storm deity called more commonly by his appellation Baal, both well known from the Canaanite epics of the fourteenth century from Ugarit. The name of the patriarchal god, *El Shaddai* (AV, "God Almighty"), recorded only in the Priestly strata, accords perfectly in the context of Patriarchal religion in flat contradiction to the views of older scholars (*cf.* § 7). *Šadday*, "Mountain One," must be associated with similar appellations: *Har*, "Mountain" (=god)," an element in the names of Hyksos chieftains who ruled Egypt in the second quarter of the second millennium, and *Ṣûr*, "crag" or "mountain," known both from the Mari letters and Babylonian records as elements in personal names—and found in the Priestly lists of princes (see § 7).

Alt, Levy, and Albright have pointed out characteristics of the religion of the Patriarchs which are particularly significant for Mosaic religion. One of these is the feeling of actual kinship of some sort which linked the Patriarch or clan to its god. A second is closely related: the practice of a clan or invidual to choose a (special) god and enter into a type of contract or covenant with him.

The old traditions of Israel preserved the coloring—political, social, and religious—of this era in remarkable fashion. While the oral tradition and old Priestly written records cannot be taken as historical in any literal fashion, since tribe and individual often blend and exchange, and since the folkloristic elements common to all ancient folk epics adorn them, they nevertheless have proved to have an historical aspect.

5. The portion of the Hebrew tribes which found itself in Egypt in the third quarter of the second millennium B.C. had passed into an even more sophisticated age and culture. It was a period of mass identification of the gods of one pantheon with those of similar attributes in another. It was an age in which Accadian served as a *lingua franca* of Near Eastern diplomacy. It was the era in Egypt which produced the solar monotheism of the Akhenaten heresy.

Moses and the leaders of Hebrew elements in Egypt, to judge from their Egyptian names, had become comparatively assimilated into this Egyptian culture. Whether or not Moses was reared as an Egyptian prince, there can be little doubt that he was cosmopolite of Tanis, the capital city of Egypt.

Perhaps a few general comments about the desert sojourn are now in order, a subject to which we shall return below (§ 6). The desert wanderings of Israel lay in the era before the effective domestication of the camel, as Albright has shown at length. The Israelites by necessity had to live on the fringes of civilization and could never live the isolated life of the true Bedouin. At the end of the wilderness wanderings, at least a portion of the tribes under Joshua stormed Canaan in concerted effort, as shown most recently by Wright.[4] Their settlement was rapid and general. Such broad considerations based on archaeological fact are fast making primitivistic views toward early Israel and its religion untenable.

A great deal of light has been thrown on the life of Israel in the period of the Judges. The admirable monographs of Alt[5] and especially Noth[6] have shown definitively, in the view of the writer, that Israel during the period of the Judges was organized in a twelve-tribe league around a central Yahweh sanctuary. Such an organization has close analogues among the ancient peoples of Greece, Italy, and Asia Minor; and, as Albright has pointed out, there were central shrines at Nippur in Babylonia, Nineveh in Assyria, the temple of Sin in Harran, etc. Noth argues that the unity of the tribes of Israel which becomes highly evident in their uniting under Saul, may be traced clearly to the earliest days of Joshua's conquest. This unity is not to be attributed to the need for defense against the Philistines purely, for many of the tribes were not hard pressed. Nor is it to be attributed to the worship of Yahweh alone. There must have been some outward, concrete expression and center of Yahwism before any unity could have come from the religious factor. Even if they had worshiped a common Yahweh in various localities, such a practice would not have been a unifying force, but rather a separating one. The conclusion must be drawn that the religious unity of the Israelite tribes was based on a common cult at a common sanctuary.

The application of new knowledge drawn from Phoenician and Israelite orthography, and the application of comparative material drawn from the Ugaritic mythological tablets, provide radically new procedures for the analysis and dating of the earliest Old Testament poetry. This method was first applied by W. F. Albright to the Oracles of Balaam, which in their original form are shown to date from the thirteenth or twelfth century. In a similar way, the Song of Deborah (Judg. 5), the Song of Moses (Exod. 15), the Blessing of Moses (Deut. 33), Psalm 18 (= II Sam. 22), Genesis 49, Psalm 68, etc., may be shown to antedate the great prophetic movement of the eighth century, and in the case of the first three mentioned, to antedate the United Monarchy. The utility of such scientific means of dating must not be overlooked. It grants scholarship a corpus of literature which reflects Davidic and pre-Davidic theology, and which can be contrasted with the early prophets, presumably the creative and formative minds in the history of Israelite theology. The results of the theological analysis of this early literature make several conclusions necessary. As long maintained by Kittel, Gressmann, Eichrodt, Albright, and other critics of evolutionary historicism, the basic tenets of prophetic religion are already present in this earlier age: the concept of the covenant, a lofty ethical level (in contrast to the essentially amoral religions of contemporary Canaan), a conception of God as righteous Judge, as cosmic Lord of nature and history; and most striking of all, a consistent tradition of the Mosaic and desert origins of Yahwism. Wellhausen admittedly had considerable difficulty in explaining the historical roots of the prophetic movement. But in light of the above mentioned results, not to mention other lines of evidence, how can such a phenomenon as early Yahwism be explained as it suddenly appears amidst the naturalistic polytheisms of the ancient Near East?

The increasing knowledge of ancient Near Eastern law-codes, together with the use of Form-criticism in analyzing Israelite law[7] grants yet another fresh avenue of approach to early Israelite religion. While the customary law of Israel fits in well with the codes of the ancient Near East, and probably reflects both Canaanite jurisprudence and the long-accumulated decisions of judge and priest throughout Israel's stay in Canaan, the so-called apodictic law (the unqualified commands of Yahweh typified by the form "Thou shalt") has at best indirect parallels. Its antiquity and conceptual pattern point to the desert as its place of origin. Moreover, as Alt has pointed out, such law seems to have been preserved and administered primarily in the covenant sanctuary of the confederacy.

The Ras Shamrah tablets, the Marseilles Tariff, and South Arabic Inscriptions have given new perspective in studies of the sacrificial system of Israel. Scholarly opinion now indicates that the Israelite system described in the tabernacle legislation of Leviticus probably goes back in its basic outlines to common Semitic practice.

6. We are better prepared now to turn to a consideration of the desert experiences of Israel, the period to which the tabernacle traditions are attributed. A few generations after the Israelites had left Egypt and stormed Canaan, they were organized in a loose confederation, indeed in a primitive theocratic system, around a central sanctuary. Both their religion and their organization were sufficiently strong to overpower, not only the decadent

Canaanites and their religion, but in time also the powerful opposition of the Philistines. Moreover, Israel's religion appears, even in our earliest sources, as a new construct. Its God, its characteristic covenant law, its system of land-tenure, and its political organization are in radical contrast to the religion and social forms of its neighbors.

Such circumstances lead to but one conclusion: the desert era was the creative and normative period of Israel's political and religious history, and this development was fomented and led by a revolutionary religious spirit, no doubt that of Moses. Such evidence has brought leading scholars of the present day to a new recognition of the scope of the Mosaic revolution. Under Moses, Israel came to worship a new God. Yahweh was a righteous and living God among the capricious and dying gods of the Near East. He was cosmic in power and abode. He possessed no consort and was of such stature that other gods were reckoned on a secondary level.

It would be incredible in the age in which we are dealing to suppose that Yahwism could be established and transmitted unless Moses had instituted a nuclear cultic system, and organized his tribes or clans into some manner of religious and political structure.

THE HISTORICAL STATUS OF THE PRIESTLY TRADITION

7. The conclusions reached above find their primary biblical witness in the Priestly strands of the Pentateuch. While the J stratum strongly emphasized the revelation at Sinai, and E describes both the disclosure of Yahweh's name and the formulation of the covenant in the desert, it is particularly the tabernacle traditions which maintain that Yahweh was first worshiped in the desert, and that the cultic institutions and the formation of the state (which P correctly identifies as being one) find their origin under Moses in the desert. While the Priestly account is schematized and idealized, and while the Priestly writers read the theological interpretations and historical developments of later ages into their system, nevertheless, Priestly tradition must be deemed an important historical witness to the Mosaic Age.

Some of the detailed information of the lists and genealogies of P must not be passed over lightly. Often the Priestly scribes placed their ancient sources in wrong contexts; but the day when their work could be universally rejected as "pious fraud" has passed. Examples are the census lists in Numbers 1 and 26 (originally a single document). Moreover, Noth is no doubt correct in regarding the framework of Numbers 26 as pre-monarchical in its historical origins.

Similarly the lists of cities of refuge and the Levitic cities (Josh. 21 and II Chron. 6) have recently been shown by topographical and archaeological studies to reflect a system of the Davidic era, but which had its roots in the earlier system of Israelite land-tenure going back to the first days of the twelve-tribe system.[8] Wellhausen is probably quite right in pointing out that there is no trace of the system in later Israelite history. No doubt it was always in part ideal and passed out of existence by the time of the Divided Monarchy. The extended lists of boundaries in Joshua 12–20 have been shown by similar methods[9] to reflect the age to which they are assigned, while the interwoven document dealing with the cities of Judah and Benjamin are probably to be assigned to the early Divided Monarchy.[10]

Even more striking is our increasing knowledge of ancient onomastica, which may be applied to the study of Priestly proper names. Such a document as the list of princes, underlying Numbers 1, 2, 7, and 10, may be used to illustrate our contention. Gray in his *Studies in Hebrew Personal Names*, the standard work of the previous generation, rejected the document as a fiction on grounds which archaeological data have now shown to be false or inapplicable.

It will be instructive to describe briefly how his arguments have been refuted. Names with a *Šadday* element, which appear no less than three times in this list and nowhere else in the Bible, were rejected as artificial constructions without archaeological parallel. We have noted in § 4 the place which *Šadday* assumes in the religion of the Patriarchs, but more striking evidence is found in the occurrence of the name *Šadday-ʿammî* (Shaddai is my kinsman) in an Egyptian inscription of the fourteenth or early thirteenth century.[11] *Šadday-ʿammî* seems to have been a Semite, roughly contemporary with Moses in Egypt! The name is almost identical with the *'Ammî-Šadday* of the Priestly list. In a similar way the element *Ṣûr*, "Mountain," was regarded as unlikely in personal names owing to the lack of ancient parallels. Those parallels have now been furnished. Gray maintained that the proportion of names with the element *El* far exceeded the proportions of the use of the name in early Israel, but matched the proportions of late times. However, the various onomastica of the second millenium had a superabundance of names with the element *El*, as our new evidence amply shows. The curve of usage which Gray drew actually reflects a resurgent popularity of the name-element. Hence the proportion of *El* names in our list now supports its antiquity! Moreover, the majority of the single elements in the Numbers lists occur in combinations in the milieu to which tradition ascribes them.[12] The elements *'am* (people, i.e., kinsman), *'aḥ* (brother), and *'ab* (father), all referring to the link of kinship felt with a god, are most common appellatives of deity, both in our list and in the Amorite onomasticon from the middle of the second millenium. As Amorite names from the Mari tablets continue to be published, the evidence grows stronger and stronger. While we are still unable to fix the precise historical origin of the name list, it is an old document which accurately reflects the name usage of Mosaic times.

W. F. Albright has recently defended the antiquity of still another old Priestly document, the list of spies in Numbers 13:4–16.[13] While the archaeological documentation of these names is not so striking, it nevertheless must be fitted into the earlier period.[14]

Martin Noth has shown that the Priestly list of stations involved in the Exodus (Num. 33:2–49) rests on an old document quite independent of the JE narrative of the Exodus and journey to Canaan.[15] This old record seems to come from the time of the early monarchy at latest, and may, as Noth gives good reason to believe, have been developed from a standard list of stations on a pilgrimage route from Canaan to Sinai. If such be the case, it is understandable how Priestly writers took such traditional

c

stations, reversed their order, and used them as supplementary data for the route of Israel from Sinai to the Promised Land.

The antiquity of these dozen or so Priestly documents warrants closer attention on the part of scholars to other written sources of P. This is especially true in the case of such a document as the tabernacle description, whose doublets and conflate condition reveal a long history of transmission (*cf.* § 11).

THE HISTORY OF THE TABERNACLE INSTITUTION

8. With the formation of a covenanted league under Moses in the desert, suitable institutions for its functioning were created. The central institution, according to the unanimous witness of the sources, was the Tent of Assembly (cf. § 16), which was utilized both for religious and for political gatherings. The "Aaronic" priesthood and a sacrificial cult (derived no doubt from the patterns of worship to which the people were accustomed) were instituted. The essential covenant law was no doubt proclaimed and fixed in liturgical forms at this period and added to from time to time when Yahweh proclaimed his will directly or through sacred lot.

There is good reason to believe that Moses instituted the aniconic tradition of Israel as argued persuasively by Wright and Albright, so that we may assume that the Ark, understood as the throne of an invisible God, was also instituted in the days of Moses. Such traditions best perpetuate themselves when embodied in concrete form.

The sources are at variance as to the place of the tabernacle in Israel's encampment. Gressmann holds that the tent-sanctuary and its precious Ark could never have stood unprotected outside the camp of the Israelites. Rather, drawing upon well-known representations of Egyptian[16] and Assyrian battle-camps, and familiar notices of Diodorus relating to a tent-shrine in the center of the camp of the Carthaginians, he concludes that the Priestly accounts are more accurate in placing the sacred cult installations in the center of the camp. However, under different circumstances, both traditions may be accurate. The heavily idealized camp of the Priestly tradition, with priests and tribes grouped in systemic order in protective array about the tabernacle, may reflect the battle formation of Israel in the ritual of "Holy War." On the other hand, the tent may have been pitched in partial seclusion among the peaceful encampments of Israel, and there is good reason to believe that the Ark led Israel as they made general migrations (cf. § 13).

9. Little is known about the early history of the tabernacle as an institution in Canaan. If Noth and Alt are correct, the first locus of the central sanctuary was at Shechem, as suggested by early records in Deuteronomy and Joshua, where the desert covenant was renewed and extended to the twelve tribes who made up the later nation of Israel (Josh. 8:30–35; 24; etc.). However, the official sanctuary during the major phase of the period of the Judges was at Shiloh. Such is the consensus of the sources, early and late. Moreover, the fact that Shiloh is given such prominence despite its insignificant size and out-of-the-way location in Palestine reinforces tradition. Shechem, on the other hand, seems to have remained under strongly Canaanite influence during most of the Period of the Judges.

At Shiloh the house of Eli continued the hereditary priesthood preserving even some of its Egyptian background in the names Hophni and Phinehas. Shiloh remained the central sanctuary until its destruction at the hands of the Philistines after the Battle of Ebenezer (*ca.* 1050 B.C.), when the Ark was captured. The destruction of the central sanctuary is amply corroborated by the excavations of Kjaer and Schmidt,[17] as well as by notices in later tradition (Jer. 7:12; 15:1; 26:6; Ps. 78:60, etc.). The earlier sources refer to the sanctuary at Shiloh as a temple (*hêkāl*), while the later sources refer to it as a tent. When the old fabric of the original tabernacle disappeared, no one can tell. Perhaps it fell apart during the vicissitudes of the Conquest.

The period following the destruction of Shiloh is largely a blank in the history of the central sanctuary. Saul's establishment of the sanctuary at Nob, only two miles from his residence in Gibeah, seems to have been an attempt to draw the strands of the old amphictyonic system together under his surveillance as well as to identify it with his own protomonarchial system.

The blood purge of Nob priests after their traffic with David is particularly indicative that certain sovereign powers, derived from the strong tradition of the old theocracy, still resided in the Nob sanctuary.

Whatever may have been the subsequent history of the institution after the fall of Shiloh, it finds its culmination in David's "Tent of Yahweh." We get ample evidence of David's political sagacity as well as his religious devotion—or that of such advisors as Nathan (II Sam. 7)—in connection with the establishment of the Jerusalem sanctuary. David brought together the Ark, chief cult object of the covenanted tribes, the hereditary northern priesthood, and the desert-born tradition of Israel's tabernacle, to form his official cultic institution in the neutral city of Jerusalem. The nimbus of the old sanctuary, the loyalty to the old system, and the cherished memories of the desert tradition were thereby transferred to the Tent of David, giving legitimacy and security to the Davidic monarchy.

10. It is well to recognize that the "tabernacle" became the symbol of the institution of the central sanctuary in later biblical thought. By telescoping tradition, the institution which served as Israel's sanctuary was conceived *ipso facto* to be the tabernacle. For this reason, one is justified in terming not only the desert tent, but also the Shiloh structure (whatever its form may have been), and particularly the Tent of David, "the tabernacle"; for in these resided the one, continuous, central, religious institution of early Israel. The motifs of the desert tent maintained themselves in these sanctuaries, arising out of the desert era, continuing into the time of David, and projected in their ideal form in the later religious thought of Israel. These sanctuaries were characteristically seats of normative Yahwism; each contained the Ark; each was a center of covenant law and judgments. They were the focus of pilgrimage customs, a dominant Priestly house, and, in varying degrees, the center of a political system.

THE PROMULGATION OF THE TENT IDEAL

11. New vistas in the ancient history of the tabernacle institution require a reinterpretation of the character and date of the

Priestly materials which promulgated the tabernacle ideal in later times. Priestly tradition seems never to have taken the form of an independent "Code." It is most easily described as a commentary or rather a systematizing expansion of the normative JE tradition in the Tetrateuch (Gen., Exod., Lev., Num.). Evidently priests of the late pre-Exilic and Exilic period collected and edited ancient written (*sic!*) documents, perhaps salvaged from temple or government archives, and thus produced what they considered a more precise and detailed picture of the desert period. That is to say, they were continuing the prophetic tendency to regard the desert era as normative for Yahwism, but were interested more in its cultic establishment.

An Exilic date for the major Priestly work seems almost certain now. Its language can scarcely be post-Exilic, since there are no Aramaisms. Its theology is clearly reflected in the writings of the oldest post-Exilic prophets, particularly Zechariah (*cf.* 2:5, 10 ff.; 8:3, 11, and *passim*). The *Nethinim*, singers, and other orthodox institutions of the Restoration have no place in its pages. It must be closely connected with the work of Ezekiel.

The theology of the Priestly strata fits into this period perfectly. The downfall of the nation with its ensuing capitivity was a catastrophe with tremendous implications for its faith. The covenant was "broken." Monotheism was threatened. The doctrine of election seemed directly repudiated. The sacrosanct temple had been sacked, and the inviolable city lay in ruins. The great historical tenets of Yahwism needed emphatic restatement. The future of Israel's religion rested upon the ability of the faithful to explain and answer the crises and problems of the time. Out of the Exile came reformulation of the faith. Ezekiel pointed the way. The Priestly writers looked to the pre-temple era, to Israel's normative Mosaic institutions, and provided a reinterpretation of the past which later became authoritative. In contrast, Second Isaiah (Isa. 40 ff.) heralded the Restoration; he was not only concerned with the return of Israel to Jerusalem, but primarily with the victory of Yahweh. He exulted over the vindication of the covenant faith. He restated the role of the Chosen People, and effectively described the meaning of the captivity. A powerful doctrine of election permeates Ezekiel, P, and Second Isaiah. In all three the memory of the golden desert era is evoked. Ezekiel and the Priestly strata, especially, are desperately concerned with the sin of Israel, which has precipitated the captivity, and they search for means of atonement. All three emphasize the cosmic and holy nature of Israel's God. Second Isaiah, however, adds a new mood in his victory paean: he sings of the downfall of the idol-gods and of the universal sovereignty of his vindicated Lord.

12. The most recent trend in the literary criticism of the Priestly writings is represented in the work of G. von Rad (*Die Priesterschrift im Hexateuch*, 1934), and M. Noth in his *Überlieferungsgeschichtliche Studien* (1943). Von Rad splits P into two separate sources, one older, less Priestly, and more historical; the other comparatively late, Priestly, and artificial. He is followed by Galling and in part by Noth, but has not gained general acceptance. Noth's work seeks to eliminate P from Joshua, cutting away all accretions to leave a source, largely narrative, which concludes with the death of Aaron and Moses. Noth's treatment, however, overlooks P's character as commentary formed from sundry old records in his insistence that P be a logical unity, later split up to form the framework of the Tetrateuch. Noth is probably correct in regarding JEP and the Deuteronomic books as separate entities. And yet, even if this is true, the Joshua lists, for example (*cf.* § 7), must derive from the same circle of documents, extant in the pre-Exilic period, as many of those in the Priestly portions of the Tetrateuch.

These recent attempts to seek out the "nuclear" Priestly stratum reflect a new respect for the historical core of P. The conflations, doublets, and additions which allow separation of Priestly materials into two or more parts also testify to the age of its sources, but at the same time to the heterogeneous character of its origin. We cannot use the Priestly materials uncritically. Priestly tradition in its present form is dogmatic and late; nevertheless, it is a valuable historical witness, often more reliable in detail than the older oral sources. In the last analysis, it can in no way represent pious fraud, but rather the best efforts of

Priestly scholars who tried to piece together the golden past from materials available to them.

THE ARCHAEOLOGY OF THE TABERNACLE

13. Old Testament scholars, taking their cue from students of Arab life as early as the turn of the century, began to compare the tabernacle and the Ark with nomad tent-shrines surviving into modern times. Gressmann, in *Mose und seine Zeit* (1913), compared the Ark to the Ruwala *'utfah,* following Musil and older scholars. In 1918, Hartmann published a study of the tabernacle and the Ark[18] in which he drew on the parallel institutions of the *'utfah, mahmal,* and *qubbah.* A most valuable study was that of Henri Lammens, which appeared in 1919,[19] and treated particularly well the pre-Islamic history of the *qubbah.* The most recent collection and treatment of modern and ancient parallels is that of Morgenstern, "The Ark, the Ephod, and the Tent."[20]

The *'utfah* is a class of tribal palladia still surviving among the modern nomad tribes. Its best known representative is the *markab* of the Ruwala. It takes the form of a camel saddle in modern times, is made of a wooden framework, decorated with ostrich feathers, and more or less resembles a tent. Traditionally, it accompanied tribes into important military encounters and led them in migrations. Some manner of "holiness" pervaded the *'utfah.* Originally, no doubt, it was associated with the tribal deity(s). Sacrifices are still made in connection with it, at which time blood is sprinkled on it.

The *mahmal* is a highly revered tentlike structure, which until very recent times was carried in various processions to Mecca. It too was borne on camel back. It was usually fabricated from highly decorated silk on a boxlike framework with a domed top. There is evidence that it was regarded formerly as having some kind of supernatural sway over the camel which carried it, so that it could guide caravans through the deserts.

Going back into the pre-Islamic period, we come upon the highly significant *qubbah,* which seems to be the ancestor of the *mahmal* and *'utfah.* The *qubbah* was a miniature red leather tent with a domed top. Some *qubbahs* were suitable for mounting on camel back, others larger. The *qubbah* generally contained the tribal idols or betyls.

The characteristics which have been noted in the *'utfah* and the *mahmal* were far more explicitly characterized in the usage of the *qubbah*. In times of war it accompanied the tribe, generally being set up close by the chieftain's tent. It had the power of guiding the tribe in its wanderings. It possessed a peculiar sacredness or physical holiness second only to the betyls which it contained. It was both a palladium and a place of worship. Moreover, priests used the *qubbah* as a place for giving oracles.

Lammens observes that the red leather of which they were constructed is most extraordinary. Black tents were characteristic from oldest times. Moreover, red exposes the military camp and the station of the chieftain. The custom is strange and implies a strong conservative religious tradition.

A number of representations of the *qubbah* come from Syria, as well as a specific mention of the institution in an Aramaic inscription. Of particular interest is the bas-relief from the temple of Bel in Palmyra (third to first centuries B.C.) portraying the *qubbah* with traces of red paint still adhering to it.

Morgenstern has pointed out that even earlier evidence for the custom of the tent-shrine comes from the fragments of the Phoenician history of Sanchuniathon (*ca.* seventh century B.C.) where reference is made to a portable shrine of undisclosed character pulled by oxen. The shrine was presumably in the possession of Agroueros, a semi-mythical figure who lived in primordial times. Better evidence for Phoenician tent-shrines, however, comes from Diodorus, who tells of a tent of sacred nature pitched in the center of a Carthaginian battle camp with an altar near by (*cf.* § 8).

The Priestly traditions also have specific mention of the *qubbah* in Numbers 25:8. The passage is somewhat obscure; but the context suggests that it is a reference to the tabernacle, or as Ingholt suggests, to the sacred enclosure.

These parallels lend striking corroboration to the Priestly tradition that the tabernacle had a covering of ram's skin, dyed red; and no doubt we must conclude that the *qubbah* institution among the Semites sheds light on the origin of the tabernacle. We must suppose that the portable red leather tent was one of the oldest motifs in Semitic religion. This it goes without saying that the tabernacle and the Ark have historical connections with their Semitic past. On the other hand, we have no right to push such parallels too hard, as has been the tendency of some scholars, particularly of Morgenstern. As the *qubbah* was radically reinterpreted by Mohammed, so no doubt the ancient Semitic tent-shrine was transformed in early Israel to suit the purpose of Yahwism.

RECONSTRUCTION OF THE PRIESTLY TABERNACLE

14. The Priestly tabernacle as it appears from descriptions in Exodus 26 and 36 is a portable temple. Two motifs run throughout its structure and installations. One derives from the desert and suggests its origin in a tent-shrine. Under this category are the tent curtains, especially the covering of red leather; the acacia wood similarly is a product of the desert, and stands in contrast to the olive and cedar wood which characterized the temple of Solomon. The other principle clearly represented in the tabernacle points to the influence of Syro-Phoenician temple architecture. The division of the tabernacle into two sections, a "Holy Place" and a "Most Holy Place" or *dĕbîr,* and the substantial structure of frames (*qĕrāšîm*) and pillars over which the curtains were draped, are particularly suggestive of temple form. It will be pointed out at a later time that some of the tabernacle furnishings surely suggest the influence of some of the environment of Canaan.

The tabernacle *par excellence* consisted of two great tent curtains (in turn composed of five smaller curtains each) made of the finest linen beautifully embroidered with winged sphinxes (cherubim). One of the curtains formed the main hall of the tabernacle, the Holy Place; the second covered the Most Holy Place, including the back of the tabernacle. Over these curtains, three protective coverings were spread, the outer of finely treated, imported leather,[21] a second a red-dyed ram's hide, and a third of goat's hair.

The curtains were spread on a framework of qĕrāšîm which A. R. S. Kennedy on the basis of biblical evidence has translated "frame" (AV, board). As scholars have long realized, the qĕrāšîm could scarcely have been solid timbers or "boards." Their ponderous size and weight alone would eliminate them from reason. The yādôt of the "frames," then, would be the vertical arms and presumably they were joined together by cross-pieces to make a lattice-work.

The tablets of Ugarit have given additional confirmation to the theory of Kennedy. Here the qrš refers to the throne-room of El at the source of the primordial rivers and the fountains of the two oceans (deeps). Presumably the throne-room was a trellised pavilion.[22]

Again we have evidence of the dual nature of the Priestly tabernacle. Apparently the qĕrāšîm framework has historical connections with the abodes of deity in historical connections with the abodes of deity in Canaanite mythology. Probably the conception of the tabnît, the "model" (Exod. 25:9), also goes back ultimately to the idea that the earthly sanctuary is the counterpart of the heavenly dwelling of a deity. There is no reason to assume with most scholars (most recently Galling) that the tabernacle framework is the fiction of late writers who wished to make the tabernacle conform more closely in structure to the temple.

The frames were to be fifteen feet high and two feet three inches in breadth. As is to be expected in the case of frames, no thickness is mentioned. Forty-eight of the frames were to make up the structure, twenty frames for each side and eight for the back, making the dimensions of the tabernacle forty-five feet long by fifteen feet high. The Most Holy Place was to be closed off from the Holy Place by a tapestry veil hung on four acacia wood supports, and in turn, the entrance was to be protected by an embroidered screen hung on acacia supports.

The symmetry of the tabernacle is clarified by the notice that the veil is to be hung under the hooks that join the two great inner curtains (Exod. 26:33). The tabernacle consisted thus of two rooms, the Holy Place of twenty by ten by ten cubits (30 x 15 x 15 feet), and the Most Holy Place, a cube ten cubits to the dimension. The Ark was to be placed in this sacred cube; the Table of Presence Bread, the Altar of Incense, and the Lampstand were to adorn the Holy Place.

The tabernacle is described as being enclosed in a court, shut off by linen curtains, one hundred by fifty cubits in size (approximately 150 x 75 feet). The Altar of Burnt Offering and the Laver were set up in the Court, no doubt before the entrance to the tabernacle.[23]

THE TABERNACLE AND THE DAVIDIC TENT

15. A number of considerations have led the writer to the opinion that the Priestly tabernacle account reflects the Tent of David. Such an opinion cannot, of course, be demonstrated, but evidence points increasingly in that direction.

It seems evident that P does not give a precise description of the tent which Moses built in the wilderness. Logically, it would seem that the Mosaic tent was simpler and more conformed to its Semetic prototypes. Moreover, it must have been almost inevitable that the Priestly writers draw their tradition of the tabernacle from the highest and most elaborate *development* of that institution (see § 10).

The dual motifs pointed out in the tabernacle description support the same conclusion. In particular the proportions of the tabernacle must almost necessarily be connected with the plans of such temples as have been excavated at Beth-Shan, Tell Ta'yinat, and of course, the temple of Solomon. The acacia wood, the tent-curtains of red leather no doubt stem from the desert tradition, but the *qereš* structure which converts the tent into a portable temple seems to have Canaanite connections. Some of the cultic implements and some of the decorations of the Priestly garments in particular suggest Phoenician influence. These dual motifs are not to be explained away entirely by supposing them anachronisms reflecting the temple of Solomon. Some influence of the temple upon the P account is undeniable.

Certain parallels in measurement are best explained as resulting from the scribes' knowledge of the temple dimensions; such influence might easily come to bear if certain tabernacle dimensions were vague. It seems totally unnecessary to dissolve the dualism of the tabernacle, however, if we assume that the Priestly sources are describing the culminating development of the tabernacle institution.

Mention has already been made of the large number of old records incorporated by the Priestly writers which are traceable to early times, particularly to the reign of David (§ 7). There can be no doubt that David organized an elaborate administrative and secretarial staff, and it may well be that certain written documents from this time were available to the priests from temple or government archives. Our suggestion is that the tabernacle account also is some such document.

The Priestly tabernacle fits in very well with what little we know of the Davidic tabernacle from earlier sources. We know that it contained "a proper place" for the Ark (II Sam. 6:7), presumably a *děbîr*. In its proximity was an altar of burnt offering (II Sam. 6:17) and there seems to have been a second horned altar inside the Tent.[24]

Finally the wealth of the Davidic court and the important part which the tabernacle played in David's political strategy (§ 9) would lead us to believe that the Davidic tabernacle was richly and ornately fabricated, in which case it would agree well with the Priestly descriptions. That is not to deny that the extreme lavishness in the tabernacle adornments (and the reckless use of gold in the Solominic temple) may be due in part to the tendency of tradition to exaggerate.

In this connection it would be well to make some comments on the most recent reconstructions, particularly that of Galling.[25] Galling, following von Rad's separation of the Priestly tradition into two strands (*cf.* § 12), segregates all the solely desert characteristics of the tabernacle, attributes them to the earlier source, and proposes by that means to arrive at the historical Mosaic tent. He considers the original account to have included different dimensions (later suppressed) and to have consisted only of the outer covering. This he drapes over poles, allowing no credence to the division into Holy Place and *děbîr*. The framework of the tabernacle, the inner curtain, and a large part of the cultic equipment he ascribes to the imagination of the later, less reliable Priestly strand.

By isolating the desert motifs in the tabernacle Galling may well reach something resembling the actual Mosaic tent. However, to throw out the remainder of the description as later fabrication is unnecessary and goes against what we know of Near Eastern scribal procedures in general, and the Priestly sources in particular.

LIGHT ON TABERNACLE TERMINOLOGY

16. *'Ōhel Mô'ēd* (Tent of Meeting), the name of the tabernacle which is found in the JE account in Exodus 33 and often in the Priestly tradition, has been explained by the occurrence of the word *mô'ēd* in the Tale of Wen-Amun (*ca.* 1060 B.C.).[26] In this contect it refers to the city assembly of Byblus called together to consider a petition of the Tjekel (a group of the Sea-Peoples who settled around Dor) for the extradition of Wen-Amun. The passage may be compared to Isaiah 14:13 which refers to the mount of "assembly" (*mô'ēd*) in the far reaches of the north. The reference is to the assembly of the gods,[27] well known from the myths of Ugarit.

From such passages we gather that the Tent of Meeting, or properly the Tent of Assembly, originally referred to the amphictyonic or political aspect of the tent. However, the Priestly interpretation is not to be dismissed too lightly: speaking of the Tent of "Meeting," Yahweh says, "I will meet with you to speak there unto you. And there I will meet with the children of Israel . . ." (Exod. 29:42, 43; 25:22; 30:36). This interprets the *'Ōhel Mô'ēd* primarily as a tent of revelation. However, it is to be observed that in the amphictyonic gatherings, Yahweh was considered to be the head of the covenant assembly, and it was He who made the important decisions in war and peace (through oracle, or by human mediation). There was no separation of church and state in early Israel.

Noth has shown that *nasî'* (AV, prince: *cf.* §7) often employed by the Priestly writers is another technical term denoting a tribal leader who took part in the amphictyonic assembly (*'ēdāh*) of Israel's early twelve-tribe system. Many other examples of the Priestly source's use of archaic terminology could be presented; however, we shall confine ourselves to two other terms which bear particularly on the theology of the tabernacle tradition.

17. The typical Priestly designation of the tent-sanctuary is the term *miškān,* "tabernacle." Evidence from Ugaritic and the thirteenth-century Balaam Oracles, especially, makes it virtually certain that the term originally meant simply, "tent." Later it became a poetic, elevated designation of a tent. In the Priestly materials it is restricted to the tent *par excellence,* the tabernacle. Still later the term was used figuratively in reference to the temple.

The associated verb, *škn* (AV, dwell), has an even more interesting history.

Underlying the massive detail of the Priestly strata is one dominant theme. This theme may be expressed as follows: under the conditions of the desert covenant, Yahweh will "tabernacle" in the midst of his people Israel (Exod. 25:8, 29:45, 46; 40:35; and often; *cf.* Lev. 26:11). The term translated "to tabernacle" (in lieu of a better rendering) is *škn.* It is generally thought to indicate a literal abode on earth. Scholars have assumed that the Priestly writers follow a grossly primitive doctrine of divine immanence. It is asserted that though they reach sublime heights in their conception of creation at the hand of God, and indeed describe their Deity in the most exalted terms of transcendence, yet they fall to a crass particularism when describing the manner in which God is present in their tent-sanctuary. By the same token, *miškān,* "tabernacle," has often been translated "dwelling."

The early usage of *škn* is closely parallel to the usage of *miškān,* "tent." It occurs in the Balaam Oracles, the Song of Deborah, the Noachic Oracle, Jacob's Blessing, the Blessing of Moses (all pre-tenth-century sources), in the earlier traditions of the Yahwist (J), in the Keret Epic of Ugarit, etc. In fact there is scarcely an ancient poem dating from the tenth century or earlier, sources which does not contain this term. In ancient poetry, *škn* is used to picture nomad life and clearly means "to encamp" or "to tent."[28] So also it is used in the earlier J traditions to describe the nomadic habits of the Patriarchs, and in the Keret epic to mean "encamp." In contrast to the abundant use of the word in materials of great antiquity—all of which appear to reflect a desert setting—we find that the term *škn,* "to tent," falls into disuse in the bulk of biblical writings until it is met again in the Priestly strata.

In the Priestly strata, the term *miškān* applies to the one tent, the Mosaic sanctuary. The word has become a proper name. So too, P restricts the meaning of the verb *škn.* Taking its connotations from a nomadic background, and more directly from the sacred *miškān,* it is used by the Priestly writers when they wish to speak of God manifesting Himself on earth in the midst of Israel. Thus in P, *škn* is used invariably and solely to specify the "tabernacling" of Yahweh—the earthly presence of Yahweh—for the purposes of revelation and atonement. Even in cases where Yahweh's Glory or Cloud settles on Sinai or before the tabernacle, this word *škn* is used.

Such usage reflects the Priestly effort to go back to a normative desert tradition for terminology. This expression becomes even more significant when we observe that not only does P always use this term to express the concept of Yahweh's immanence, but it never uses the term *škn* in any other sense. Priestly tradition has taken a concrete, archaic term, associated with Israel's desert tradition, and used it as an abstract term to express a theological concept.

Still another line of evidence can be drawn upon. The common word in the Priestly materials, and throughout the Old Testament, which means "dwell" or "inhabit" is *yšb.* P uses the term *yšb* whenever it wishes to speak of men "dwelling," but never of Yahweh, or any manifestation of Yahweh to Israel. Moreover this distinction is held more or less throughout the Old Testament. When Yahweh is said to "dwell" (*yšb*), the place of dwelling is never on earth, in the temple or the tabernacle, but *in heaven alone.* The only exceptions, apparently, are in places where *yšb* or its derivatives are used in the sense, "to enthrone," or "throne," particularly in the expression, "He who is enthroned on the cherubim."

The Priestly writers were struggling with the problem of divine immanence and transcendence, in other words, the problem of the covenant-presence of Yahweh in the sanctuary. Israel's cosmic and omnipotent God could not be confined to an earthly sanctuary. Yet the supreme object and benefit of the covenant relationship—of Israel's election in the great events following the Exodus—was God's new "closeness" in the tabernacle. It seems clear that this old word *škn* has been taken as the technical theological term to express this paradox. The Priestly writers retrieved a "desert" terminology that was genuinely archaic. Yahweh does not "dwell" on earth. Rather he "tabernacles" or settles impermanently as in the days of the portable, ever-conditional tent.

We may observe in passing that the Deuteronomists sought in a different way to solve the problem of the covenant-presence of a transcendent God. They bluntly state that Yahweh's abode is in the heavens, not the temple. Rather His "Name" may be said to be in the temple (see esp. I Kings 8:27–31).[29]

Conforming the Hebrew evidence is the usage of the Septuagint. There the term *škn* is generally translated by *kataskēnoun,* "to encamp." or *skēnoun,* "to tent," and *miškān is* commonly translated *skēnē,* "tent." This is particularly the case among the more literal translators. Allusion should also be made to the *šĕkînāh* doctrine which grew up shortly after the Old Testament writings were completed. *Šĕkînāh* probably is an older word, however, and is to be very closely related with the Priestly use of *miškān* and *škn.* In early intertestamental writings, the *šĕkînāh* is the restricted or local manifestation of Yahweh, later coming to have a wider meaning. It also plays a part in the theological background of the New Testament.

CONCLUSION

18. In the preceding pages, we have endeavored to describe the place of the historical tabernacle, both in its relation to the desert origins of Israel, and as it played the role of covenant sanctuary

in Canaan. We have found it to be the seat of Mosaic institutions, the preserver of vigorous desert Yahwism, and the center of an inherently theocratic political system. With these concepts as a background, we have turned to the tent ideal of later times, particularly the Priestly description of the tabernacle. The Priestly tabernacle appears in this perspective to be the culminating tradition—schematic and ideal to be sure—of themes which had seminal beginnings in the Mosaic tent.

As for the contemporary and future generations to which the Priestly writers addressed themselves, no doubt the tabernacle account was to be an explanation for the past and a plan for the future. Theologically speaking, they strove after a solution to the problems of covenant theology; the means through which the breached covenant might be repaired, and the conditions under which a holy and universal God might "tabernacle" in the midst of Israel. It may be added that the writers of the New Testament were intimately concerned with the same themes, that is, the forgiveness of sin and the self-revelation of God. Christian theology may thus be said to continue, and, from a Christian point of view, to resolve these Priestly problems of the Old Testament, through the Word which "became flesh and 'tabernacled' among us full of grace and truth . . ." (John 1:14).

NOTES

1. For recent syntheses of the historical background of the Old Testament, see particularly Albright, *From the Stone Age to Christianity* (Baltimore, 1940), and Frankfort, Frankfort, Wilson, Jacobsen, and Irwin, *The Intellectual Adventure of Ancient Man* (Chicago, 1946).

2. *Cf.* the recent review of De Vaux, "Les patriarches hébreux et les découvertes modernes," *RB,* LIII (1946), 321–48; LV (1948), 321–47; LVI (1949), 5–36.

3. The element *Jacob* also appears in the name of a Hyksos chieftain (Ya'qub-har), and in a contemporary Palestinian place name recorded in Egyptian lists.

4. G. Ernest Wright, "The Literary and Historical Problem of Joshua 10 and Judges 1," *JNES*, V:2 (1946), 105–14.

5. A. Alt, *Die Staatenbildung der Israeliten in Palästina* (Leipzig, 1930).

6. M. Noth, *Das System der zwölf Stämme Israels* (Stuttgart, 1930).

7. See particularly, A. Alt, *Die Ursprünge des israelitischen Rechts* (Leipzig, 1934).

8. See Albright, "The List of Levitic Cities," *Louis Ginzberg Jubilee Volume* (1945), pp. 49 ff.

9. *Cf.*, especially, Noth, *Das Buch Josua (Handbuch zum A.T.* [Tübingen, 1938]), pp. ix–xv.

10. For the assignment of the sources of the Joshua lists, *cf.* § 12.

11. M. Burchardt, *Die altkanaanäischen Fremdworte und Eigennamen in Ägyptischen* (1909). The name was called to my attention by Prof. Albright. *Cf. From the Stone Age to Christianity*, p. 185.

12. Reuel (*Re'um-el* in the Mari Letters), meaning "God (El) is a Shepherd," is a particularly interesting example of a congruent name.

13. *ARI*, 201, note 13.

14. In the same connection, it may be pointed out that the name Bezalel (one of the traditional fabricators of the tabernacle) now has good parallels from old Amorite usage.

15. "Der Wallfahrtsweg zum Sinai," *Palästina-jahrbuch*, XXXVI (1940), 5–28.

16. Especially the contemporary reliefs of Rameses II (1300–1234), presumably Pharoah of the Exodus, which shows the Egyptian camp drawn up in rectangular form with the tent of the divine king and various sacred objects in the center.

17. Albright, *ARI*, p. 104.

18. *ZAW*, XXXVII, 209 ff.

19. "Le culte des bétyles et les processions religieuses chez les arabes préislamites," *Bulletin de l'Institut Français d'Archéologie Orientale*, XVII (1919), 39–101.

20. *Hebrew Union College Annual*, XVII (1943), 153–265; XVIII (1944), 1–52.

21. *Taḥaš* leather (AV, badger skins) has caused unending speculation on the part of scholars. An Assyrian word supposedly meaning "sheepskin" seemed to satisfy for a time. However, Landsberger has maintained that the word in question, *taḥšu*, is to be read dušu, "sheep-skin" (?). Efforts to etymologize on the basis of Arabic *tuḥas* have led to weird results, the latest being that of Aharoni who concludes that *taḥaš* means *monodon monoceros*, "narwhale"! By far the most reasonable suggestion is that of Bondi who connects *taḥaš* with Egyptian *tj-ḥ-s*, Middle Kingdom *t-ḥ-s*. As Albright pointed out to the writer, the phonetic equation is quite proper, and the word was borrowed during the second millennium to judge from the laws of phonetic change, thus fitting perfectly into the desert milieu. Egyptian *tj-ḥ-s* is found as early as the Old Kingdom meaning "to stretch or treat leather." This would suggest then that the mysterious *taḥaš* skins were actually an imported (?) specially finished leather.

22. The occurrence of the word in Ugaritic was called to my attention by Prof. Albright.

23. For the best recent attempt to reconstruct the tabernacle from the biblical data, see A. R. S. Kennedy, "Tabernacle," *Hastings Dictionary of the Bible*, IV, 653–68. Kennedy takes up the many tedious problems not mentioned here.

24. I Kings 1:50; 2:28–30. The words "come out" seem clearly to suggest that the altar was within and thus may have been either an altar of incense or a Table of Presence-bread. It is possible, however, that Benaiah was calling from outside an enclosed court, in which case the altar would have been an altar of burnt offering. Neither possibility injures the parallel to the Priestly tabernacle.

25. Beer-Galling, *Exodus* (*Handbuch zum A.T.*, [1939]), pp. 128 ff.

26. The discovery was made by Wilson and was published in *JNES*, IV (1945), 245.

27. *Cf.* J. H. Patton's discussion of the assembly of the gods and parallel usages of *mô'ēd* in the Psalms (*Canaanite Parallels to the Book of Psalms* [1944], p. 24).

28. A few remarks may be made here on the stem *škn*. *Šakânu* in Old Akkadian is already a true root meaning "to place" or "to set down." In Assyrian it is often used in idiom to mean "pitch or set up camp" (esp. with *mâdaktu*, but also with *karâšu*, etc.). From comparable usage, the derived noun *maškanu* seems to have been specialized in Northwest Semitic to mean camping-place or particularly in the plural, "encampment." Hence the singular, "tent." It is interesting to note that *maškanu* in East Semitic was specialized to mean "a grain storage place" or "grain shed" (so Albright in modification of Goetze) which was later borrowed in Hebrew in the form *miskĕnôt*, "storage places." The two specializations of the derived noun are almost identical in semantic development to German *Lager*, "encampment" or "storage-place."

The specialization of the very *škn* in Northwest Semitic probably did not derive directly from such idioms as mentioned above. Rather it seems to have derived its nuances in denominative fashion from the use of the noun *maškanu* or *miškān*, "tent," and hence came to mean "to tent" or "to encamp."

29. *Cf.* Wright, pp. 181–83.

4

THE ROLE OF ORAL TRADITION
IN THE OLD TESTAMENT

Eduard Nielsen

The older scholarship, with its analysis of the Pentateuch into the four main strata, J, E, D, P, dealt preeminently with the supposition that at different junctures there were writers who wrote. A profound challenge to such assumptions has come from the so-called Scandinavian school, of whom Professor Nielsen may be taken as more or less representative, thought the Scandinavians have some deep inner differences. Within the common views of the Scandinavians, oral tradition is regarded as more significant than the hypothetical sources of the Graf-Wellhausen school. Indeed, Professor Nielsen spends several paragraphs on the relative rarity of writing in ancient Israel. Germane to his argument, too, is his exposition of the role of writing in the case of the literary prophets.

In general, the Scandinavians have regarded the written Pentateuch as very young, but the oral traditions behind the written as extremely old. Even though these scholars are prepared to argue for the great antiquity of the oral material, they do not equate this great antiquity with historical reliability, but regard the latter as a separate and distinct problem. Central in much of the Scandinavian scholarship is a motif virtually absent from the older scholarship, namely, the important place which the cult observances on the holy days occupied, and, accordingly, the significance of cult practices in preserving and transmitting the oral tradition.

It scarcely overstates the case to declare that in effect the Scandinavians reject totally both the strata in the Graf-Wellhausen hypothesis and the reconstruction of the history of the religion of Israel which such strata implied to the Graf-Wellhausen school. Professor Nielsen's essay may be somewhat difficult for the beginning student. It can be helpful to bear in mind that Professor Nielsen is pursuing two related facets of a single contention, namely, that the older scholarship—with its bondage to the written sources, some coming from the pre-exilic specific ages— is wrong, and that the views on oral tradition serve to correct that wrongness. Consistent with this double contention, he inquires into the extent of pre-exilic writing and allusion to it in the Bible, and he asserts that the age of abundant writing was relatively late; hence, he argues, the transmission of materials in the earlier period was primarily oral.

THE POINT of departure for this chapter is taken from Nyberg's words: "The written Old Testament is a creation of the post-exilic Jewish community; of what existed earlier undoubtedly only a small part was in fixed written form."[1] That is to say, the Old Testament as *written* literature may in all probability be ascribed to the period between the destruction of Jerusalem in 587 B.C. and the time of the Maccabees.

In what follows we shall attempt to demonstrate the tenability of this thesis, firstly, in a negative manner, by establishing the subordinate role of writing in pre-exilic Israel; secondly, in a positive manner, by tracing the more direct evidence of oral transmission in the Old Testament itself; and finally, we shall briefly touch on the problem how a written canon can come into existence in an age that demonstrably still venerates the spoken word.

Let us begin with a few fundamental remarks. The principal source of our knowledge of pre-exilic Israelite culture is the Old Testament itself. Those who maintain the generally recognized conception of the unreliability of oral tradition will deny that anyone taking Nyberg's thesis of the origin of the written Old Testament in post-exilic times seriously has the right to say anything of importance about the pre-exilic culture on the basis of the Old Testament itself—always excepting that which in the

Old Testament itself is expressly indicated as being taken from written sources, "the Book of Songs," "the Book of the Upright," "The Book of the Wars of YHWH" and above all that which must be presumed to originate from the Israelite and Judahite annals.

We have attempted [in previous writings] to create a new attitude to tradition, a favorable one, characterized by faith in the reliability of this method of transmission, or at least in its possibilities in this respect. Not only was there a different technical mastery of tradition from any that exists in our culture; the desire to disregard tradition was also absent. The individual's sovereignty over the materials handed down from his fathers was foreign to the ancients. On the basis of Old Testament literature we can therefore hopefully begin to point out where and when writing was used in pre-exilic Israel, and where and when the spoken word was employed.

Naturally we are obliged to consult modern Palestinian archaeology to see if it can supplement, or merely confirm, or even perhaps revise, our conception of the culture of ancient Israel in this respect.

1. Statistics of the occurrence of words such as *kathabh* (write) *sepher,* (book), etc., demonstrate as clearly as could be wished that the use of writing for really literary purposes belongs essentially to the exilic and post-exilic period. But at the same time such statistics show that writing was used to a considerable extent for more practical purposes, and if the Old Testament had not been a collection of texts chosen from a religious standpoint, but more especially composed of political, juridical, profane, poetical, mercantile, and grammatical elements, the statistics would certainly show a still more widespread use of writing in pre-exilic Israel than is now the case.

In the Tetrateuch ("four books": Genesis, Exodus, Leviticus, and Numbers) we find that there is no testimony to the use of writing either in Genesis or in Leviticus. In Leviticus, which does not really contain narrative portions, there is perhaps not so much reason to expect any reference to the use of writing. As to Genesis, the Jewish commentator B. Jacob has drawn attention to the fact that is more likely a literary fiction than a true tradition, that the use of writing was unknown in pre-Mosaic times, a fiction which it was not possible to carry through entirely; *cf.* the term *sepher toledhoth* (book of generations) (Gen. 5:1), and the mention of Judah's signet (Gen. 38:18).[2] The fiction becomes apparent in Genesis 23:1–19, Abraham's purchase of the field with the cave of Machpelah. At this "oral" stage of Israelite culture *no* document is drawn up, although the business world was the largest employer of clerks then as it is now.[3]

In Exodus we come across the verb *kathabh* (write) eleven times, nine of them in Exodus 24 and 32–34, referring to the tablets of stone with the Decalogue, and one of them, Exodus 24:4, to the book of the Covenant. The two remaining instances are Exodus 39:30, which mentions the inscription "Holy to JHWH" on the frontlet of the High Priest, and Exodus 17:14—the only place in the Tetrateuch that mentions a really *literary* activity of Moses—the recording in a document of the victory over the Amalekites. In Numbers, evidence of writing is given five times: in the mention of Aaron's blossoming rod, Numbers 17:17 f. (the use of writing as a mark of ownership); the station catalogue, Numbers 33:2; 11:26, which states that the names of the seventy elders were written down; and Numbers 5:23, where the letters seem to possess a supernatural power, in the text which provides for the ordeal for a woman suspected of unfaithfulness, Numbers 5:11–31. Finally, we must mention Numbers 21:14, which speaks of a *sepher milhamoth YHWH* (the book of the wars of Yahve), a passage we shall return to later.

As to Deuteronomy and the Deuteronomistic history the matter stands thus, that the use of writing (from a statistical point of view) is concentrated on (a) "this Book of the Law," "the Book of the Law of Moses," "the Book of this Covenant" (the last expression from II Kings 23:21), and (b) the annals, which are mentioned for the first time towards the end of the account of Solomon, I Kings 11:41, and for the last time regarding the northern kingdom, II Kings 15:31 (Pekah b. Remaliah), and regarding the kingdom of Judah, II Kings 24:5 (Jehoiakim). The formula with which the Deuteronomist refers to these annals is usually: "Now the rest of the history of X, and all that he did, is it not written in the book of the Chronicles of the kings of Judah [Israel]?"

Even though we may surmise that written law-codices were very well-known in pre-exilic Israel,[4] we refrain from treating group (a) as pre-exilic material. The question of the transmission of the laws will be dealt with in connection with Joshua 24:25 and I Samuel 10:25.

As to the annals, the most divergent views have been expressed in the course of time. At one end we have Hölscher with his conception of the book of the Chronicles of the Kings of Judah, or Israel, as one great epic work continuing the Pentateuch, or rather those parts of the Pentateuch which are separated as the source E and are supposed to have been composed after 586 B.C.[5] At the other end stand Eissfeldt and Noth with the view that is a question of semi-official or private publications, published after the deaths of the kings in question, since two things are apparently presupposed by the Deuteronomist: 1. that anyone who desires to do so can read more in the works referred to; and 2. that the reign of each king is presented as a completed whole, a fact that is not at all characteristic of annals which are added to year by year.[6] It is, however, questionable whether these conclusions can be drawn from the well-known quotation formula. It may merely be that the Deuteronomist wished to provide his work with a stamp of guarantee and hence informs us that he has made use of the best sources, and that he has chosen the material which in his opinion was of essential importance. It would seem that the only necessary supposition is that the annals—both those of the northern kingdom and those of Judah—in some way survived the downfall of the kingdoms. The fact that Pekah and Jehoiakim are the last kings mentioned in the annals also supports this supposition. The collection of the northern annals must thus have been saved from destruction after the death of Pekah, but before the fall of Samaria, by being transferred into the kingdom of Judah, which at this time had inherited a large number of northern traditions, e.g., the legends of Elijah and Elisha, the prophecies of Hosea, etc.

In Deuteronomy itself, we find writing used for other purposes, in the administration of justice. Deuteronomy 24:1 ff. contains the decrees regarding divorce; here it is laid down that the man who wishes to be divorced must have a bill of divorcement drawn up—a practice which naturally dates from pre-exilic times, judging from the metaphorical use of the bill of divorcement in the prophets (Jer. 3:8; *cf.* also Isa. 50:1).

In Joshua 18:4 ff. we read that Joshua sent men out to survey the remaining parts of the West Jordan country. He instructs them to note down the results of their survey so that these can be used in the division of the land between the tribes that as yet had received no territory. The text may be attributed to the most recent strata in the book of Joshua.[7]

The political central administration could not dispense with writing. From the time of David one or more *sōphĕrīm* (scribes) make their appearance at the royal courts, but these are evidently high officials and not merely clerks; otherwise we should hardly have been told their names. In any case it is well worth-while to try to get a clear understanding of the functions of these men. Jeremiah 52:25 mentions a *sōphēr sar haṣṣābhā)* (scribe of the military commander) or, judging by the phrase, a man who might be secretary to the general, but the parallel passage in II Kings 25:19 has *hassōphēr sar haṣṣabha)*, which furnishes this man with direct military authority. In both recensions of the text it is said of him, that it was he who "caused the people of the land to be mustered," i.e., levied them for military service.[8] In the letters from the royal archives at Mari[9] a military person is mentioned by the little DUB.SAR=Acc. *ṭupšarru*, i.e., tablet-writer. In *TCL*, xxiii, No. 13, 29, he is mentioned between the "magnate of the West" (GAL.MAR.TU) and "captain and picked soldier"; his name was *Mašum*[10] and his special duty was to attend to the *tēbībtum*, a species of muster. This was held for each district[11] and served several purposes; first of all the one of ascertaining the number of men fit for service in the district concerned, and thus determining the contingent the district could provide. The conscripted soldiers had their names put down on lists and were obliged to remain in their home districts.[12] If the "scribe" *Mašum* is identical with the sender of letter No. 131 from *TCK*, xxiii, he also had regular military functions, for in this letter he describes his relief of a town which was threatened by 2000 Habiru.[13] In this connection it is interesting to note that a *sōphēr* (scribe) appears in one of the oldest texts in the Old Testament, the Song of Deborah, Judges 5:14, and that he evidently has a purely military function. But this can hardly surprise us when we consider that the Amorite culture, as it is revealed in the Mari texts, in many ways points forward to the culture of the invading Israelites.[14] Nevertheless it is significant that *sōphēr* as a regular institution first makes its appearance in the time of David, II Samuel 8:17; in the sanctuary legend of Jerusalem, II Samuel 24, we have a description of a census of the people remarkable as something quite new, a quite un-Israelite action; but it should be pointed out that David does not execute it by means of a *sōphēr* but with the aid of Joab and his men. The census has a military purpose; it is to muster the genuine Israelite citizens, *gibbōrē-hayil,* those who are to appear at the king's summons and who are subject to taxation.

It is characteristic of every ancient Near Eastern kingdom that its correspondence with the neighboring kingdoms was extensive, and even though the Old Testament sources relate nothing whatever of such a diplomatic correspondence, *from* the Israelite kings, we may surmise by analogy that, for instance, Solomon's messengers to King Hiram of Tyre were provided with letters, but in true oriental style as an aid to, and a means of control over, the orally delivered message.

The writing of letters is, however, expressly mentioned in the case of messages of a more private nature, but the known instances are all of a distinctly macabre nature. This is true both of David's letter written to Joab, the contents of which it was impossible to let the messenger deliver orally (II Sam. 11:14), and of Jezebel's letters to the elders of Jezreel expressing a desire to have Naboth slandered (I Kings 21:8). Jehu's letter to the elders of Samaria (II Kings 10:1 f.) also belongs to the sphere of the nefarious and could not at that time be proclaimed in public with its exhortation to the leading men of the city to make an end of the ruling dynasty. Here the *written* message evidently plays a considerable role and therefore the letters are expressly mentioned.

Before leaving the Deuteronomistic historical compilation we must examine some passages a little more closely. These are some phrases in connection with the Song of Moses (Deut. 31 f.) and Joshua 24:25 f. (Joshua gives the people statutes and ordinances and writes "these words in the book of the law of God") and I Samuel 10:25 (Samuel publicly recites the *mishpat* of the kingdom before the people and enters it in a book which he lays before the face of YHWH, i.e., in a YHWH sanctuary); further the well-known passages that expressly cite a written source for the lines quoted. These passages are Numbers 21:24, citing "the Book of the Wars of YHWH"; Joshua 10:13 and II Samuel 1:18, citing "the Book of the Upright," as well as I Kings 8:13, citing "the Book of Songs" (only in LXX, III Kings 8:53), which commentators often propose to change to "the Book of the Upright."[15]

The first group of passages is in literary critical circles typically enough referred to different sources: Joshua 24:26 to E, I Samuel 10:25 is considered a later addition, Deuteronomy 31:9 ff. is denoted Dt with the exception of the portion of this chapter dealing with the Song of Moses which is referred to a special source X. By mentioning *hok ū-mishpāt* (statute and judgment), Joshua 24:25, the group of passages clearly reveals its connection in tradition with Exodus 15:25, where it is stated that Moses at one of the springs in the Kadesh oasis gave the people *hōkū-mishpāt,* a passage which is normally referred to as J. We will here ignore the distinction between sources, and instead indicate the significance in the fact that these references do not appear at chance points in Old Testament tradition, but at crucial moments in the history of Israel where one epoch succeeds another.

As the first point in the history of Israel's law, the Sinai-Kadesh tradition is mentioned with its fundamental revelation. The next point is Moses' farewell to the people in the country east of Jordan; the conquest of the land and then the assembly in Shechem form the third milestone; and finally as the fourth link in the chain comes the decisive step which makes Israel a state and introduces the monarchy. It is characteristic of all these traditions that the law is promulgated publicly and orally, and that it is afterwards written down and that this document is deposited in a sanctuary of YHWH. So the tradition of a lawbook found in a temple of YHWH, II Kings 22 f., does not come upon the reader of the Deuteronomistic historian without the necessary preparation.

More interesting to us in this connection is the fact that the law-tradition is of a double nature. When once the law has been ratified in an assembly of the people on the basis of an oral promulgation, it is written down and deposited in the holy place. But this does not mean that the oral recitation of the law ceases. In Deuteronomy 31:9–11, the responsible leaders of the people are commanded to see to it that the law is orally promulgated in the assembly of all Israel when the people are gathered together every seventh year at the feast of tabernacles before the face of YHWH in the place where He lets His name dwell. This double method of tradition reminds one strikingly of the mode of tradition of the Homeric poems.

Let us dwell a moment on the fact that this text has become a point of departure for an interesting hypothesis as to the function of the "minor" Judges as "law reciters." The latter designation is taken from a culture which is geographically as well as historically quite remote from the Israelite, viz., that of ancient Iceland, which has parallels with ancient Israelite culture in other fields, too. The credit for first making such a comparison between these two cultures belongs to A. Klostermann.[16] He finds points of similarity between the old Icelandic law-book "Gragas" and Deuteronomy: they must both be considered largely as a reduction to writing of the public recital of the law, and in reality they are both old law plus commentary. The literary form of the Icelandic law-book, which betrays its oral past by the mnemotechnic arrangement of material, is explained by the position of law in life. After Ulfliot had established an initial constitution and judicial system, the transmission of the laws was attended to by men chosen for this office; these "logsogumaor" had the office of reciting large portions of the law at the annual assemblies (called "things"). With the changing times modifications and additions are introduced, "Nymaeli" are added, but the law remains itself in its essence.[17] As to Deuteronomy, we have from the surrounding texts the rule cited above which clearly states that the law is to be read every seventh year at the feast of Tabernacles. Moses' own oral declaration of the law is expressly designated in Deuteronomy 1:5 as an explanation of the words of the law; according to tradition he combines in his person the function of both the law-giver and the law-reciter. He also resembles the Icelandic law-reciter in that the more intricate legal decisions are reserved for him, Deuteronomy 1:17, Exodus 18:22. Joshua must likewise be considered a law-reciter, and he and Samuel are both said to have added "Nymaeli" to the Mosaic codex (Josh. 24:25 f. and I Sam. 10:25). Between Joshua and Samuel we have the "minor" judges,[18] men who were neither priests nor heroes, but who are remembered because they "judged Israel." We must regard these men as being full of understanding and well versed in the true tradition, and it was their privilege to convene and to lead general assemblies of the people. Almost thirty years later this hypothesis has been endorsed by Alt[19] and it is shared by Noth,[20] who in this context denies that the monarchy had any influence on the framing of Israelite law, as we find it in the Old Testament—a view which a closer analysis, however, will prove to be illusory.

The other group of passages seems to bear unmistakable witness to the fact that writing was already used for real literary purposes in early pre-exilic times. We have at least two different literary works mentioned by name, "the Book of the Wars of YHWH" and the "Book of the Upright."

From the "Book of the Upright" comes a verse which refers to Joshua's war against the Southern Canaanite coalition under the leadership of Adoni-zedek, king of Jerusalem (Josh. 10:13), and David's lament for Saul and Jonathan (II Sam. 1:18); and possibly also Solomon's words at the dedication of the Temple at Jerusalem (I Kings 8:13). Already the fact that these poems— between the origin of which there may be several centuries—here stand side by side in the same work, so that an author writing in the sixth century can refer to them, must demand our attention and caution. Which is more likely, that at the time of Joshua, one began to compile a work called "the Book of the Upright," and through the centuries continued to add new material to it, or that the poems from the time of Joshua and later generations lived on the lips of the bards, until at some unknown time and from motives as to which we can only conjecture, these poems—chosen in the course of tradition and time—were collected into a book, and called "the Book of the Upright"? I have no doubt but that the latter is the more probable. Perhaps our conception is substantiated in another way, by the words connected with David's lament for Saul and Jonathan. We read in II Samuel 1:17 f.: "And David made the following lamentation over the bodies of Saul and his son Jonathan, and he commanded them to teach the children of Judah a bow [?]." *Kesheth* (bow) seems very peculiar here; it is omitted in LXX and this has given rise to doubts as to the integrity of the text.[21] The Hebrew Massoretic text, which is *lectio difficilior* (harder reading) and is further supported by the Syriac version, the Peshitta, must be retained; it might be possible to understand *Kesheth* as the name of the poem in which the picture of Jonathan's bow occupies such a prominent place. The words *lelammēdh benē-Yehūdhāh* (to teach Judah's sons) do not in any case belong to the usual late heading with which the Old Testament Psalms are so well supplied. It is only to be found in one case, Psalm 60; more recent study of the Psalms has attempted to move this Psalm back some 800 years, from the time of the Maccabees to the time of David. *Lammēdh* means "to impress upon others by oral teaching"; the word is especially characteristic of the framework of Deuteronomy.

Thus the texts mentioned here can hardly *prove* that writing was in use for literary purposes in early pre-exilic times, and it is hardly advisable to *surmise* a literary activity of this kind until the approach of the time when the culture as a whole tended to a written fixation of its tradition.

In reality Numbers 21:13–14 points in the same direction: "From thence they removed and pitched camp on the other side of Arnon, which is in the wilderness that comes out from the territory of the Amorites. Rightly is it said in the book of the wars of YHWH, 'Waheb in Sufa and the gorges, Arnon and the slope of the gorges, which goes down to the seat of Ar and leans toward the territory of Moab.' " The quotation is evidently cited because of the last three or four words which show that Arnon is the boundary river of Moab. It is clear that there is no inner connection between a quotation from "the Book of the Wars of YHWH," a travel record which gives the route from the wilderness of Sinai to the East Jordan country, and the account of the battles between the Moabites and the Amorites. This fragment of a song of victory[22] must—since it is an Israelite one—refer to the boundary between *Israel* and Moab. YHWH has given the people possession of the land of the Amorites; this is the narrator's presupposition and that is why he gives the quotation here. But typically enough he has not yet related that YHWH had given the land of the Amorites to Israel; this is first mentioned in verses 21 f. Seen from the narrator's viewpoint—and still more from that of the traditionists—these events belong to the distant past; the "territory of the Amorites" has long ago become the East Jordan possessions of Israel, and therefore it is affirmed on the evidence of the Book of the Wars of YHWH that the boundary of Moab really is Arnon. This quotation which establishes a boundary presupposes two things: (1) Israel must have become settled, and (2) the Moabites must have been forced back beyond Arnon. This situation does not arise in the time of the Judges, as the Moabites still possessed land beyond the Jordan, Judges 3:12. It is only under David that the Moabites are subdued (II Sam. 8:2), and subsequently by Omri (II Kings 3:4 f., and Mesha inscription, 11. 4–8). During or after the reign of Ahab, Moab advances again, and it is an open question whether still another Israelite king, *viz.,* Jeroboam II, about the middle of the eighth century (II Kings 14:25), succeeded in driving the Moabites back beyond the Arnon.[23] At least after his time the Moabites rule the territories north of the Arnon, for Isaiah 15 mentions Nebo, Medeba, Heshbon, and Jahaz as towns of Moab. Thus, the quotation in Numbers 21:14 can originate from any of three epochs in the history of Israel, the time of David, Omri, or Jeroboam II. Now II Kings 14:25 states expressly that the victories of Jeroboam to the north-east and the south-east were accomplished according to the word of a prophet of YHWH;[24] is it not natural, then, to see a connection between this quotation from "the Book of the Wars of YHWH" and Jonah b. Amittai? Perhaps the objection will be raised that it is a strangely reversed method of procedure to try to "confirm" older traditions by younger ones. Quite apart from the fact that such things may be pointed out in other cases too in the Old Testament,[25] one must remember the Israelite's attitude towards tradition. It is to him a world from which his life has drawn nourishment; he lives in it, is strengthened in it, and it gives him a goal for his exertions. Therefore it is only a half truth that in Numbers 21 it is the old traditions that are supported by a new; it is just as true that it is the present situation of the Israelite which is supported by the traditions of the past, "Rightly is it said in the book of the wars of YHWH. . . ."

There remains the question of the character of this book from which the quotation is taken. If it is true that the quotation is rhythmical, that we here have a fragment of a song of victory or a song of derision, "the Book of the Wars of YHWH" may to a certain degree be considered a parallel to "the Book of the Upright." The latter is a collection of songs, apparently of southern, Judaean origin, while "the Book of the Wars of YHWH" according to the presentation above must be considered a collection of north Israelite poems. It can presumably at the earliest have been completed towards the end of Jeroboam II's reign, and at the latest before the fall of Samaria. This brings us to a time disturbed by the onslaught of Assyria in the West, and it is quite possible that a feeling of crisis spread in some circles of the Israelite people, and that the glorious traditions and oracles slowly began to be written down.[26]

There is no room here for a comprehensive account of the use the prophets made, or did not make, of writing in the pre-exilic times . . . But in connection with what we have said above about the importance of a feeling of political crisis as a motive for the increase of literary activity, we would like to raise the supplementary question: Why does "written" prophecy begin with precisely Amos and Hosea in the northern kingdom and with Isaiah in the southern kingdom? The consummate literary form of their books shows clearly they cannot be regarded merely as an incipient beginning of something completely new. And yet since the victory of the historico-critical method of Bible research in the last century the most common conception is that with Amos something new and exceptional comes into being in world history, personality-religion is fashioned by these men's experiences of God in a world and a community, the religion of which might be characterized as "static nature religion."[27] Due only to the circumstance that the prophets themselves saw to it that their works were published,[28] we have a large portion of their preaching preserved. An attempt has been made to prove their creative contribution in the *literary* field, but our increasing acquaintance with the literature of the ancient Near East as well as our revised conception of the date of the origin of, e.g., the Israelite psalms, together with our changing conception of the relation of the prophets to the cult,[29] is a definite argument to the contrary. The prophets were supposed to be revolutionary in their *ethical* preaching. This viewpoint is, however, only tenable so long as one regards the Israelite *laws* as late pre-exilic literature, reflecting the prophetic message in many points. But who in our days dare acknowledge the view that God as a God of righteousness is a theological tenet created by the later Israelite prophets? The prologue to Codex Hammurabi (1:32 f.) says that the gods have made Hammurabi king "in order to let righteousness shine forth in the land, to abolish the wicked and the criminal, so that the mighty shall not abuse the weak," and in the epilogue we read (24: 59–62): "in order that the mighty shall not oppress the weak, and that orphans and widows may receive justice." Hence the new contribution of prophetism was thought to consist in the fact that these men were so imbued with righteousness on behalf of YHWH that they had to preach the *uncompromising judgment* of the apostate people. Their entirely unique message was thought to be this: YHWH had finally rejected His people

D

because of their sins. But this interpretation can only be maintained by first casting suspicion on the "positive statements" in
Amos (9:11–15), Hosea (2), Isaiah (2:1–4, 9, 11, etc.) and
Micah (2:12–13, 4–5), or re-interpreting them (Isa. 7). Instead
one ought to try to find something that is common to at least
the main portion of the collections of prophetic oracles which
have been handed down to us, something that in a characteristic
way distinguishes the preaching of these men from that of such
men as Ahijah of Shiloh (I Kings 14), Micaiah b. Imlah (I
Kings 22), Elijah (I Kings 17 ff.), and Elisha (I Kings 19 ff.),
as well as from the prophets in the countries surrounding Israel.
This is the line that has been attempted by scholars in modern
times. I may here refer to Engnell's paper on "Profetismens
ursprung och uppkomst,"[30] where he points out that the common
ground for prophets such as Amos and Hosea is their preaching
of Jerusalem's YHWH and their struggle for the Jerusalem kingship. Their preaching may be called genuinely Israelite in so far
as they stand in the main current of Israel's own religious history,
that of Jerusalem and Deuteronomy. As a genuinely Israelite
prophet in this sense Amos is "perhaps . . . not the first but
the first we have any certain knowledge of."[31] And now we
proceed to the answer to our question. If this Jerusalem-Deu-
teronomic tendency can be discovered also in the written prophets
from the time before the exile, it is comprehensible why the
words of just these prophets have survived; especially considering
the fact that the centuries in which they were active are remarkable for the fall of the northern kingdom, its destruction as an
independent state and, as a consequence of this, the rising hope
of the Judaeans for the re-establishment of the kingdom of David
under the leadership of Jerusalem[32] (Amos 9:11 ff.; Mic. 5:2 ff.;
Isa. 7; Jer. 3; etc.). This does not imply that the preaching of
Jeremiah, for instance, is exhaustively characterized. He preaches
judgment and righteousness as well, and as poet and lyricist he
represents the acme in Old Testament literature. But the fact
that his prophecies have been preserved is presumably due not
so much to these factors as to the fact that the "Deuteronomists"
were able to use his message because his hopes of a reunion of

the two brother-nations merely represents the leading thought of the Deuteronomist, expressed in another way.

We conclude this section on the use of writing in pre-exilic Israel by inquiring whether archaeology has anything to say in confirmation or refutation of our thesis.

So far no inscriptions, tablets, or documents from pre-exilic times have been found in Palestine which might be designated as Israelite literature. The epigraphical material we have is easily surveyed: Ostraca from Samaria, informing us of the Israelite court household of the time of Jeroboam II, and from the time cf Hezekiah the Siloam inscription which relates an episode from the completion of this undertaking. Above all we have from the last days of the kingdom of Judah the Lachish letters, ostraca sent to the Judaean commander Ya'ōsh in Lachish, the present Tell ed-Duweir.[33] These letters are indeed not without importance for our subject as they seem to give us some notion of the ability to read and write in this period. Letter No. 3, lines 8–13,[34] has been variously interpreted and this is true of the letter as a whole. We cite one of the earliest and one of the most recent translations, by Torczyner and Albright.

On Torczyner's rendering,[35] Ya'ōsh, the commandant of Lachish, has sent a letter to the sender of this letter, Hōsha'yāhū, and dwelt on the fact: "that he says: My Lord, I do not know to read a letter. Yahweh lives (to punish me) if anybody has tried to read to me a letter for ever. And also, whatever letter came to me I have not read it and not even seen anything of it." On this Torczyner makes the following remark: "It is certainly not a matter of course that everybody could read and write at that time." To a passage in Letter No. 4, which was presumably sent by the same Hōsha'yāhū and reads: "I have written on the page according to whatever my lord has sent to me," Torczyner remarks: " 'I have written' must certainly not be meant as 'written by my hand,' but may well be 'made (my scribe) write' as in many similar examples in the Bible and in all ancient literature" (see Jer. 30:2, 36:19, 51: 59–62).[36]

The rendering of *ydth* by the first person singular has, however, been disputed and is hardly correct. Albright's translation

reads thus: "And as for what my Lord said, 'Dost thou not understand?—call a scribe!' As Yahweh liveth no one hath ever under-
taken to call a scribe for me; and as for any scribe who might
have come to me, truly, I did not call him nor would I give
anything at all for him!"[37] Here *lo ydth* is construed as a question,
sphr is vocalized sōphēr (scribe) instead of sēpher (book). Both
these interpretations show clearly and unmistakably that writing
belonged to the craftsman, even when it was a case of the relatively simple Canaanite alphabetic writing (in which the Lachish
letters are written), and that even men of authority[38] were—or
could be conceived of as—illiterate. Could one wish for any
better confirmation of Nyberg's words: "The art of writing was
the business of the *ḥaṣṣat* (specialist) and not that of the *āmmat*
(layman), as it always has been in the east."[39]

2. We may now briefly consider the other side of our problem,
and seek the positive evidence for the existence of an oral tradition in Israel. In the case of the legal material we have already
touched on the importance of oral tradition in connection with
Klostermann's hypothesis regarding Deuteronomy and the minor
Judges. To be sure we regard it as impossible to consider the
Deuteronomy we know as a sample of pre-exilic literature—for
instance, as being identical with Josiah's law-book from 622 B.C.
It should, however, be possible to speak of a Deuteronomistic
trend in the culture of pre-exilic Israel, and its first origin should
be sought—in agreement with Noth—in the sacred institution
which constituted itself under the name of Israel as a union of
twelve tribes, an amphictyony, in central Palestine (*cf.* Josh. 24).
The Deuteronomic laws may in the course of time have developed
from the oral recitation of laws, periodically held in the Israelite
assemblies. If we consider Deuteronomy itself it is immediately
and forcibly impressed upon us that the introductory as well as
the concluding parenetical (hortatory) sections were based on the
oral recitation of the laws.

(a) Deuteronomy 1:5 itself indicates the entire following work
as Moses' own oral, expository recitation of the law. Deuteronomy 4:1 depicts the situation: "Now therefore hearken, O Israel,
unto the statutes and judgments, which I teach you, to do them,

that ye may live and go in and possess the land which YHWH, the God of your fathers gives you." Or 4:8: "And what nation is there so great, that hath statutes and judgments so righteous as all this law, which I set before you *this day*?" Furthermore, 4:20: "But the Lord hath taken you and brought you forth out of the iron furnace, even out of Egypt, to be unto him a people of his own inheritance, as ye are *this day*." Or again, 4:38–40a: YHWH led the people forth out of Egypt "to drive out nations from before thee greater and mightier than thou art, to bring thee in, to give thee their land for an inheritance as it is *this day*. Know therefore *this day* and consider it in thy heart, that YHWH is God in heaven above and upon earth beneath; there is none else. Thou shalt keep therefore his statutes and his commandments which I command thee *this day*. . . ." The entire fourth chapter with its ever recurrent "this day" reflects its use at the assemblies.

(b) But we can define a little more precisely the cultic aspect of this "assembly" which in Deuteronomy 31:11 is expressly stated to take place at the feast of Tabernacles, or in other words at the New Year festival, the autumn festival, which after the introduction of the monarchy was the royal festival proper in Israel. In the slightly historicized introduction to the Decalogue we still clearly perceive the cultic actualization of the creative deeds of the past: "And Moses called all Israel and said unto them: 'Hear, O Israel, the statutes and judgments which I speak in your ears this day, and ye shall learn them and keep them so that ye do them. YHWH our God made a covenant with us in Horeb. Not with our fathers made YHWH this covenant, but with us, even us who are all of us alive this day' " (Deut. 5:1–3). If Psalm 95 is an enthronement psalm, the passage "Today when ye hear his voice, harden not your hearts as in Meribah . . ." (vv. 7–8) throws an interesting light on this festival of the covenant and popular assembly.[40] A festival of the covenant coinciding with a royal festival must certainly be interpreted this way: the king is recognized as being responsible for God's law to the people. Seen against our knowledge of the religious conditions of the kings of Israel and Judah, influenced as it is by the Deuteronomist, this may seem strange to us. Yet it is no more remarkable than that Hammurabi holds the same position as an intermediate between Marduk—or Shamash if one prefers—and his subjects.[41]

(c) But the Old Testament also assumes a transmission of the law which is not connected with the great festivals or sanctuaries alone, the father's oral teaching of his household, and especially of his sons. There is direct evidence of this in our texts, and there is not the slightest reason to deny that such a teaching in the home took place in a community permeated to the core by patriarchal ideas. The home is a miniature national community. Just as the people may be said to be concentrated in a single individual, the chieftain or the king, who in himself bears the destiny of the people and whose acts have consequences for the future of the whole people, so too the *paterfamilias* is "the centre from which strength and will emanate through the whole of the sphere which belongs to him and to which he belongs."[42] Just as the community on certain occasions is confronted by the fundamental principles of its existence, so too is the family (*cf.* Exod. 12:26; 13:8, 14; Deut. 4:9–10; 6:7, 20 f., etc.).

In this connection it would be natural to glance at the Wisdom literature, by which the teacher's fatherly relation to his pupil reveals a spiritual affinity to the father's teaching of his sons. It becomes more and more apparent that this type of literature extended through the whole ancient Orient and was exceedingly old; it was especially cultivated in the schools as a special type, and was thus presumably from the very first intimately connected with the art of writing and the scribes.[43] If we examine the book of Proverbs with this in mind we shall undoubtedly be surprised to note that in one place only in all these collections is the use of writing directly affirmed, Proverbs 22:20: "Do I not write to thee 'thirty,' with counsel and knowledge?" and that this passage in all probability refers to the Egyptian book of Wisdom, which bears the name of Amen-em-ope. For this book contains exactly thirty chapters, and a portion of their contents is given in the immediately following section of Proverbs. On the other hand, we find the expression "to write upon the tablets of one's heart" in several places (3:1 and 7:1 f.). This phrase must be compared with the Arabic expression about the Qurân, that it "lives in the hearts of the believers," i.e., they know it by heart.[44] Besides this, Proverbs contains direct evidence of the oral form of teaching, as when we read in 1:5:

> The wise man shall hear and increase his knowledge,
> The man of understanding shall attain unto the art of living . . . .

and also in 2:1 f.:

> My son, when thou receivest my words
> and hidest my commandments with thee
> by opening thine ear to wisdom,
> and applying thy thought to understanding . . . .[45]

Finally we may briefly mention that the book of Proverbs ends with a poem, the stanzas of which are arranged alphabetically, i.e., according to the initial letter of the stanza. This is interesting evidence of the fact that the circles that were familiar with the art of writing did not reject the oral method of transmission. For it is difficult to imagine any other reason for an alphabetical composition and arrangement of the stanzas in this manner than the wish to procure a mnemonic aid.

The views that are here applied to the Proverbs are undoubtedly also valid to a certain extent for the Israelite Book of Psalms. Since we are so fortunate as to possess parallel [repeated] psalms in the Book of Psalms, and these are not quite identical in their present textual form, we can by examining these variants establish errors of hearing and thus prove that the oral tradition played its part in the composition of the Israelite Psalms.[46]

As to the prophetic and historical literature I shall [later] to make some analyses which should demonstrate what is characteristic of the traditio-historical method. Among recent traditio-historical discussions of the Old Testament historical books we may especially mention A. S. Kapelrud, *The Question of Authorship in the Ezra Narrative,* 1944.

3. We have attempted to establish the insignificant role of writing in pre-exilic Israel, and we have drawn forth some more or less unmistakable testimonies to the importance of oral trans-

mission, testimonies taken from the Old Testament itself. And at the same time we have indicated reasons for the fact that writing at a certain epoch in the history of Israelite-Judaean culture gains an importance as a preserver of tradition which it had not earlier had in even approximately the same degree. To conclude we will briefly sum up these indications.

The change from oral to written literature does not take place because cultural summits have been reached, nor because the ability to read and write has become common property, but because the culture itself is threatened—from within by syncretism, and from without by political events. This change occurred, for Judah, presumably towards the end of the seventh century or at the beginning of the sixth; for northern Israel, perhaps a century and a half earlier. But it is neither consummated all at once nor does it put an end to oral transmission. To be sure there is a characteristic difference between the way in which Jeremiah is entrusted with the words of YHWH and the way in which Ezekiel is charged with them (Jer. 1:9; Ezek. 2:8–3:9); and certainly it is symptomatic that it is precisely in Ecclesiastes that we find a phrase such as: "And further, my son, be admonished! there is no end of the many books that are written, and much study wearies the flesh," and that the book of Esther alone contains one and a half times as many allusions to the use of writing as the whole Tetrateuch, though the latter fills twenty times as much space in the Hebrew Bible. Nevertheless, scarcely any other period can equal the oral tradition of Judaism as it has been deposited in the Talmud.[47]

It would lead too far here to demonstrate what forces and motives cause the formation of a written canon and a "supplementary" oral tradition in one and the same period. One has the feeling that when once society has been somewhat consolidated through the incipient formation of a written canon, there is again room for oral tradition, and in this case its task will be to adjust an authoritative basis for the life of the community—which is now fixed in writing—to living conditions that have changed in the meantime. In this way history has evidently repeated itself many times; the Church and Islam are both outstanding examples of this. When one comes to think of it, it is a strange phenomenon that a writing or a collection of writings at some period in the history of a movement, a community, a confession, or a church, is canonized and that in the future it maintains the character of a binding authority. Judaism, which has formed a school in this field, may perhaps have remembered forerunners of the canon from the earlier history of Israel. But whether the absolute validity which is attached to writing in theology—and which is practically manifested by the care of the Massoretes for the text—can be explained by Israel's own history, is perhaps rather doubtful.[48]

NOTES

1. *Studien zum Hoseabuche*, 1935, p. 8.

2. *Genesis*, 1934, p. 320.

3. In Accadian culture it was the rule that only the agreement that was fixed in writing was juridically valid. *Cf.* O. Weber, *Die Literatur der Babylonier und Assyrer*, 1907, p. 249. A comparison between Genesis 23 and Jeremiah 32 forces itself upon us. Jeremiah has to have a written contract drawn up and has to conclude the bargain before witnesses, which again goes to show that the written word evidently did not have the same independent position that it has in our culture. With this one might compare, for instance, Codex Hammurabi §§ 122–124, which deal with the depositing of movables in the care of a fellow citizen. This must be done before witnesses and with a written contract, but the fact that the witnesses are the main point, psychologically speaking, is evident, since they are named first and the contract is not mentioned at all in § 124 (though naturally implied). The juridical contracts of daily life were furnished with the seals and (or) names of the witnesses.

4. Hosea 8:12: "Though I wrote my commands by the myriad for him, they were counted as a strange thing"; Isaiah 10:1: "Woe unto them that issue decrees of wickedness, and unto the scribes that always write anguish"; Jeremiah 8:8: "How canst thou say, We are wise and the law of YHWH is with us? Verily, the lying pen of the scribes has brought forth lies."

5. "Das Buch der Könige . . . ," in *Eucharisterion*, 1923, p. 181.

6. Eissfeldt, *Einleitung*, 1934, p. 322; M. Noth, *Überlieferungsgeschichtliche Studien*, i, 1943, p. 73.

7. *Cf.* Noth's commentary on the passage.

8. *Cf.* Gesenius-Buhl *s.v. ṣābhā', Hiph.

9. The present Tell Ḥarīri on the middle course of the Euphrates. The archives which date from the eighteenth to the seventeenth centuries, and contain correspondence with Hammurabi of Babylon, are being published by G. Dossin, C.-F. Jean, and J. R. Kupper.

10. *TCL*, xxii, No. 60, 6.

11. *TCL*, xxii, No. 62, 5 f.

12. *Cf.* W. von Soden, "Die altbabylonische Briefarchiv von Mari," *Die Welt des Orients*, 1947, pp. 187–204. I am grateful to Mr. Laessøe of Copenhagen University for the above references to *TCL*. on *tēbītum, cf.* C.-F. Jean in *RA*, 1948, pp. 140 ff., and especially pp. 196 f., and J. R. Kupper in *Studia Mariana*, 1950, pp. 99–110.

13. The letter has recently been translated by Albright in Pritchard, *ANET*, 1950, p. 483. It is particularly interesting on account of its mention of signalling by means of light, a species of telegraphy which is recorded in the O.T., Jeremiah 6:1, as well as in Lachish Letter No. 4, and in the Jewish tradition; *cf.* Rosh ha-Shanah, 2:2 f. See H. Torczyner, *The Lachish Letters*, 1938, p. 83.

14. *Cf. banū-jamina* and Benjamites; the concluding of a covenant by sacrifice, in Mari by the killing of an ass; *cf.* the name of the leading clan in the covenant town of Shechem, *benē-Hamōr;* the mention of a military leader with the title *dawidum,* with which the Meša inscription's *dwdh* (l. 12) may be compared; and finally the mention of the bands of Ḥabiru operating in several places, *cf.* the Hebrews of the Passover legend.

15. *Cf.* Kittel, *Bibl. Heb.*, 3rd ed., *ad loc.*

16. *Der Pentateuch*, N. F., 1907, esp, pp. 348–428. Buhl says of Klostermann as a scholar in *Det israelitiske folks historie*, 7th ed., 1936, p. 15: "He went his own ways far from the usual main paths of modern research."

17. *Op. cit.*, p. 415.

18. Judges 10:1–5 and 12:7–15. They were six in number, were of distinguished rank and well-to-do. Jephthah, a half-blood, probably only attained to the dignity because he had previously been the deliverer. Shamgar did not belong to the "minor" judges.

19. *Die Ursprünge des isr. Rechts*, 1934, p. 31.

20. *Die Gesetze im Pentateuch*, 1940, p. 48. Noth urges the connection between the religious league of the twelve tribes which came into existence after the conquest, the amphictyony, and the O.T. laws.

21. Cf. Kittel, *Bibl. Heb.*, 3rd ed., and Gesenius-Buhl, *Handwörterbuch, s.v.* Ḳesheth.

22. Or a song of derision? Cf. Eissfeldt, *Einleitung*, 1934, pp. 99 f.

23. Amos 6:14 indicates the extent of the kingdom at the time of this

king in this way: "From the entering in of Hamath unto the stream of Arabah," and II Kings 14:25 reads: "He [Jeroboam II] restored the territory of Israel from the entering of Hamath unto the sea of Arabah, according to the word of YHWH, the God of Israel, which he spoke by his servant, the prophet Jonah b. Amittai, who was of Gath-ha-Hepher." While scholars are agreed that *yām hā'arābhāh* is a designation of the Dead Sea, it has been difficult to reach an agreement as to the location of *naḥal hā-'arābhāh* (*cf.* Hammershaimb, *Amos,* 1946, pp, 104 f.). It is most reasonable to surmise that *naḥal hā-'arābhāh* must be a stream or river flowing into the Dead Sea. When it is used as a designation of the southern boundary of Israel in such a lapidary passage, it must be a stream of some significance in the minds of the people, and it was perhaps considered the ideal boundary for Israel; *cf.* the parallel text in II Kings 14:25: "He *restored.* . . . ." I therefore suggest that *naḥal hā-'arābhāh* should be considered a poetic circumlocution for the Arnon, especially as Amos in his threats against Moab only mentions one Moabite town (Amos 2:2), probably the capital of Moab proper, Qeriyoth, presumably identical with the Ar of Isaiah 15:1, and certainly situated south of the Arnon, but he does not mention either Mēdebā, 'Ataroth, or Dībōn, all situated north of the Arnon. According to his inscription (11:9 f.), Mesha recaptured these towns from Israel. If these towns had belonged to Moab, when Amos was active in Bethel, he would surely have mentioned them in the passage above; the analogy with the other words of Amos in chapters 1–2 go to prove this. At any rate we venture to conclude that Jeroboam II really had succeeded in driving the Moabites out.

24. *Cf.* the preceding note.

25. Thus the episode Jeremiah 26:20–24 can hardly have taken place before the events mentioned in 26:1–19. But the episode is related in order to throw the risk Jeremiah ran into relief. *Cf.* also Acts 5:34 f.

26. In *ZATW,* N. F., xii, pp. 130–152: "Hat es ein israelitisches National-alepos gegeben?" Mowinckel assumes the identity of these two collections. His argument rests on an assumption which it is easier to refute than to prove; that Numbers 21:17 is also a quotation from "the Book of the Wars of YHWH." In his article he emphasizes the oral tradition as well as the late composition of the work.

27. That this conception has lasted until our own time is evident from a chapter which is strangely "out of fashion" in many regards, "Jeremia og Religionshistorien," the introductory chapter to H. Birkeland's book on Jeremiah, 1950 (in the series *Religionens stormenn*). He overlooks almost entirely the connection between the later Israelite prophets and the earlier Israelite prophetism and prophetism in the surrounding countries, and thus obscures the structure of later Israelite prophetism.

28. Birkeland, op. cit., modifies this and says there were at least some who understood, or thought they understood, these new men, and therefore passed on their words until they were finally written down.

29. It should be superfluous to point out that a new departure in this field was made by S. Mowinckel in his Psalmenstudien, I–VI (1921–24).

30. In Religion och Bibel, 1949, pp. 1–18.

31. Op. cit., p. 18.

32. As long as the northern kingdom existed as an independent kingdom these hopes were in vain; cf. II Kings 14:8 f. (Amaziah of Judah and Joash of Israel).

33. The letters are edited by H. Torczyner, The Lachish Letters (1938). The relevant literature is becoming quite voluminous.

34. Torczyner, op. cit., plates on pp. 46–47.

35. Torczyner, p. 51, commentary, p. 65.

36. No. 4, plates on pp. 76–77, 11. 3–4, commentary, p. 81.

37. In Pritchard's ANET, 1950, p. 322.

38. Hōsha 'yāhū presumably held military rank.

39. Studien zum Hoseabuche, p. 8.

40. On the connection of Psalm 95 with the festival of the covenant and the transmission of the law, see for instance Mowinckel, Le Décalogue, 1927, pp. 121–133.

41. On the king as the bearer of the law, see e.g., Östborn, Tōrā in the Old Testament, 1945, ch. 3. Cf. too my article: "The Righteous and the Wicked in the Book of Habaqquq," Studia Theologica, VI, i, 1953, pp. 54 ff.

42. Johs. Pedersen, Israel: Its Life and Culture, I–II, 1926, p. 63.

43. There is a detailed monograph on this subject by L. Dürr, Das Erziehungswesen im Alten Testament und im Antiken Orient, MVAG, xxxvi, 2, 1932.

44. Johs. Pedersen, Den arabiske Bog, 1946, p. 14.

45. Cf. further 4:1–5; 5:1–2; 6:21; 8:1 f.

46. An analysis of this nature is H. Ringgren, "Oral and Written Tradition," Studia Theologica, III, i, 1951, pp. 34–59.

47. For literature, cf. Nielsen, Oral Tradition, p. 21, note 2.

48. It is a well-known fact that Mohammedan theologians consider the Qurân an earthly copy of the heavenly book. Related conceptions may be found in the Old Testament, most clearly in Ezekiel's vision at his call where the prophet describes how a book is given to him to eat, and in it sighs and woe were written. This is of course the prophecy of doom for which he was to be the mouthpiece in the ensuing days. The Old Testament also speaks of heavenly books in quite a different way: of God's own book of doom in which the iniquities of every man are entered (Isa. 65:6 f.), and of the heavenly census-paper in which the true worshippers of YHWH are written, and where their names can be

blotted out if they turn aside from Him (*cf.* Ezek, 13:1 f.; Exod. 32:32 f.; Isa. 4:3, Mal. 3:16: Pss. 40:7, 69:28). In "Mesopotamian Theology III," *Orientalia*, xix, No. 2., 1950, pp. 155 ff., A. Leo Oppenheim refers to the conclusion of the Irra myth as a proof that Mesopotamian theologians were not unacquainted with the conception of a heavenly book. The god Išum showed the poet in a vision the poem about Irra, and in the morning the poet wrote it down without adding or omitting a single word. The already mentioned colophon from a hymn to Ea, Shamash, Marduk, and Sin contains the technical word for a canonical, authoritative text, GAB.RI,la-bi-ru. Cf. *AfO*, xii, p. 245. This reference I owe to Mr. J. Laessøe.

5

THE HAGGADA WITHIN SCRIPTURE

Samuel Sandmel

"Haggada" is the term used in rabbinic literature for the embellishments of, and additions to, the narrative accounts of the biblical personalities. The title of the essay is its thesis, namely, that such embellishments of and additions to the content of the tradition did not await the postbiblical period, but arose within Scripture itself.

My essay represents a reaction away from the particulars of the Graf-Wellhausen hypothesis, in which I too was systematically trained, in the direction of the Scandinavian school. It represents, however, a reaction away from the Scandinavian emphasis on oral tradition, this in reasserting the significance of the written, as over and against the oral. The essay, though, affirming the high antiquity of some of the narrative materials, rejects the view of J as an ancient unified document; it sets forth that there was never an E source or an RJE. It ascribes the double, and occasional triple, traditions to purposeful recasting of a written source by a later hand, rather than the existence side by side of divergent, ancient accounts. The essay does not touch directly on the issue found in the two essays of Noth and Bright as to whether or not the presettlement period is prehistory. My opinion inclines more to Bright's than to Noth's, for I believe, against Noth, that Israel was an entity of some kind prior to the settlement. I would diverge from Bright in the following way, that with him I am prepared to argue for the presence of tenable history in the patriarchal material, yet I have found no satisfying method by which to disentangle the historical from the nonhistorical. The materials, in my judgment, were not created out of thin air, or solely out of an etiological purpose, but it is impossible for me to distinguish in any broad way between historical kernels I believe present, and the embellishments which for me obscure these kernels.

I

This essay* may seem to some an effort to drive still another nail into the coffin of the Graf-Wellhausen hypothesis, but that would be an indirect result rather than a deliberate purpose. So as not to be misunderstood, I should state a truism which unhappily seems to need frequent restatement in our day, namely, that to abandon the Graf-Wellhausen hypothesis is not the same as rushing into the comforting arms of an orthodoxy, authentic or neo.

The Graf-Wellhausen hypothesis emerged from phenomena in Scripture, not from the caprice of scholars. Were the phenomena not present in Scripture, the hypothesis would not have been put forward. Since they are present, the Graf-Wellhausen hypothesis was an effort to account for the phenomena. That effort could have been right or it could be wrong; or, to say this more judiciously, it could have been adequate or inadequate. It came into the public arena of biblical scholarship out of the curiosity and the learning and the *Zeitgeist* of respected and respectable scholars, who still have much to teach us.

In the 1960's it is scarcely necessary to recapitulate in other than broad terms the main objections to the Graf-Wellhausen hypothesis. A Hegelian view of history dominated its originators; they presumed that religious developments (that is, evolution) necessarily follow a prescribed pattern, as though development is

*I record my deep gratitude to my friend and colleague, Dr. Julius Lewy, for both a critical reading of this essay, and for certain references found in the notes. Needless to say, the opinions herein are my own, and not necessarily Dr. Lewy's.

rectilinear; they appear to have assumed that once a religious idea
was expressed, it emerged to obliterate those ideas which it encountered; and it rested on a painstaking analysis of strata alleged
to exist in what for the adherents was the proper unit, the Hexateuch rather than the Pentateuch.

Since the adherents worked largely prior to, but essentially
divorced from, archaeology, both artifacts and also the tremendous
yield of linguistic data and texts, their primary tool was literary
analysis. Most of us have used, or at least seen, the text published
with the various layers distinguished either by the font prescribed
for the printer or else by the use of many colors, as in the
Polychrome Bible.

In the past two decades there have risen to prominence theories
of oral tradition which can necessitate a rethinking of what a
stratum or a document might imply. Explanations which allude
to cultic legends have attracted attention. One scholar, Ezekiel
Kaufmann, has suggested that P is the oldest rather than the
youngest stratum. Two scholars, Volz and Rudolph, have denied
that there ever was an E document.

It can be appropriate, therefore, for still another suggestion
to be put forth. But the context for what I here propose must not
fade from view: The explanations offered emerge not from caprice,
but from phenomena in the text. Whether an explanation seems
right and gains acceptance, or seems wrong and fades into a mere
footnote in a book like Pfeiffer's, in no way makes the phenomena
in the text disappear. The explanations may vary, the phenomena
remain constant.

II

If a personal word is not out of order, what I here set forth
emerges from a return to Tanak[1] studies rather than from an
unbroken preoccupation with them. The disadvantage may lie
in the recession from one's memory of the details, especially the
tiny ones, of the exercises in source analysis which I once did.
Perhaps, though, to leave Tanak alone and then return to it
presents some advantages. Before reverting to Tanak studies, I

did considerable work in NT, rabbinics, apocrypha, and pseudepigrapha, and in Philo. The phenomena in these literatures unquestionably array themselves in particular ways in the mind of the student, and thereafter he can find himself perhaps unduly influenced by them. Yet perhaps even in missing some occasional trees in the Tanak, he might feel that he now sees the forest better than he did.

III

Several near axioms in the study of the literary history of the Tanak have periodically bothered me. Two of these I mention here.

One is R^{JE}. This symbol stands for the hypothetical editor, compiler, or whatever one calls him, who combined the J and the E accounts. Pfeiffer tells us (*Introduction to the Old Testament,* p. 283) that "this redactor was no mere hack writer." Yet when I read Pfeiffer's description of the four methods allegedly used by this redactor, to me the epithet hack rushes to the tip of the tongue, for Pfeiffer makes him at best only a copyist. Pfeiffer attributes to him four methods: preserving intact valuable stories; omitting a story found in one source through the inclusion of the same story from the other; giving one story in full and supplementing it from the other source; or reproducing two stories, making the identical appear to be reports of successive incidents. None of these four implies a viewpoint or any creativity. Lods, on the other hand, attributes to R^{JE} no brilliance, no originality, and no profundity of thought. How come such diverse judgments?

But with what do we deal in R^{JE}? Were there two divergent documents, J and E? Did R^{JE} sit at a desk, copying now from J, and now from E, adding a phrase here and there? A hack such as Tatian did this with four gospels, but by Tatian's time these gospels were virtually canonized; why should a Hebrew Tatian have spent time blending two accounts, but without himself having any discernible motive or viewpoint? To me, this whole matter of R^{JE} makes no sense.

But the phenomena of blending are present, at least if for the moment we accept that doublets imply divergent sources. Yet suppose that R^{JE} was a writer, not a redactor, and that he had before him one account, not two, and suppose that he rewrote the one account, though supplementing it both by utilizing extant older material and also by creating new material? To me it makes sense to conceive of someone who rewrites something older and does so for a purpose; the mere copyist seems to me inhuman, and an impossibility.

But suppose Volz and Rudolph are right, and there was never an E code?[2] What happens to R^{JE}? Then we could no longer speak of blended documents, but of a source that underwent rewriting; we would deal not with two documents, but with two stages, or more, of the one document.

The second near axiom troubles me even more. On at least twelve occasions in the annual teaching of the same course, I have stated that Genesis 1:1–2:4 is P, and 2:4 ff. is J. From at least Philo on, the dissimilarity in these two accounts has been public property. Assuming that a priestly editor inserted this J account into a P framework, then was this P editor completely oblivious to the dissimilarity so clear to modern scholars? Was he less perceptive, less intelligent, than we? How is it that we can see what he was blind to? Must I not try to understand this putative blindness on his part and to explain it, at least to myself?

IV

That important line of research which begins with Gunkel and extends into the modern Scandinavians such as Nyberg, Mowinckel, and especially Engnell has properly alerted us to oral tradition. Yet I sometimes have the feeling that some exponents of oral traditions so stress the oral that they forget that their pursuit is what lies behind documents which are written; and while one can overlook their scorn of literary critics, it seems a little more difficult to forgive their scorn of written documents.

Does oral tradition remain constant and unchanged within the oral stage? Such is the implication of the modern oralists. Are the men who transformed the oral into the written mere recorders? Again, this is the implication of the oralists. I have myself written enough, and taught enough students who have written, to believe that no one ever wrote without having a viewpoint or a purpose. The latter may not be so marked as to constitute what in NT is called a *Tendenz*,[3] but I find it a priori impossible to believe that a writer can abstain from letting at least some tiny facet of his personality enter in.

From a different viewpoint, I confess to becoming weary of a typical Ph.D exercise: the discovery of the sources alleged to exist in documents. Stated absurdly, the premise behind such studies, now that scientific biblical scholarship is at least 160 years old, seems to be that nobody ever wrote anything: he only copied sources. There has been a spate of studies embracing source and derivation: What Philo tells, he got from the rabbis; what Jesus taught, he got from the rabbis; what Paul taught, he got from the rabbis (or the Wisdom of Solomon). What NT teaches is derived from the Dead Sea Scrolls. It is certainly legitimate to ask, Are there discernible sources behind this document? But the issue is prejudiced when the question is put, What are the sources behind the document? And when the searcher for the sources forgets the particular document allegedly containing a source, the student has embarked on an egregious tangent!

An obliviousness to the text itself seems to me the greatest defect in present-day biblical scholarship. I say this at the same time that I express the view that the Graf-Wellhausen set of documents is incorrect.

V

The hypothetical documents, J, E, D, and P, as most usually they are called, are the result of the discernment in the text of doublets or triplets and of contradictory narratives. On the supposition that a single writer would scarcely repeat himself, or flagrantly contradict himself, these phenomena were explained as resulting from the blending together of different sources.

To illustrate beyond the creation accounts, Abraham's sojourn in Egypt (Gen. 12:9 ff.) is J, while the account in 20 is E; that Beersheba (21) means *seven* is J, but *oath* is E; the first expulsion of Hagar in Genesis 16 is J; that in 21 is E.

Is a theory of diverse documents, written as suggested in the case of the Graf-Wellhausen hypothesis, or oral sources the only conceivable explanation? I do not think so. Rather, there exists an easier, simpler explanation.

A good approach to the explanation presently to be offered begins with postbiblical Judaism on the one hand and the gospels on the other hand. From the latter, let us take three individual items. First, Mark relates that Jesus was baptized by John, Matthew appends to the narrative that John would have prevented him, while Luke relegates the matter to a subordinate clause; John omits it entirely, possibly deliberately. The apocryphal Gospel of the Hebrews (James, *The Apocryphal New Testament*, p. 16) provides a brief scene of Jesus and his mother discussing whether or not he should go to be baptized. Do we deal with these accounts of the same thing with divergent and multiple sources? Next, the so-called rejection in the synagogue at Nazareth discloses that Mark attributed to Jesus an inability to work miracles, a motif altered by Matthew from *could not* to *did not do,* and absent from Luke; Luke, however, has transposed the position of the rejection so that it comes virtually at the beginning of the events, rather than almost midway, as is the case with Matthew, and a third of the way as in Mark. Moreover, Luke portrays Jesus as citing events about Elijah and Elisha which have in common a benefit wrought for a gentile. The incident at Nazareth is not found in John. Again, have our authors utilized divergent sources? Third, the money-changers incident occurs in Mark on what seems to be the second day of Jesus' entry into the temple; Matthew allocates the event to the first day, this in a prolonged account, while Luke relates the event very briefly, yet adds that Jesus was daily in the temple teaching, thus greatly de-emphasizing the narrative itself. In John, the incident is found, not as an event of Passion Week, but in the second chapter. Were the sources multiple?

In view of these divergencies, which can be multiplied by

countless other examples, how much fixity can be attributed to gospel tradition, whether it is oral or written? Does the *Tendenz* of the evangelist in any way affect his allocation of this material, or his manner of relating it?

I have cited from the apocryphal Gospel of the Hebrews to suggest that while canonization can act to crystallize tradition, it does not fix it beyond change. If illustration is needed, consider the narrative in Genesis 12:9 ff. of Abraham's sojourn in Egypt. Philo so recasts the account as to depict a base king guilty of the grossest disregard to regulations of hospitality. Josephus embellishes the account by relating that Abraham went to Egypt to convert or be converted by the Egyptian priests, and coincidentally taught them mathematics, which they in turn taught the Greeks. The rabbis embellish the story by having an angel present in the bedroom to administer beatings to Pharaoh when his lust prompts him to make advances toward Sarah. The narrative in Genesis 12 in no way explicitly states or implicitly suggests that Sarah's virtue was not violated; to the contrary. But all these embellishments unite in the conclusion that her virtue was unsullied.

Or, to take another example, the early history of Jacob is that of a deceiver who takes from his brother both the *beracha* (blessing) and the *bechora* (primogeniture), so that Esau says of him, Did they call him Jacob because he, as now, has "Jacobed" me twice? But how do the postbiblical narratives treat these incidents? In them Jacob is the righteous hero—the pious scholar of soft voice—while Esau is the villain whose strong hands impel him to horrendous sins of violence.

Such exegesis, when it is narrative, is called by Jews haggada; the word means narration, a term used in contradistinction to halaka, the term for legal matters. Haggada, in short, is the fanciful retelling of tales.

The acquisition of the status of canonicity not only did not impede haggada, but spurred it on, even to the point where the haggada contradicted facets of the content of the canonical.

The bare incident of Genesis 12:9 ff. relates that Abraham took Sarah to Egypt, passed her off as his sister; she was taken to Pharaoh's harem, and, postprandially Yahve wrought a plague on Pharaoh and the latter sent Abram away. In Genesis 20, Abimelech similarly takes Sarah to his domicile. But now Elohim appears to Abimelech in a dream, warning him that he may die because of this married woman. We are told explicitly that Abimelech did not approach her. Indeed, Abimelech defends his having Sarah with him on the grounds that he understood her to be Abraham's sister. Elohim attests to Abimelech's purity— a strange attestation, for are sisters to be considered as readily available?[4]—and advises Abimelech to restore Sarah to Abraham, for the latter is a prophet who could pray on behalf of Abimelech. What Abraham is to pray for is not yet clear; that comes at the very end of the story: Abraham prays that the sterility of the Philistine women be cancelled, for the deity had brought about the sterility.

What embellishments do we see? The random plague of Pharaoh becomes now the plague of sterility; the deity has intervened, and Sarah's virtue is unimpaired. Not only has Abraham not committed a prevarication, but he is a prophet. Abraham was not lying; Sarah was his half sister.

Were we to find this story in Genesis Rabbah instead of Genesis 20, we would promptly recognize it as a haggada based on Genesis 12:9 ff.

As for the Hagar story, Genesis 16 relates that after Hagar became pregnant, she was disrespectful to Sarah. At Sarah's bidding Abraham permitted her to send the maid away. An angel of Yahve found Hagar in the wilderness, and assured her that her offspring would be the progenitor of a mighty people.

Neither Sarah nor Abraham appears admirable in this account.[5] Rabbinic exegesis rescued them. So, too, Philo escaped from his embarrassment at their character by means of his allegory. He states that Scripture has no intention of portraying two women in a domestic quarrel. Rather, when Abraham married Hagar, the meaning is that Abraham went to college. Hagar represents the encyclical studies, while Sarah is true wisdom.

The second story of the expulsion of Hagar tells us that Ishmael is now born, and is guilty of some misconduct toward or with Isaac—the text here fails us—and that is why Sarah is indignant.

Abraham is, properly, distressed at Sarah's demand that Hagar be expelled. At this juncture, Elohim advises Abraham to hearken to Sarah, for Ishmael is to be the progenitor of a great people. This time Abraham gives Hagar bread and wine to take with her into the wilderness. She puts Ishmael on her shoulder. (The P chronology establishes, as the rabbis noted, that Ishmael was a lad of sixteen, but the rabbis inform us that Ishmael was smitten with a disease that shrank him to the size of a babe.) When the water gave out, Elohim was true to his promise to Abraham, and he provided water for Hagar.

In this second version, it is Ishmael who evokes Sarah's displeasure, not Hagar; Abraham is distressed, rather than compliant; and it is Elohim who responsibly decides what is to be done and how.

Again, this is exculpating material which is familiar to us from the midrash.

There is a third version of the patriarch and his wife. It is related of Isaac that he told Abimelech that Rebekah was his sister. In this version the king does not take the patriarch's wife to his harem; one wonders why the fib. The truth of the relationship is revealed to Abimelech not by the deity, but by his looking out the window and seeing Isaac and Rebekah *in flagrante delicto.* Some scholars have taken this version to be the oldest of the three stories. I doubt this. To my mind the narrator, having named his Philistine king Abimelech, simply retold the story. In this version, the deity is not needed, for Abimelech is not lustful; now no plagues are required, for it is only to Isaac that Rebekah belongs. Indeed, the rebuke of Abimelech to Isaac states simply: one of the people might have lain with her—but didn't.

Or, why did Jacob go to Paddan-aram?[6] Genesis 27 motivates the trip through Esau's threat to kill Jacob. But Genesis 26:34 has told us that Esau married two Hittite girls, thus embittering Rebekah and Isaac; accordingly, Rebekah, in 27:46, expresses anxiety that Jacob may also marry a Hittite, so that Isaac in 28:1 tells him not to marry a local girl, but to go east and get a proper wife. This latter version is termed P, while the former is JE. I do believe that there was a P code; I am not sure that this is in reality P. But with regard to labels, haggada has again entered in to recast an older account in terms favorable to the patriarchs.

Why must this rewritten account of Jacob's motive in going east for a wife be P? The analysts ascribe Genesis 24 to J— usually J². There underlies this latter account the same viewpoint which supposed that Jacob must go east to marry, namely, that a good Jew should not marry, as it were, out of the faith. But in those early times where were there Jewish girls? The narrators solve this problem by having Abraham, Isaac, and Jacob all marry girls from the east. (They seem oblivious about Jacob's eleven sons and they allow Joseph to marry an Egyptian!) Are these eastern wives history or haggada?

To move to the Joseph story, there are variations as to whether it was Reuben or Judah who alone among the brothers had some sense of conscience; and whether it was at Judah's suggestion that Joseph was sold to Ishmaelites, or, instead, rescued and kidnapped by Midianites. Are these variant traditions, or a story and a haggada? Reuben in Genesis 35:22, a story begun but not finished, had an affair with Bilhah, Jacob's concubine, earning Jacob's scolding in Genesis 49:3–4. Why then retain him as a hero, especially in the time when his tribe had died out? What is more natural than to make Judah the hero in place of Reuben? And is it not intended as an accolade that Jacob takes the initiative, admirable in the situation, of saving Joseph by selling him into slavery, whereas Reuben passively returns to the pit to find it empty? No, the Judah passages are a haggada on the Reuben passages; they are not a separate source.

Similarly, the account in Genesis 34 of Dinah and Shechem is "composite." In one aspect, Dinah has been raped, but Shechem proposes to marry her. Obliged by Dinah's brothers to be circumcised, Shechem is killed, along with his father, by Simeon and Levi, and for this action Jacob rebukes them. In the other aspect, Dinah has been seduced, not raped, by Shechem. The latter's father seeks out Jacob, proposes marriage, and indeed, subsequent intermarriages; he is told that circumcision is a necessary preliminary. Every male in the city was circumcised; thereupon the sons of Jacob slew them all and plundered the city. The second account is termed E, indeed E²; the former is J.

To my mind the relationship is the reverse, that the older aspect is that of seduction, of a dignified marriage proposed through the father, and of a destruction of an entire populace by all of Jacob's sons. I take this earlier account to be a late anti-Samaritan passage. As for the other account, it is a series of corrections, calculated to soften what would otherwise necessarily be a harsh judgment. Seduction becomes rape; the proposal of marriage is made by Shechem rather than, properly, by his father; the slain are only Shechem and his father, not the whole city; the slayers are only two of the brothers, Simeon and Levi, conforming to Genesis 49:5–7; and Jacob rebukes them for their deed.

Lastly, for our purposes, we may turn to the so-called E account of the revelation of the divine name in Exodus 3:13 ff. A parallel account in Exodus 6:3 is attributed to P. To J is attributed Genesis 4:26b, against whose natural meaning the ancient versions struggle desperately; this verse attributes to Enos the initial knowledge of Yahve's name. The translation of Genesis 4:26 (Targum Onkelos, Pseudo-Jonathan, and LXX) attempts to deprive Enos of the credit for this discovery of the divine name, for by the time of the translations it was standard Jewish haggada, found in the midrash, Josephus, and Philo, that it was Abraham who had made the momentous discovery.[7]

The passage Exodus 3:13–15 can be ascribed to some ancient document only by ignoring the high good humor of the haggadic passage. The "I am who I am" is simply a good-natured pun, the humor of which has escaped the long-faced grammarians who have disputed whether *ehye* in verse 14, *"ehye sent me,"* is a qal or a nif'al; or a Gressmann who dutifully cites Wellhausen that the third person, not the first, is *erwartet*. A wag could write *I am sent me*; an ancient source scarcely. The wag was indulging in his very early times in the by now age-old pursuit of giving a supposed etymology of Yahve, and has done so almost as well as modern scholars.

A point to be stressed is that a tradition which includes the ascription of the discovery of God to Enos, Abraham, and Moses is thereby reflecting its living quality. And if one replies that these items are contradictory of each other, then notice how in Genesis Rabba the age of Abraham at his discovery of Yahve is given variously as one, three, ten, or forty-eight. Moreover, the ten plagues—the dividers into J and E are pushed to say that the E "narratives have evidently in some cases been abbreviated or omitted"—grow in miraculous nature through haggada within Scripture, and then in number in rabbinic exegesis from ten to fifty to two hundred.

The Chronicler reflects a haggadic approach to Samuel-Kings; but even within Samuel-Kings haggada is present.[8] This is the case not only with the pro- and anti-monarchy sentiments attributed to the man Samuel, but haggada can be illustrated typically from two quite separate stories. First in I Samuel 24, while Saul is defecating in a cave, David cuts off a part of Saul's skirt.[9] This legend, or version of a legend, was told to create laughter (as was the legend that David brought a dowry of a hundred Philistine foreskins to Saul!); a haggadist, with a deep hostility to Saul, here retold the story found in 26; there David, with Abishai, steals into Saul's encampment and makes off with his spear and canteen. Second, in David's slaying of Goliath (an act done really by Elhanan, II Sam. 21:19; see the Chronicler's harmonization, I Chron. 20:5), a legend told that David, as yet unknown to Saul, came to the front lines to visit his brothers, and then slew Goliath. After David's fame as a musician had become legendary, a haggadist recast the beginning of the Goliath incident: Saul was prone to melancholy (a haggadic strand consistently disparages Saul), so that David was brought to court so as, by his lyre, to lull Saul into moments of normalcy; so David was already known to Saul.

We deal not with sources blended, but with haggadic recastings of a single source.

Sometimes the recasting converts a secular story into a religious story. Such is the case with the rollicking account of Ehud in Judges 3:12 ff., and of Samson, the consorter with prostitutes, in Judges 13 ff. When once Samson is made a battler for Yahve, he acquires from a haggadist a wondrous birth, as in 13:3 ff. Indeed, the haggadists so work in Joshua-Judges as to try to persuade us that conquest and settlement were two separate stages; but simultaneously Scripture gives us a picture of slow penetration and conquest in Judges 1:1–2:5. In Joshua we read of an easy and total conquest under Joshua's leadership (with a temporary setback only at Ai); but passages in the Pentateuch give us the haggada that the true conqueror is the hornet.

The usual disquisitions on E (and P) tell us that these sources increase the miraculous elements in J, and increase the theological. Such is the bent of haggada. But it is haggada, not documents. While P is to be regarded as a document (but embodying a considerable amount of older material), E never was a saga and never was an extended document.

Was J a document? Was it a saga? To the first question the answer is no. To the second, if we mean a long, connected document, the answer is again no. If by the symbol J we mean a level of narration relatively free from theological interpretation, and in that sense "secular," then J was a group of early legends and myths. In very early form, such a group included an account of the origin of circumcision in Moses' time, the truncated narrative in Exodus 4:24–26. This is treated in a totally different way by a haggadist in Genesis 17 who traces circumcision to Abraham. The Eden traditions—the etiologies—may be termed J, in a loose sense.

But J never was a long, connected document. If we will exclude the brief Isaac material (Gen. 25–26), the very ancient story of Tamar (Gen. 38), and the account of Dinah (Gen. 34), Genesis falls into four major parts, the last three of which are the traditions, respectively, about Abraham, Jacob, and Joseph; the first would lend itself to subdivision into Adam and Noah. But a survey of the supposed J accounts in these four segments would lead necessarily to the conclusion that this J was never a unified document. If it was, how account for the character of Jacob in Segment III and his totally different character in Segment IV? Does the honored Jacob in the Joseph cycle exhibit any affinity with the deceiver in the Jacob cycle? Of course not. If one says in rebuttal that the Jacob of the Joseph cycle is the reformed character Israel found at the end of the Jacob cycle, then this is tantamount to conceding that the Joseph cycle lacks that primitive quality which J ought to possess by the mere description which the scholars give of J as a saga.

An open-minded appraisal of the Jacob cycle must recognize that at its kernel lies a folk tale of incalculable antiquity.[10] It is the story of a clever deceiver, whose exploits delighted and tickled the risibilities of generations ancient beyond measure. But subsequent generations began to have reservations about the moral character of the supposed ancestor. One haggadist tries to divert from Jacob as a deceiver by having us suppose that his name means "ankler." Another haggadic aspect intervenes into the narrative to "nationalize" Jacob and Esau. Rebekah has two *nations* in her womb; *nations* will serve Jacob (Gen. 27:29) and Esau will also, though not forever (Gen. 26:40).

In the Jacob cycle we can see a folk character of low moral attributes who needed to be transformed from a mere ancestor into a respected ancestor, and from a respected individual to a national symbol. Since I have no great quarrel with the P code, I am content to use this symbol; but in my own teaching of the Jacob cycle I speak, not of J and E, but of primitive "secular" elements, of "respected ancestor" materials, and of "nationalizing" materials.

The nationalizing is evident in the Abraham cycle (Gen. 12:2–3; 15:5, 18). But what is absent from the Abraham cycle is material primitive enough to be called J. Genesis 12:1–9 is a tendentious account; God gave the Hebrews Palestine through his gift of it to Abraham. Genesis 12:10–20 is the nearest thing to a J-type story; its purpose is to relate the source of Abraham's wealth. Genesis 13 is part and parcel of Genesis 18–19, to which we come in a moment. Genesis 14 relates the military prowess of Abraham (he conquers four eastern kings with 318 "home-trained" soldiers; that the data conforms with what archaeologists can tell us about the 19th or 16 pre-Christian century in no way alters the necessary conclusion that in its present form the chapter is a late haggada).[11] Genesis 15—supposedly the first appearance of E in Genesis—is haggada, an expansion of Genesis 12:1. (The ancient rabbis tell us this in the form of stating that the incident described in Genesis 15 occurred in Ur!) Genesis 16 is the work of the "nationalizer," explaining the kinship of the Hebrews and the dwellers in wilderness (Gen. 16:9 is a gloss to account for the two versions of Hagar's expulsion). Genesis 17 is P's account of the origin of circumcision, now a covenant symbol.

Genesis 13:18–19 is an elaborate and sophisticated account. Since Abraham lived long, long ago, it must have been at the time of the vaunted destruction of the four cities, Sodom, Gomorrah, Admah, and Zeboiim; our account mentions only the first two. Abraham is brought into relationship with these cities through his nephew Lot,[12] and he is made to intervene and to bargain with the deity on behalf of pure justice. The story grew by the addition of a story giving the etymology of Isaac's name, infelicitously ascribing a lie to Sarah (Gen. 18:15); the P account (Gen. 17) salvages her reputation by ascribing the laughter to Abraham, a laughter not denied in this haggadic recasting and hence not fibbed about. Genesis 20, as mentioned above, is a haggadic retelling of Genesis 12:10–20. Genesis 21:1–7 is a P summary; 8–21 is, to repeat, a retelling of Genesis 16; 22–33 is the etymology of Beer-sheba, whether *seven* (29–30) or *oath* (31). (Another haggadist tells it about Isaac, Gen. 26:15–33.)

Genesis 22:1–19, in which is discerned a preachment against child sacrifice, is in its present form embellished by making a didactic tale into the story of a man who withstood a test.[13] (The rabbis embellish the account into a Joblike narrative; and they increase the test from this one incident to a total of ten.)

Genesis 22:20–24 belongs with Genesis 24. Genesis 23 tells of Sarah's death—Abraham graciously bought her burial place even though Yahve had previously given him the land. Genesis 22:20–24 and Genesis 24 convert an old, old story of a marriage arrangement into an account of how Isaac managed to marry within the fold. The haggadist is at his best here, for the narrative is first-rate. The nationalizer's hand is present in 24:60. The P editor tells us (Gen. 25:20) that Isaac was forty when he married Rebekah; the rabbis note that Rebekah was three; they reflect no apparent surprise at this age which they ascribe to her. Genesis 25:1–18, the conclusion of the Abraham material, reflects the nationalizer.

As this survey suggests, virtually the only primitive aspect of the Abraham material is the supposition, coming from later times, that he dwelled in primitive times. He is not the folk character that Jacob is, in need of transformation into respectability. He is, except for Genesis 12:10–20, respectable at all times. There is a relative sophistication in the Abraham material, this emphasized by both the succeeding Jacob stories and the preceding Adam-Noah stories.

The proliferation in the scholarly literature of exponents to accompany code symbols, yielding J^1, J^2, J^3, and E^1, E^2, E^3, and the like, are in their own way testimony to the absence of persuasive evidence that Genesis is only a pedestrian amalgam of some ancient source or sources. We shall presently need to consider the difference between the viewpoint argued for herein and the more traditional view. But for our immediate purposes the recognition is essential that the four cycles do not present that kind of unified, cohesive material of the same kind and level which could reasonably lead to conceiving of J as a long, connected saga, stretching from Genesis 2 into Joshua or even further.

The material in the Adam-Noah cycle has lent itself to a usual interpretation which is dependent on the supposition that the author (whether single or plural) of the P code was a complete moron. The aspersions of the P writer are many and invariably wrongheaded, but they have never been this explicit. Preliminary to any comment on the Adam-Noah cycle J material imbedded in P is the question of P's procedure. It is fairly universally conceded that P starts on a broad canvas: creation and the origin of mankind, and then a gradual narrowing of the focus to only Israel. If P apparently decided on this course, and was bent on amplifying his framework by adding extant material, what sorts of material could there have been conceivably available to him? He might have borrowed from the Babylonians and gone from cosmogony into theogony, but his theological premises of monotheism barred such a step. Rather, he chose a series of etiological legends which have a common base in that they explain the origin of human ways and institutions, not the origins of God. Thus, man is the result of Yahve's fashioning, trees of his planting. Men die, but mankind learns; hence, the two trees, of life and of knowledge, were available, but man ate of learning, not of immortality. Woman—so kindred to man—came from man's rib. Animals received names because man gave the names to them. Why is a serpent legless? Why does woman travail in childbirth? Why must man toil for his livelihood? Why are clothes worn even beyond any need for protection? How did the earth get populated, and how did the trades and occupations develop? What prompts murder, and how do men regard the murderer?

Are these not etiologies whose relationship is to mankind, not to the Hebrews in particular? What other kind of material would P have introduced, once it was his decision to introduce material? For Lamech he found a poem available; for other persons or events he called on folk tales. Are these folk anecdotes of the same level as the Abraham material? Of course not. Then were they part of the same saga? Of course not. Rather, these tales were the floating property of men, and introduced as such with editorializing more prone to exclusion than to inclusion. Explicit myth has been winnowed out of these stories except at one point. Genesis 6:1–7, the union of the sons of the gods with women, somehow escaped the pruning scissors, and its presence suggests that P might easily have provided a whole spate of mythological anecdotes. Whether P drew on oral or written sources is a matter merely for conjecture; what is certain is that he was highly selective in the bits and pieces which he utilized.

The so-called narrative of the flood reveals its advanced character when it is contrasted with the Gilgamesh epic. The P editor felt called on to annotate it rather than simply reproduce it, probably because he was dealing with a written document which he was winnowing. He recognizes that men live under laws; so he attributes a revelation of a limited number of laws to Noah.

Since P, through using the flood, has gotten the world depopulated, he must now account for the repopulation, through Noah's three sons; he pauses to tell only that Hamites are slaves. Having cited the genealogies of nations in Genesis 10, he resorts to a legend to account for a world divided into nations speaking different languages, reaching his climax in a pun on *babel* and *balal*. And having succeeded in telling how humanity came to be divided into nations and tongues, he is ready to address himself to his prime topic, a particular nation and tongue.

The so-called J materials in the Adam-Noah cycle are the result of a sophisticated use of comparatively naïve materials. They can scarcely be regarded in the same light as the folk tales of Jacob, or the novelette of Joseph, or the didactic tales about Abraham.

Yet a question can be raised about P. Respecting the Abraham and Joseph materials there is very little of the so-called J that P need have objected to. There is little in these two cycles he could not have believed in. The question, then, is this, did P believe this assembly of etiological tales? Did he believe creation took place as he himself described it, or as J described it? Was he aware of contradictions, discrepancies, anomalies, and the like? And if he was not, shall we term him a moron?

A factor which is relevant to the discipline of Bible study is the resiliency of the religious mind. A Tatian could blend together four gospels which modern scholars prefer to print in parallel columns; these days they limit the parallel columns to three, ruling John to be too distant. Once one spoke of a harmony of the gospels, today one speaks of gospel parallels. Yet Tatian wove all four together. Do we not all know OT scholars who are opaque to problems so clear to the rest of us in NT, and Rabbinic scholars unable to discern, let alone confront, problems in the Tanak? Do we not all know of biblical archaeologists who are blind to the textual and literary problems of Scripture? This, in general, is what I mean by the resiliency of the religious mind.

Did P believe the folk tales he interpolated into his *Grund-*

schrift? Of course he did, for he read and understood them in the light of his own beliefs, and for him Genesis 2:4 ff. was not out of accord with Genesis 1.

But here the interjection might be made that I have described the haggadic materials in the Tanak as reflecting correction as well as embellishment, refinement as well as elaboration. It could be supposed that I am here contradicting myself.

Such is not the case. It is phenomena in Scripture which I am describing, and these phenomena are there. What needs to be clear is a peculiarity in the literary methods of the biblical authors. I shall initially describe it as a disinclination to expunge. Just as Genesis 6:1–7 attests to the deliberate winnowing out of the mythological materials, so too Genesis 35:22a underscores the disinclination to expunge. Here we have the beginning of a narrative known to some redactor in a longer version. The amount told us is no more than that in absence of Jacob, Reuben lay with Bilhah, his father's concubine, and Israel heard of it. Any reading of this verse is its own persuader that something has begun which is not fully narrated; moreover, Genesis 49:4 discloses that the incident was in circulation. Why did the redactor not retell the whole story? And if he was going to expunge, why expunge the end, but retain the beginning?

The redactors turn out to have counterbalanced the disinclination to expunge by adopting what we may call a process of neutralizing by addition. The haggadic item once added, meant to the redactor that that which he was emending had the same meaning as that which was the result of the emendation. The Abraham of Genesis 20 thus determines the character of the Abraham of Genesis 12:10–20. The disenchantment with kingship of I Samuel 8 means to the haggadist that all of Samuel-Kings reflects this disenchantment.

The P editor could set forth his own religious calendar in Leviticus 23 and still reproduce the discrepant calendars in Exodus 23:14–19 and 34:21–24, for he understood these calendars as in accord with the revised and precise list he was himself devising.

E

In this same fashion, the author of Jubilees in rewriting Genesis provides a calendar of a pentacontad (units of fifty days, or years) type completely at variance with the solar-lunar calendar of P. This freedom on the part of Jubilees has led an occasional scholar to suppose that Jubilees must be as old or older than P; this view is based on the wrong premise that canonicity produced rigidity.

Reverting to the Tanak, the redactor could and did object to this or that. But his way of handling the objectionable was to append something, a verse or an incident, or a new version, but without removing that which bothered him. The redactors of the Pentateuch did not feel that need which the Chronicler felt to create a new work; nor to create, as did the church, a series of gospels, instead of one redacted and re-redacted gospel. (Tatian, who combined the four, is described by Eusebius as an Assyrian; perhaps something in the Semitic psyche accounts for Tatian's being a combiner rather than the author of a new eclectic and selective gospel.)

Were these haggadic additions oral before they were written? Quite possibly. What is important to recognize, however, is that when they were written down, it was not disinterested writing, not mere automatic copying.

No writer ever writes without some purpose. The Scandinavians and the Dibeliuses go far astray in disregarding in surviving literary documents the personality, interests, and motives of the writer.

By redactor I have not meant to imply a person who worked on the totality of a writing; it might have been one single item which he added in the margin of his text, or included on a piece of parchment sewn on to his scroll. The haggadist was that person who felt the need to embellish or modify. By a redactor I mean a writer who either recorded an oral haggada which became his by conviction, or else gave birth to his haggada when his pen touched paper.

Such stages of redaction seem to me not only truer to the *genre* of Scripture; but the theory of the blending of diverse sources an invitation to the improbabilities which mark the pages of so much 19th-century scholarship. The premise of blended sources leads to the conceit that the sources involved can be disentangled, and that, by and large, they are blended together in equal quantity. As a result, a disentangler feels the need to end up with two or more self-contained entities. No such obligation rests on him who searches for haggadic additions; and hence he is free from the absurdity of those analyses which ascribe 1a, 2b, 3c, and 4a to J; 1b, 3ab, and 4b to E.

Moreover, if a Scriptural chapter is recognized as containing both ancient tradition and also subsequent haggadic expansion it is unnecessary to strive, as do some few archaeologists,[14] to attribute historical reliability even to the haggadic elements. Nineteenth-century scholarship was too skeptical of that reliable history coincidental to Samuel and Kings. Some scholars of the past decades have been too credulous of the haggadic elements which encase the reliable history. And for the Pentateuch they bring criteria for fixing historical accuracy which overlook the unhistorical *genre* of the literature.

The haggadic tendency makes of Scripture a literature which grew by accretion. This seems to me exactly the way in which literary reflection of a live religious tradition would grow. From the oral to the written, and from the book to canonicity, and from canon to midrash, represents a continuous process.

In the first Christian century this midrash took two major turns (along with some minor ones). One midrash resulted in Mishna and Gemara, *The* Midrash, and the targumim; then Saboraim and the Gaonim and then philosophers, Aristotelian and neo-Platonic. The other resulted in gospels and epistles, and ultimately a NT; there were in addition Apostles, Fathers, and Ante-Nicene Fathers, and Post-Nicene Fathers, and then philosophers, Aristotelian and neo-Platonic.

The Graf-Wellhausen hypothesis remains the point of departure for scientific biblical scholarship. This is the case not because its answers are right, but because they have reflected an awareness of the right questions. Scripture remains; the hypotheses come and go. For the Graf-Wellhausen hypothesis to merit the high accolade of being the point of departure implies the need to depart from it.

NOTES

1. Tanak (which Jews pronounce *tanach*) stems from the abbreviations of the three divisions, Torah, Nebhi'im, and K'tubhim, of the Hebrew Scriptures. Tanak seems to me more desirable a term than OT, which Jews could object to, or Bible, which Christians could object to if limited to OT.

2. In *Der Elohist als Erzähler ein Irrweg der Pentateuchkritik*, BZAW, 63 (1933). They repudiate E not so much as a code, but as a *narrator* comparable to J. In Volz's portion of the monograph, he gives four objections to the usual source analysis (pp. 14 ff.): 1. A writer copying from two parallel narratives—here and there a word, or a half sentence, or a sentence—is a scholarly artifice, not a reflection of real life. 2. The criteria for determining the source divisions rest on improper criteria. 3. The Pentateuch should be approached like other Scriptural books, and not unlike them. If so, tiny repetitions, contradictions, etc. are discernible as glosses; longer such items represent J's use of divergent materials, all brought into J's long narrative; extensive items of this kind represent an edition of the long narrative, or of this narrative's being put into a new *Verband*. 4. The source analysts destroy the artistic beauty of the unified account.

Neither Volz nor Rudolph, however, supplies any positive hypothesis to replace the repudiation of E as a narrator. Martin Noth, *Überlieferungsgeschichte des Pentateuch*, pp. 22 ff., scarcely meets the challenge of Volz, but simply hews to the old line that parallel materials must necessarily mean parallel sources.

3. *Tendenz* as an explanation of textual phenomena is, of course, not unknown in OT scholarship. To my knowledge, however, it was never raised to the critical eminence which in NT scholarship is associated with C. F. Baur and the Tübingen School. I counted, in my *The Genius of Paul*, pp. 146–48, that the Tübingen School correctly noted that there is *Tendenz* in Acts of the Apostles, but Hegelianism blinded them from a proper characterization of it.

4. We know of the practice in Nuzian society whereby a man could live with his sister in concubinage, and yet not be averse to having her marry someone else, this in consideration of a sum of money. The late biblical recaster may have known of this practice; see H. Lewy, *Orientalia*, 10 (1941), pp. 211 ff.

5. The behavior of Sarah and Abraham conforms with the treatment of slave girls such as Hagar. See Codex Hammurabi, ## 145 ff., and Driver and Miles, *The Babylonian Laws*, 1, p. 305.

6. That he went eastward, and not south or west, reflects group historical memory, as of Haran. The issue is not where he went, but the motivation which the Tanak supplies for his going.

7. See my "Gen. 4:26b," in *HUCA*, 33, 1961.

8. A full assessment of the succession of Deuteronomic writers is deliberately withheld here, out of considerations of space. I deal with the subject in my *The Hebrew Scriptures* (Knopf, 1963). In brief, if it is just to label Job, Proverbs, and Ecclesiastes as wisdom literature, then the D writings can be put into this same loose category. The D writers represent neither the priesthood nor the prophets, despite friendliness to both, but are rather sages-teachers who inferred lessons, and taught them, from Israel's history. So strong in D is didacticism that while it is proper to credit the D writers with more accurate history than scholars did at the turn of the century, it is improper to make secular historians of them. Especially suspect are the fortuitous appearances of prophets, named or unnamed; and a more reliable history of prophecy can be written solely from the literary prophets (all of whom except Isaiah the D writers neglect) than from coalescing them with the accounts of prophets, including Elijah and Elisha, in Samuel and Kings. Moreover, it can be suggested, though the connection cannot be traced, that the post-Tanak descendants of the late P writers are the Sadducees and of the late D writers the scribes—Pharisees—rabbis.

9. The cutting of the skirt has symbolic force, as Julius Lewy notes, *RHR*, 9 (1934), pp. 31 ff. My comments are on the late setting of the anecdote, Saul in a cave, and not on the significance of the ancient symbol.

10. Professor Julius Lewy believes the stories may well have been current among Western Semites in Mesopotamia already in the 19th and 18th century.

11. Historical memory could be called on to reproduce in the Abraham material recollections of these early times. Thus a conformity to early historical conditions could emerge, to be blended with a late sophisticated assessment, of the patriarch. The conformity to early historical conditions does not in itself establish the historicity of the particular narrative. Scholars, in an eagerness to trace the background of a text, have often been neglectful of the text.

The ascription to Abraham of having given a tithe to a priest at Salem is not so much historical as a lesson taught by example. As yet there were no Israelite priests, as yet Jerusalm was not Israelite. But if Abraham could offer a tithe at Salem, the precursor to Jerusalem, to the precursor to the Aaronites, how much more should his descendants! Moriah of Genesis 22 became identified in II Chronicles 3:1 and in the rabbis with Mount Zion, for where else would the patriarch have offered a ram? Note that in Genesis 14 the author is careful to tell us that Melchizedek was a priest, not of the *ba'al*, but of the vague *el elyon*. That is, the author of this didactic section skillfully avoids the pits he might have fallen into.

12. The nationalizer ascribes the origin of Ammon and Moab to incestuous relationship (19:38); rabbinic exegesis in part condemns Lot's daughters, and in part, with Josephus, praises a motive ascribed to them of wishing to repopulate the world. See my *Philo's Place in Judaism*, p. 69, n. 303.

13. In its present form the accentuation in Genesis 22 is on Abraham's character rather than on the incident. This seems to me to represent a deviation, through accretion, from a simpler state in which the events, climaxing in the desisting from the act of child sacrifice, were the principle focus. An even more ancient folk tale may underlie the account; see H. Lewy, *Symbolae Hrozny* (1950), p. 353, n. 106.

14. The archaeologists have often been the victims of popularizers. Occasionally an archaeologist has made statements which, taken from context, have been misconstrued. This latter has been the experience of my intimate friend, Nelson Glueck, who learned to his dismay that there was being attributed to him a quasi-fundamentalism which his colleagues know is remote from him; curiously, he was unjustly attacked from quite a different quarter on the basis of phrases lifted out of context from his *Rivers in the Desert*. Wright's sober study, "Is Glueck's Aim to Prove that the Bible is True?" *BA*, 22 (1959), should now set the record straight. It may also clarify for literary analysts the position held by responsible archaeologists. See also Glueck, "The Bible and Archaeology," in *Five Essays on the Bible*, p. 66: "Although there is much which can be archaeologically confirmed, there is much more which cannot and need not and never will be historically substantiated." I do not hereby imply that archaeologists will, or should, espouse the viewpoint in this essay; I only suggest that this viewpoint is in full potential harmony with archaeology.

Introductions to Chapters VI and VII

In the nineteenth-century scholarship, the view obtained that the sources J, E, D, and P reflected the ages in which they were composed. Toward the turn of the century, the scholarship, continuing to hold on to these four sources, began to doubt that they reflected only the ages of composition, and suggested that older materials, whether oral or written, lay behind each of the written documents. Professor Noth, still largely working with the four documents, has sought to clarify what has lain behind them.

The impression of the Hebrew conquest of Canaan in Joshua is that of a single successful expedition, and that in Judges of a complex series of disconnected events and of sporadic settlement. Beyond this major problem as to what took place, there is an almost endless series of subordinate problems. Professor Noth sets forth his view of the history of the conquest and settlement. It is consistent with his broader approach, and represents one method of writing Hebrew history today, with which is associated the term "Tradition-History," the translation of a German term, Überlieferungsgeschichte. First Albrecht Alt and then Martin Noth, though dependent on predecessors, inquired into the ways in which Scripture has transmitted the traditions which have been recorded, for example, in the various strata, JEDP, of the Pentateuch. The important distinction is essential, however, between the history contained in the transmitted traditions and the history of the transmission. In principle one could possibly be sure he knew how the traditions were handed down, but declare that the traditions do not reflect credible history. For Noth the period before the settlement is prehistory, and the conquest as related in Joshua largely without history. The materials of the Pentateuch are primarily etiological, folkish explanations of origins, and without firm historical kernels. Indeed, Israel, the collective people, did not arise before the settlement in Canaan, but emerged only out of the growing unity among the separate tribes, this unity representing an amphictyony or loose federation.

Prior to the conquest, so Alt and Noth suggest, certain portions of the Pentateuchal materials were the property of certain tribes, rather than a totality of tradition possessed by all the tribes. Noth's view is expressed in his Überlieferungsgeschichte des Pentateuch *(alluded to as UG in Professor Bright's essay); this title might be translated as "Tradition-History of the Pentateuch." There Noth isolates five major themes, each of which he asserts had had a separate and distinct history, and originally there was no genuine contact of any one of the five with the other four. They are the exodus, the entrance into the Palestinian environment, the promises to the patriarchs, the Wilderness wanderings, and the revelation at Sinai. These five themes, originally separate, were blended together in the Pentateuch, but history as such, or precise history, is scarcely to be derived from any of these five themes, and certainly not from the relatively late period of their assembly into the Pentateuch.*

I have chosen Professor Noth's chapter on the tribal homes as illustrative of his treatment of the period in which he believes reliable history is discernible. The painstaking care in his work should impress the student.

Next, I have selected Professor Bright's essay because it is marked by the equally painstaking care and by an eminent fairness in the criticism which he makes of Noth and of Alt.

Respecting Professor Bright, the student will notice that though like Noth he accepts J, E, D, and P, he nevertheless challenges Noth's methodology, and, as a consequence, he also challenges Noth's conclusions which dissolve the history of the pre-settlement period.

6

THE HOMES OF
THE TRIBES IN PALESTINE

Martin Noth

"ISRAEL," which, according to Old Testament tradition, was an association of twelve separate tribes, cannot really be grasped as a historical entity until it becomes a reality living on the soil of Palestine. Naturally, the Old Testament tradition is unquestionably right in regarding the tribes not as indigenous to Palestine but as having entered and gained a footing there from the wilderness and steppe at a definite point in time. Even if the event had not been recorded in so many words, it would be possible to infer that it had taken place from the location of the areas occupied by the tribes in Palestine and from their mode of living and dwelling there. It goes without saying that the tribes had a history of their own before they entered Palestine and in the Old Testament certain tribal traditions from that early period have been preserved which are undoubtedly genuine. We shall deal with them later on in greater detail. On the other hand, these traditions were first given their definitive form within an Israel that was already united in Palestine and they were conditioned by its point of view. Together with the historical events on which they are based they made a contribution of basic import-ance to the self-consciousness and faith of Israel when it was living in Palestine, but, at the same time, in their existing form they are based on presuppositions which did not exist until the tribes had already settled on Palestinian soil. Above all, as will be seen in a moment, the fusion of the tribes into the entity "Israel" only became a final and enduring reality in Palestine; and the individual tribes only became consolidated into permanent historical entities in the process of their occupation of the land. The traditions are an essential and decisive part of the heritage of the Israel that we know in Palestine and it is in this context that we must regard them as a historical fact of fundamental significance, having its roots in the prehistory of Israel. On the other hand, the history of Israel, in the strict sense of the history of a more or less definable entity, only begins on the soil of Palestine.

To define this entity with precision it is necessary first of all to establish the actual list of tribes reckoned as Israel and the areas which they inhabited. This can be done by using all the various data which are scattered about in the fragments of narrative tradition, as preserved, above all, within the framework of the great collective work of the Deuteronomist and to some extent also, in that compilation of traditions, the Pentateuch, which evolved on Palestinian soil. The most important source of all is provided by a few traditions which deal specifically with individual tribes. A comprehensive description of the tribal geography was later inserted in the Deuteronomistic writings (Josh. 13–19, 21) incorporating an old list of the borders of the tribal areas, which probably derives from the period before political organization took shape and which states the various dwelling-places of the individual tribes in the form of an enumeration of the permanent boundary marks. It is true that it does not simply reproduce the tribal territories at a particular historical date but describes the areas to which the individual tribes laid claim, in accordance with the theory that the *whole* land of Palestine was to belong to the united tribes of Israel. Obviously, however, the territories actually inhabited by the tribes form the basis of the list;[1] to eliminate the purely theoretical elements we are not reduced to mere surmise and supposition, for in Judges 1:21, 27–35 we have a list the basis of which also derives from the pre-monarchical era and which, at least as far as the tribes of central and northern Palestine are concerned, briefly states which Canaanite city-state territories they were in fact unable to occupy, although here too the supposition is that they were really entitled to them.[2] In addition, there are one or two further traditions which, whilst they do not deal with the geography of the tribes, do contain some

information about the continued existence and make-up of the tribes
of Israel. In Numbers 26:4bβ–51 we have a list of the families belonging to the tribes which is presumably fairly old, although it is impossible to give it a precise date;[3] and in Genesis 49:1b–27/28 and
Deuteronomy 33:6–25 we find collections of brief aphorisms about
the individual tribes which were later inserted in the Pentateuch
narrative in the form of "The Blessing of Jacob" and "The Blessing
of Moses"; such sayings had probably been in circulation among the
tribes for a long time, some expressing praise, others chaffing or
mocking. They were compiled unsystematically and derive from
various, no longer precisely definable, periods. The description of the
behavior of the various tribes of central and northern Palestine
contained in the Song of Deborah (Judg. 5:2–30) is based possibly
not so much on the single event here commemorated as on the way
the tribes habitually acted.

The tribes of Israel fall into a number of geographically correlated groups. As far as one can see, the tribe of *Judah* always
played the leading part among the tribes of southern Palestine. It
inhabited the southern part of the mountains west of Jordan, south
of Jerusalem, and its area extended southwards almost as far as the
city of Hebron. Bethlehem, at the Amarna period, "a city of the
land of Jerusalem,"[4] was its centre. It is now impossible to say how
this city, which was probably only temporarily subject to the rule of
Jerusalem and had itself been a minor centre of government, came
into the possession of the tribe of Judah. To the north the territory
of Judah was bordered by the city-state of Jerusalem and the territories of the other city-states in its vicinity; to the east the "wilderness of Judah," sloping down to the Dead Sea, formed a natural
boundary. The few oasis settlements on the west bank of the Dead
Sea may also have been inhabited by Judaeans. As far as these
borders are concerned, the descriptions contained in Joshua 15:1–12
correspond to the facts, but, for reasons which we shall discuss later,
southwards and westwards they greatly extended the frontiers of
Judah. In fact the mountains south of Judah were inhabited by other
tribes, which will be mentioned directly, and even the city of Hebron
belonged to one of them and not to the tribe of Judah. In the west,
however, the southern part of the Palestinian coastal plain was in the
hands of the initially powerful Philistines, who had subjugated the

old Canaanite city-states formerly situated there; and only in the hill country between the mountains proper and the plain, in which there were comparatively few city-states, was there room for new settlements. This was the only direction in which the powerful tribe of Judah could expand; and in time Judaean clans did in fact advance into this hill country and apparently entered into normally peaceful relationships with the Canaanites already residing in some of the cities there.[5] The name Judah (*yᵉhūdā*) is not related to any well-known type of Semitic personal name and can hardly have been a personal name originally: in any case it cannot be explained philologically as a compound of the name for God (*yhwh*). On the other hand, we have evidence of a number of similarly constructed place-names[6] and the probability is that it was originally used in the phrase "mountains of Judah" (*har-yᵉhūdā*) to describe part of a mountainous district south of Jerusalem[7] and in the phrase "wilderness of Judah" (*midbar-yᵉhūdā*) to describe the area sloping down to the Dead Sea, to the east of the mountains.[8] It is probable that the clans which settled in this area called themselves later the "people of Judah," "Judaeans" (*bᵉnē-yᵉhūdā*), and thus became the "tribe of Judah."

From various scattered references in the Old Testament we know that a few other tribes or clans resided south of these Judaeans in the most southerly part of the mountains. Hebron (in the area of the modern *el-khalīl*) which was probably already a Canaanite city, was in possession of the *Calebites* who belonged to the kindred of the Kenezites,[9] other parts of which were represented among the Edomites.[10] The traditions behind Numbers 13–14 and Deuteronomy 1:22–45 and Joshua 14:6aβb–15 are an attempt to explain how it came about that Hebron, a city of blessing and importance, was assigned to Caleb, the *heros eponymus* of the Calebites; they therefore presuppose the possession of Hebron by the Calebites. How far the area of the Calebites extended it is no longer possible to say with any certainty. According to I Samuel 25:1–3 a Calebite was living in Maon, which was about 10 miles south of Hebron (the modern *tell ma'īn*), and, according to I Samuel 30:14 the tribe of Caleb had a share in the Negev, the somewhat indeterminate region of steppe south of the mountains west of the Jordan. The area occupied by the Calebites appears to have extended southwards from Hebron.

The *Othnielites* were another Kenezite tribe: according to Joshua
15: 15–19 = Judges 1: 11–15 they owned the city of Debir, which is
said formerly to have been called Kiriath-Sepher. Unfortunately
its situation is not known for certain.[11] But in all probability it lay
south-west of Hebron, presumably on the heights of the mountains
west of Jordan. We have no information at all as to how far the land
of the Othnielites extended in this area.

The most southerly part of the mountains was also inhabited by
the *Kenites* whose *heros eponymus* Cain appears in Genesis 4: 1–16.
If it is correct that in Joshua 15: 56–57, the words *Zᵉnōaḥ haq-gayin*
belong together[12] and are to be translated by "Zanoah of the Kenites," then the Kenites lived south-east of Hebron; for in Joshua 15:
55–57 this Zanoah is mentioned along with a number of other places
in this district. In any case we may take it that the Kenites lived somewhere in the southern part of the mountains west of Jordan, since
in I Samuel 30:29 "the cities of the Kenites" are referred to in
connection with other well-known places in the southern part of
the mountains. They, too, had a share in the Negev; in I Samuel
27: 10 there is a reference to the "Negev of the Kenites." The
Kenites do not appear to have become completely domiciled until
relatively late and possibly only a part of the tribe settled permanently. In Judges 4: 11, 17; 5:24 we hear of a Kenite nomad
pitching his tent somewhere or other in Galilee. It is true that,
according to Judges 4: 11, he had "separated himself from the (other)
Kenites," but probably there was quite a number of such "separated" Kenites. On the other hand, according to I Samuel 15:6, in
Saul's time the Kenites still regarded themselves as belonging to the
nomadic kindred of the Amalekites. Perhaps, therefore, only a
section of the Kenites established themselves in a small area south-
east of Hebron near the border[13] between the cultivated land and
the steppe, whilst other sections maintained their nomadic way of
life in the steppe and wilderness and in isolated cases even in the
heart of the cultivated land.[14]

Finally, we know very little about the *Jerahmeelites* who must
also be mentioned in this connection. In I Samuel 30:29 "the cities
of the Jerahmeelites" are mentioned beside "the cities of the Kenites"
and in I Samuel 27: 10 the "Negev of the Jerahmeelites" is referred
to alongside the "Negev of the Kenites." In a later list Jerahmeel

appears as the brother of Caleb (I Chron. 2:9, 42). Although it is impossible to determine their territory very accurately we must also place the Jerahmeelites in the most southerly part of the mountains.[15]

The tribe of *Simeon* evidently dwelt entirely in the far south; we know little about it, for in the list of the tribal boundaries in Joshua 13 ff. it is not mentioned at all, and in the historical tradition of the Old Testament it plays no part whatsoever. Only in the fragmentary narratives of unknown origin dealing with the occupation of land by Israelite tribes, contained in Judges 1:1 ff., which were subsequently taken into the Deuteronomistic compilation, does the tribe appear (Judg. 1:3) alongside Judah, and in Judges 1:17 we are informed, in the only concrete statement we have about it at all, that the tribe took possession of the city of Hormah, formerly called Zephath (the modern *tell el-mushāsh* east of *bīr es-seba'* = Beersheba); and the fact that the Simeonites resided in this southerly frontier area caused a late redactor to assign the most southerly district of Judah (Josh. 15:21–32) at any rate in part to the tribe of Simeon (Josh. 19: 2–8). In the system of tribal frontiers Simeon's area was simply made a part of the larger unit of Judah (*cf.* also Josh. 19:1, 9); and in the narrative in Judges 1:1 ff. Simeon also appears entirely in the shadow of Judah. It seems, therefore, that the tribe of Simeon, living as it did entirely on the periphery of the Israelite territories, was in no position to play an independent role in the historical period known to us. Its name was almost certainly originally a personal name (*cf.* Ezra 10:31); it was therefore named after one of its ancestors.

The most important tribes historically were those of central Palestine. First among them was the "*house of Joseph.*" This term, which has a very original and ancient ring about it,[16] gives special prominence to the significance of "Joseph" within the totality of the tribes of Israel and appears to indicate that in reality more than a single tribe was concerned. It has its counterpart in the expression, "the house of Judah," and the latter is used precisely when not merely the actual tribe of Judah but the whole group of south Palestinian tribes is concerned, which were united under the name of "Judah" and then combined in a kingdom of their own called "Judah."[17] In fact the "house of Joseph" was a particularly large association of clans holding the whole of the central part of the mountains west of Jordan and thereby possessing a more extensive area than any of the other tribes. If this part of the mountains, particularly in the northern half, was relatively intensely wooded, so that clearings had to be made before it was available for settlement,[18] this was hardly less true of the mountainous areas in the south and north of the country where more numerous tribes lived side by side. According to the description of the frontier in Joshua 16:1–3, to the south the "house of Joseph" occupied the area west of Jordan as far as the latitude of the city of Bethel[19] (the modern *bētīn*) and including this city; in the north—an exact description of the northern border of the tribe of Joseph is not given in the book of Joshua—its area extended as far as the southern edge of the great plain of Jezreel, which interrupts the course of the mountains west of Jordan. To the east, the slopes leading to the Jordan Valley were probably very sparsely inhabited and in the valley itself there were no settlements west of the Jordan worth mentioning at all in this period. The coastal plain in the west, however, was and remained in the hands of ancient city-states, as far as this partly marshy area was capable of being inhabited at all (*cf.* Judg. 1:29).

The great association of the "house of Joseph" (obviously originally a personal name) was in fact divided in Palestine itself into two tribes, Manasseh and Ephraim,[20] of which *Ephraim* was the greater and the more important. In Joshua 16:5–8 the territory of Ephraim is specially marked off within the larger area occupied by the house of Joseph. According to this description Ephraim was the southerly neighbor of Manasseh and its territory extended northwards from Bethel in the south almost as far as the city of Shechem (the modern *tēll balata* east of the city of *nāblus*) which itself fell to the area occupied by Manasseh.

The name "Ephraim" is obviously not a personal name, but the name of a place, as is already indicated by its ending, which often occurs in the names of places and countries. According to II Samuel 18:6 there was in the country east of Jordan a "wood of Ephraim" which was probably named after a particular district: it certainly has nothing to do with the Ephraim west of Jordan. The latter presumably appears in its original connotation in the term "Mount Ephraim" (*har-'eprāyim*) which often occurs in the Old Testament. This term usually denotes the whole of the great central part of the mountains west of Jordan—beyond the land of the tribe of

Ephraim.[21] But it may be that this is a later extension of the original meaning, which may have been restricted to quite a small area. According to II Samuel 13:23 the sanctuary of Baal-hazor, which is usually placed, probably correctly, on the mountain summit now known as *el-'aṣūr* a bare 6 miles north-east of Bethel, was situated "beside[22] Ephraim"; and here "Ephraim" most probably denotes a village.[23] But again, it is questionable whether in this case "Ephraim" as a place-name was in fact original and not rather "Mount Ephraim," that is, a closely confined mountainous district in which a village which grew up there was given the name of Ephraim.[24] However that may be, it at any rate seems to be certain that as a designation of a locality Ephraim originally had its real home in the extreme south-east part of what later became known, in a wider sense, as "Mount Ephraim" and that it arose in the extreme south-east part of the area inhabited by the tribe of Ephraim. The tribal name of Ephraim would then appear to have come about by clans which settled in this area being called "Ephraimites" (*bᵉnē-'eprāyim*), just as the clans which settled on "Mount Judah" acquired the name of "Judaeans" (*bᵉnē-yᵉhūdā*). Thereafter kindred clans further away to the west and north-west were probably included in the designation "Ephraim," when a tribe was constituted in this area, and, with the name of Ephraim, that of "Mount Ephraim" was also extended, until in the end it stretched far beyond the territory colonized by the tribe of Ephraim.

Quite early on, the vigorous tribe of Ephraim was no longer satisfied with the territory west of the Jordan which could only offer limited scope for expansion, since in the mountains to the north and south other tribes of Israel were settled and, to the west, Canaanite city-state territories blocked the way to the coastal plain.[25] And so Ephraimite families went over the Jordan Valley into the central part of the country east of Jordan. Here, on both sides of the Jabbok (the modern *nahr ez-zerka*), was a well-wooded mountain country which had hardly been opened up at all. Admittedly it was not particularly inviting country, but it did offer scope to a land-seeking tribe not afraid of the hard labor of clearing the forest. Coming from their dwellings west of Jordan the Ephraimites reached the district south of the Jabbok which was the original home of Gilead, a name which still survives in the place-names of the district. The people that settled there called themselves "Gilead-ites" (*gil'adī*) or "people of Gilead" (*'anšē gil'ad*)[26] and the "Gilead" mentioned in the Song of Deborah (Judg. 5:17) is a reference to them. That they were of Ephraimite descent we learn from Judges 12:4 where it is stated that in the course of a violent and dangerous quarrel they were contemptuously called "fugitives of Ephraim" by their fellow-tribesmen from the land west of Jordan. They initiated the settlement of the area in the centre of the land east of Jordan. Admittedly, their territory was not at all large and scarcely capable of further extension, since any expansion worth mentioning was prevented by the deep incision of the Jabbok Valley to the north and by the neighboring Ammonites to the east and south-east.

The other tribe which established itself within the framework of the "house of Joseph" as Ephraim's northern neighbor, seems to have had a rather complicated history. The Song of Deborah, one of the oldest passages in the Old Testament, mentions (Judg. 5:14) *Machir* as well as Ephraim and the strangely tortuous formulation of Joshua 17:1 seems to suggest that the old system of tribal borders described in Joshua 13–19 also assigned to Machir the remnant of Joseph's territory that remained after the territory of Ephraim had been subtracted.[27] But the tribe of Machir—or at any rate the main part of it—then migrated to the land east of Jordan, where it is usually located in Old Testament tradition; the people who remained in the land west of Jordan on the northern borders of Ephraim formed the tribe of *Manasseh*, which is clearly a personal name. Manasseh occupied the northern half of the central range of the west Jordan mountains from Shechem in the south. To the north its territory was still fairly intensely wooded and in the west, north and east it was encircled by the city-state territories in the coastal plain, in the plain of Jezreel and the Jordan Valley, which made expansion beyond the mountains impossible (*cf.* Judg. 1:27–28). Machir, how-ever, that is, the main constituent of the clans which to begin with had been Ephraim's northern neighbors, had meanwhile migrated into the opposite section of the land east of Jordan, into the moun-tain country north of the Jabbok, where they had become the northern neighbors of the east Jordan Ephraimites. From the first constituent of east Jordan colonial territory south of the Jabbok the name Gilead was now extended to the area north of the Jabbok and thus Machir became the "father of Gilead," this being the almost stereotyped expression used in the Old Testament (Josh. 17:1 and elsewhere). Numbers 32:39-42 contains a few scanty notes about the process by which the land north of the Jabbok was occupied. This land was fairly extensive and was probably only sparsely populated in the more accessible areas. With advancing colonization the name Gilead also travelled further. The occupation reached a limit only where the arable land passed over into desert in the east and where the existence of numerous Canaanite city-states in the north-east and north in the area around modern *irbid* (Arbela) made further expansion impossible. The greater importance of the west Jordan possessions compared with those east of Jordan was marked by the fact that "Manasseh" now became the real tribal name and—without regard to the actual historical process—Machir was subordinated to Manasseh genealogically and made its son (Num. 26:29 and elsewhere).

The southern neighbor of the house of Joseph and specifically of the tribe of Ephraim was *Benjamin*, a small tribe occupying a not very extensive area north-east of Jerusalem which still belonged to Canaan. Its borders are described very precisely in Joshua 18:11-20. According to this account, its lands included not only Jerusalem, which, according to Judges 1:21, Benjamin was unable to occupy, but also a group of Canaanite city-states north-west of Jerusalem which only subsequently entered into closer relationship with the tribe of Benjamin. The territory which the tribe of Benjamin actually inhabited was limited to part of the southern end of the Jordan Valley, west of the Jordan, around the oasis of Jericho and as far as the adjacent western section of the land rising to the summit of the mountains where a few villages on the great road north to south across the mountains between Bethel and Jerusalem belonged to the Benjaminites. Most probably the name itself means "he (who lives) in the south" and refers to the situation of the settlements in the land within the framework of the central Palestinian group of tribes. If this is so, the tribe of Benjamin also acquired its name as a direct result of its occupation of the land.[28]

Finally, the tribe of *Gad* which lived in the land east of Jordan and, alone among the tribes of Israel, probably made a permanent settlement there from the very beginning, has to be reckoned among the tribes of central Palestine. At any rate there is no reason to suppose that Gad, like other parts of the house of Joseph, only migrated later into the land east of Jordan from an original home west of Jordan. A description of the borders of Gad appears to be contained in the very complicated passage in Joshua 13:15 ff. where this tribe seems to have been assigned a strip of the mountain east of the Jordan from the Arnon (the modern *sel el-mōjib*) in the south as far as the Jabbok in the north and, in addition, the whole of the eastern half of the Jordan Valley. On the other hand, according to an older and more concrete tradition, it had established itself on the pasture land of the "land of Jazer" (*ya'zēr*) (Num. 32:1). Admittedly, it has so far only been possible to define the position of the town of Jazer approximately; but this much is certain: the "land of Jazer" must have been somewhere in the east Jordan mountains north-east of the northern end of the Dead Sea.[29] Gad therefore occupied only a small area, which was hemmed in on the east by the possessions of the neighboring Ammonites and also provided little scope for expansion in the direction of the wooded mountain country to the north; whilst in the south-east the cities on the tableland north of the Arnon set a limit to peaceful expansion, so that the only outlet· was southwards along the outer edge of the mountains on the eastern side of the Dead Sea, and the tribe of Gad did in fact gradually expand in that direction.[30]

In the Old Testament references to tribal territories the tribe of *Reuben* is always mentioned in connection with Gad (Num. 32:1 ff.; Josh. 13:15 ff.); but the details indicate that these references are not based on any clear-cut conception of a particular territory belonging to the tribe of Reuben but rather that the land of Gad was always theoretically divided in various ways, half of it being allotted to Reuben. The old inventory of the tribal borders does not seem to have contained anything about Reuben but only to have recognized the territory belonging to Gad in the land east of the Jordan. It is difficult to believe, however, that there was not some concrete reason for the later attempts to find a place for Reuben alongside Gad in the tribal geography. Probably there were clans in the vicinity of Gad which called themselves Reubenites, though we know nothing for certain about their homes. Originally the tribe of Reuben resided, not in the land east of the Jordan, but somewhere or other west of the Jordan. The Song of Deborah still appears to connect Reuben with residences west of the Jordan (Judg. 5:15b-16);[31] and in other places too there are at least traces of Reubenites formerly living west of the Jordan. According to Joshua 15:6; 18:17 there was a place in the district on the lower edge of the mountains south of Jericho which was called "stone of Bohan the son of Reuben." This stone had originally been called "thumb-stone," and the word "thumb" had been mistaken for a personal name and its bearer for a Reubenite, evidently because Reubenites had once lived in the district in question—immediately opposite the territory of the tribe of Gad on the other side of the Jordan Valley. The formulation of this local name evidently took place at a time when the tribe of Reuben was no longer known in the borderlands of Judah and Benjamin, and all that survived was the memory of the earlier presence there of parts of the tribe. West of this "thumb-stone" lay the plain of Achor (Josh. 15:7) with the pile of stones to which was linked the tradition of Joshua 7 telling of Achan, of the family of Carmi (Josh. 7:1, 18), which is probably identical with the Reubenite family of Carmi (Num. 26:6). It is true that Achan and the family of Carmi are expressly assigned to the tribe of Judah in Joshua 7:1, 18, but the only point that arises from that is that Reubenites who resided in the vicinity of the tribe of Judah finally joined the latter tribe. The fact that the name Hezron occurs among the clans of Reuben in Numbers 26:6 and was, according to Numbers 26:21, also the name of the subdivision of a Judaean clan, can be explained in the same way. Consequently, as far as we can tell from Old Testament tradition, the tribe of Reuben had no real territory of its own. There are merely slight traces of an earlier presence of Reubenites in the district of the Judaean–Benjaminite border on the eastern slopes of the mountains west of the Jordan, and there is also the traditional view that Reuben lived with Gad exactly opposite in the land east of the Jordan. From this it may be inferred that the tribe of Reuben had once had its real territory somewhere in the land west of Jordan. All that tradition tells us for certain, however, is that disintegrated elements of the tribe, in so far as they were not simply absorbed into Judah, finally retreated, apparently mainly into the land east of the Jordan, to the very periphery of Israelite territory. Thus, the tribe of Reuben leads as shadowy an existence in the tribal geography as the tribe of Simeon which has been discussed above.[32]

The north Palestinian tribes resided on the edge of the mountains which we call the mountains of Galilee, which rise northwards from the plain of Jezreel to the highest eminences of Palestine. The description of the borders contained in Joshua 19:24–31 assigns an extensive territory to the tribe of *Asher*, including the northern part of the coastal plain and Carmel with its foreland. In fact, according to Judges 1:31, 32, the Asherites did not occupy the city territories in the plain, their actual possessions being limited to the western rim of the Lower Galilean mountains east of Acco and of the Canaanite towns situated in the plain around Acco. The little tribe of Asher, whose name could, but need not inevitably, be the name of a god,[33] apparently had no necessity to expand eastwards and northwards into the almost empty lands in the interior of Lower and Upper Galilee; it was satisfied with the attractive hills and mountains above the plain of Acco. On the south-eastern edge of its territory on the western side of the great plain of *sahl el-baṭṭōf* which is set deep in the mountains of Lower Galilee, Asher came into contact with its Israelite neighbor.

This neighbor was the tribe of *Zebulun*, whose borders are described fairly exactly in Joshua 19:10–16. According to this account, the tribe resided in the mountains on the southern edge of Lower Galilee between the plain of Jezreel in the south and *sahl el-baṭṭōf* (which we have just mentioned) in the north, in the vicinity of the later city of Nazareth, the modern *en-nāṣira*. Zebulun was also a small tribe, and its territory not very extensive. In the west it bordered on the coastal plain north of Carmel, into whose city-state territories Zebulun found no access (Judges 1:30); in the south was the great plain of Jezreel, the soil of which was, and remained firmly, in possession of the Canaanite city-states. Zebulun does not appear to have needed the large-scale extension of its territory which could only have been effected by penetrating into the interior of Galilee. The name Zebulun cannot be explained for certain; it could originally have been a personal name.[34]

In Deuteronomy 33:18–19 Zebulun and *Issachar* are mentioned together, the main point being that they used to celebrate a sacrificial feast together "on a mountain." The mountain referred to

must be Tabor, which towers up impressively like a dome in the
north-eastern corner of the plain of Jezreel: for the sanctuary on
Tabor was a border sanctuary between Zebulun and Issachar in the
south-eastern corner of Zebulun and the north-western corner of
Issachar. From the details of the territory of the tribe of Issachar in
Joshua 19:17–23 it may be gathered that Issachar occupied the
southern spur of the Galilean mountains, which is bordered in the
west by the plain of Jezreel, in the south by the broad valley of the
nahr jālūd with the old Canaanite city of Beth-Sean (the modern
tell el-ḥöṣn near *bēsān*) and in the east by the Jordan Valley. We
shall discuss later in greater detail the special conditions under which
Issachar had been able to gain a footing here.[35] They explain the
tribe's curious name, which arose after its occupation of the land.
Issachar means "hired labourer" and the name was evidently first
given to it as a nickname, in connection with the satirical line about
Issachar which has come down to us in Genesis 49:15 in the blessing
of Jacob where Issachar's status is also referred to as that of a
dependent labourer.

On Mount Tabor Zebulun and Issachar bordered on the tribe
Naphtali whose territory, according to Joshua 19:34, also reached as
far as Mount Tabor and, according to Joshua 19:32–39, lay along
the eastern border of the Lower and Upper Galilean mountains. The
fact that, in this description of the borders, the territory of Naphtali
is made to extend fairly deep into the interior of Galilee and as far as
the territory of Asher, is presumably merely due to the theory that
the whole land was divided up among the tribes of Israel. The real
centres of Naphtali will have been above the Sea of Tiberias and the
adjacent northern part of the Jordan Valley. It is true that from that
base Naphtali could, if necessary, have acquired further land to the
west which was still in part wooded and uninhabited; but it is hardly
to be supposed that the tribe made any extensive use of this possibility. The name Naphtali does not look much like a personal name
and is altogether rather obscure; in this case too the point has at least
to be considered whether it did not originally refer to a particular
geographical region, in fact to the "Mount Naphtali" (*hār-naptalī*)
mentioned in Joshua 20:7,[36] though, according to the existing tradition, the mountain is supposed to have acquired its name from
the tribe. In fact the mountain may have given its name to the clans

that settled there, as happened in the case of Judah and Ephraim. The tribe of *Dan* lived on the very periphery and in a rather isolated position, near the sources of the Jordan in the highest reach of the Jordan Valley. Its center was the formerly Canaanite city of Laish (the modern *tell el-ḳāḍi*) mentioned in the Palestine list of Thothmes III. According to Judges 18:27, the tribe had acquired this city by military conquest and had given it the new name of Dan (Judg. 18:29) after its own name. The tribal name could originally have been a personal name.[37] A part of the section referring to Dan in the old inventory of the borders is probably contained in Numbers 34:7–11, where its borders, as those of the most northerly tribe, are introduced to establish the northern frontier of the whole territory of Israel, just as in Numbers 34:3–5 the southern frontier of Judah described in Joshua 15:2–4 serves to determine the southern frontier of the whole area. According to this, Dan had possessed not only the uppermost part of the Jordan Valley, but also part of the adjacent thickly wooded mountains to the east in the region now called *jōlān*; and this may in fact have been the case (*cf.* also Deut. 33:22), since the adjoining mountains westward were in the hands of the neighboring tribe of Naphtali; in the north, however, the rather uninviting mountains of central Syria and, in the south, the marshes around the northernmost lake of the Jordan Valley were unsuitable for settlement, so that the opportunities for the tribe to expand lay in the east.

In this remote area Dan had found a home after a first attempt at occupation in quite another part of the country had failed. According to Judges 1:34–35, the Danites had first tried to gain a footing in the hill country between the mountains and the coastal plain west of Jerusalem. But the earlier inhabitants[38] who ruled the country from their towns had not allowed the tribe of Dan to acquire the necessary land for settlement: an instructive example of the fact that the Israelite tribes found no room in the parts of the country which were already crowded with Canaanite cities and were usually not in a position and probably did not even attempt to make space for themselves by force of arms. So, according to Judges 18, the tribe of Dan withdrew again from this area and, as the hitherto unoccupied land in the vicinity had meanwhile been taken over by other Israelite tribes, it made a permanent home for itself in the remote area in the far north, employing force—and in this being an exception—to occupy a small Canaanite city. Apparently it was thereby the last of the tribes of Israel to achieve a permanent settlement for itself.

THE OCCUPATION OF THE LAND BY THE TRIBES OF ISRAEL

When one looks at the whole range of the Israelite settlements in Palestine it is immediately obvious that the tribes of Israel entered those parts of the country that had only been inhabited sparsely or not at all in the Bronze Age.[39] They occupied the various parts of the mountains west of the Jordan as well as the central section of the highlands east of the Jordan whilst the plains on which nature had bestowed its blessings remained in the hands of the older Canaanite population which was concentrated in cities and alongside which the tribes now lived as a new element in the population. This fact in itself shows very clearly that the Israelite occupation did not ensue from a warlike encounter between the newcomers and the previous owners of the land. In the parts of the country occupied by the Israelites there were only a few scattered Canaanite settlements, though the tribes may have occupied some of these by military force sooner or later. But such minor military conquests did not involve any conflict with the main mass of the Canaanites, who did not inhabit the region occupied by the tribes of Israel; and where, in the mountains, there was a series of Canaanite cities in one neighborhood, as in the vicinity of Jerusalem, no large-scale conflict occurred either: on the contrary, the tribes did not advance any further than the immediate vicinity of these city territories. The special case of the tribe of Dan, with its unsuccessful attempt to gain a footing in the hill country on the inner edge of the coastal plain, may be regarded as an example of the way the tribes were incapable of venturing, and in fact did not venture at all, to challenge the firmly established cities of the Canaanites with the dreaded chariots of iron of their rulers (cf. Josh. 17:16; Judg. 1:19; 4:3), to a large military conflict.

It is clear that, to begin with, the occupation of the land by the tribes took place fairly quietly and peacefully on the whole and without seriously disturbing the great mass of the previous inhabitants. We may think of it as having proceeded rather in the way in which even today semi-nomadic breeders of small cattle from the adjoining steppes and deserts pass over into a settled way of life in the cultivated countryside, the only difference being that at that time there was more uninhabited space available than there is today. Usually such semi-nomads make contact with agricultural land in the process of the so-called change of pasture: in the dry summer time when their flocks of sheep and goats can no longer find enough fodder outside, they come by an explicit or tacit arrangement with the inhabitants into agricultural country where the fields have been harvested; and here their easily satisfied flocks find fodder enough. Unlike the camel nomads of the desert with their proud contempt for a settled way of life, these peaceful semi-nomads always hanker after a more settled life in the coveted agricultural countryside; and as soon as there is an opportunity, whether owing to gaps in the previous settlements or access to inhabitable but previously uninhabited districts, the day comes when they do not return to their winter pastures in the steppe and desert but settle down permanently in the agricultural countryside. The Israelites were land-hungry semi-nomads of that kind before their occupation of the land: they probably first set foot on the land in the process of changing pastures, and in the end they began to settle for good in the sparsely populated parts of the country and then extended their territory from their original domains as occasion offered, the whole process being carried through, to begin with, by peaceful means and without the use of force.

This means that the Israelitish occupation was a process that lasted for a good time, not merely in the sense that each individual tribe needed a certain time to occupy its own territory but also in the sense that the tribes did not all settle in the land at the same period. We know for certain that the tribe of Dan did not move into its final domains until after most or all the other tribes had already found their new homes. It may be that this was a unique case, since this tribe had first tried to gain a footing in an area that was particularly unfavorable because of the presence of Canaanite cities; and we have no information to indicate that other tribes attained the ultimate possession of their territory only after unsuccessful attempts to establish themselves. But various details concerning the distribution of the tribal areas in Palestine show that the total occupation by the tribes of Israel was a complicated process which must have passed through several stages and covered a fairly long period of time.

In this connection the situation of the tribe of Reuben, which was discussed on pp. 131 f., and which always appears at the head of the list in the traditional enumeration of the tribes, is specially noteworthy. In the old tradition no special area was assigned to this tribe. If there were Reubenite clans in the neighborhood of the tribe of Gad, they had apparently only migrated later on to the land east of Jordan; in the opposite part of the land west of Jordan there were also a few traces of the former presence of Reubenites who had been absorbed to some extent in the association which made up the tribe of Judah. We have evidence therefore only of the remnants of the former tribe of Reuben, which must have dwelt somewhere in the central part of the land west of Jordan. But in the period of which we have more exact knowledge, this area, in so far as it was available to the Israelites at all and was not occupied by Canaanite city-state territories, was already in the hands of other tribes which were only able therefore to take possession, or at any rate, full possession, of their territories after the tribe of Reuben, for reasons unknown to us, had disappeared altogether, with the exception of a few insignificant remnants. It follows that Reuben must have been established before the other tribes completed their occupation.

This inference is confirmed by an evidently quite similar situation in the tribes of Simeon and Levi, which usually follow Reuben in the traditional list of the tribes. The old tradition does not assign any particular district to Simeon either; and there is only a brief record of the fact that Simeonite clans lived in the extreme south of the land and were counted as part of the greater whole of "Judah." Tradition has nothing to relate, however, of the areas occupied by the tribe of Levi and it is impossible to find any area where it could have dwelt in the same region as the other tribes.[40] But Simeon and Levi certainly once had their homes in Palestine since they are mentioned in the list of tribes; and the tradition of Genesis 34 originates in the fact that both tribes once lived in the vicinity of the formerly Canaanite city of Shechem in the central area west of Jordan. But it was there that the "house of Joseph" resided later on, and, again, we have to conclude that the "house of Joseph" was unable to occupy its new home until after Simeon and Levi had departed, and that it entered Palestine later than those two tribes. In the reference to Simeon and Levi in the blessing of Jacob both tribes are cursed to be "scattered in Israel"

(Gen. 49: 5–7) on the traditional basis of Genesis 34, and Reuben also receives a curse (Gen. 49:3–4). This refers to the later situation of these tribes and also indicates that the situation was not the same from the beginning. This being "scattered" was the precondition, however, of the entry of other tribes into their domiciles in Palestine.

This also demonstrates that the prehistory of the tribes of Israel and their occupation of the land were more involved than appears from the Old Testament tradition that was only evolved in a later age. This tradition proceeded from a situation in which the tribes were already living side by side in Palestine in an orderly way and had already accumulated some common historical experience. The assumption behind the tradition is that the events which led up to this situation were simultaneous and similar for all the tribes, in fact that Israel had been associated as a single unit in Palestine from the very beginning. Under the influence of a conception based on the development of large families and clans it thinks of the tribes and the whole of Israel as having arisen by propagation and ramification from the family of a common ancestor and having formed a unity based on blood relationship from time immemorial and being bound together by a common destiny. Thus the tribes were derived each from one ancestor who also gave his name to the tribe; and these ancestors appeared as brothers, as sons of a man called "Israel" from whom the name of the whole derived.[41] It is quite true that in the building up of the tribes and also in their mutual connections the element of blood relationship did play an important part. But in addition to that there were usually particular historical circumstances which led to the amalgamation of certain more or less related clans into a tribe and to the association of a particular number of tribes into a tribal confederation.

That the Old Testament tradition took too simple a view of the events which led to the development of Israel as a totality is obvious from the fact, already mentioned, that the tribes of Israel did not all settle on the soil of Palestine at the same time but, judging from various statements in the tradition that has come down to us, their occupation of the land was divided into at least two distinct phases. The data are scanty and only incidental to the main stream of a tradition which was shaped by the conception of a common prehistory and a joint occupation of the land. We have to reckon with the possibility that the settlement of Israel in Palestine was an even more confused and complicated process, but owing to the lack of information, it is impossible to come to any firm conclusion one way or the other. But we know enough to infer that the individual tribes each had their own particular prehistory and that their mutual relationships were at best loose and fluid before they entered into a solid and lasting association one with another on the soil of Palestine under the collective name of Israel. Thinking again in terms of later conditions, the Old Testament tradition also simplified the facts by assuming that the individual tribes were firmly established as clear-cut entities from the very outset. Some of the Israelite tribes bear names that were originally place-names and derived from the areas in which the tribes in question settled;[42] in another case a tribe derived its name from the particular circumstances in which it had acquired its land.[43] These tribes cannot have been given their names until their arrival on the soil of Palestine, which means that they were not finally constituted until their arrival there. The clans that were combined in these tribal units did not apparently bring a common tribal name with them which would have made the renaming which took place in Palestine unnecessary. It follows, therefore, that these tribes had not been self-contained units at all before their occupation of the land, but consisted of clans which did not form themselves into tribes until they began living together in Palestine. The same may be assumed to apply to the tribes from whose names nothing precise can be deduced and which perhaps adopted the name of their leading clan, which in its turn might have been called by the personal name of an ancestor.[44] The Old Testament tradition therefore not only goes beyond the facts by tracing back the names of the tribes beyond the period of the occupation, but also by assuming that the tribes had long existed as self-contained units. This too suggests that the process of the occupation must be reckoned to have lasted a long time, in the course of which the tribes were formed definitively, and that this process consisted of very many different and geographically widely separated movements of population.

It is true that the Old Testament records the conquest of the land of Palestine as the "promised land" by the whole of the tribes of Israel, as a single, self-contained operation. The older strata of the Pentateuch narrative originally led up to such a presentation of the conquest, though it is impossible to reconstruct it in detail as only its beginnings are preserved in Numbers 32:1ff., whereas its continuation was dropped in the final editing of the Pentateuch. But it is possible to infer from Numbers 32:1ff., that, according to this presentation, the united tribes set out for their subsequent domiciles, presumably all at the same time, from the southern part of the land east of Jordan. This accords in substance with the account of the occupation of the land in the Deuteronomistic narrative offered in Joshua 1-12 on the basis of an old source which consisted of a series of separate narratives. According to this account, the combined tribes conquered the land west of the Jordan by force of arms and took possession of it after crossing the lower Jordan, that is, approaching it from the southern part of the land east of Jordan. But on closer analysis the old nucleus of Joshua 1-12 proves that the stories related in those chapters did not deal with Israel as a whole at all but—apart from the specifically Ephraimite tradition in Joshua 10:1ff. and the specifically Galilean tradition in Joshua 11:1ff.— exclusively with the tribe of Benjamin. Geographically the whole thing takes place within the small territory of the tribe of Benjamin; the special tradition of the neighboring tribe of Ephraim links up with this quite well, whereas the special Galilean tradition stands completely on its own, quite unconnected geographically with what has gone before. But the Benjaminite tradition originally consisted of a series of aetiological narratives, which were collated on the asumption that it was from the east, across the lower Jordan, that the tribe of Benjamin entered into its territory around Jericho and the adjoining western part of the mountains.[45] This assumption represents the tribe of Benjamin's own living tradition about its occupation of the land; and we have here a concrete example of the fact that an individual tribe possessed its own special tradition concerning the way it came into possession of its land.[46] But what is true of the tribe of Benjamin will also be true of the other tribes; and if the tribes each had their own occupation tradition in very early times, they will certainly each have moved into their subsequent territory in Palestine in their own special way. Almost all these special traditions of the tribes have been lost, however, because within the Old Testament tradition already, they were replaced by the conception of the joint conquest of Palestine by Israel as a whole, and only the Benjaminite narrative has been preserved because, for special reasons which we still have to discuss, it was specially suitable as a basis for the concrete version of the joint Israelite occupation of the land west of Jordan and was therefore developed and supplemented with this in mind; the Benjaminite foundation is still quite apparent, however.

We must therefore attempt to throw some light on the complicated process of the occupation by considering the situation of the various tribal territories and a few scattered particulars in the Old Testament. As far as the group of central Palestinian tribes is concerned we are on relatively safe ground. For Benjamin we have the hypothesis already mentioned of the sequence of aetiological narratives in the first half of the Book of Joshua; and this accords so well in content with the situation of the tribe's places of occupation that it is no doubt historically accurate. According to this account, the clans which formed the tribe of Benjamin made their way from the east or south-east through the southern part of the land east of the Jordan over the lower Jordan, established themselves in the territory belonging to the city of Jericho (the modern *erīḥa*)[47] and from there they climbed the west Jordan mountains up to the heights where the Canaanite cities north-west of Jerusalem put an end to their further advance to the west.[48] The "house of Joseph" came from the same direction; for it evidently occupied the area in which it subsequently settled, from the south-east corner. Those clans which formed themselves into the tribe of Ephraim first gained a footing on "Mount Ephraim," from which the tribe derived its name, and this "Mount Ephraim" is presumably to be sought slightly north of the Benjaminite area above the lower Jordan Valley.[49] Since the "house of Joseph" appears in the Old Testament tradition as a coherent association of fair size, it is at least probable that not only the parts which joined to form the tribe of Ephraim but also the other parts of this association came from the same direction, and then occupied the whole of the great central part of the west Jordan mountains without a break.

The territory of Gad lay north-east of the Dead Sea along the route on which all these groups advanced through the southern land east of the Jordan; it may therefore be assumed that the Gadite clans carried out their occupation of the land as part of the same migration. They remained in a small area east of the Jordan Valley, either because they found homes there straight away with which they were so delighted that they were able to save themselves the journey through the Jordan Valley,[50] or because they found the west Jordan territories which were accessible from the southern land east of the Jordan already occupied and had to be content with the modest space available east of the Jordan Valley.

It is no accident that the Benjaminite tradition contained in Joshua 1–12 was later used as the basis of the description of the combined Israelite conquest of the land west of the Jordan, since, independently of that tradition, the older strata of the Pentateuch narrative made the united forces of Israel advance to their occupation of Palestinian soil through the southern land east of Jordan. In time, therefore, the specific and historically accurate memories of the occupation of the land by the important central Palestinian tribes were imposed on all the tribes of Israel. When the conception of a common history of Israel existing even before the occupation of the land was developed in the light of later conditions, it was the specifically central Palestinian traditions which determined the picture of the total occupation of the land by Israel as a whole.

Before the tribes we have mentioned established themselves in the central part of Palestine, the tribes of Reuben, Simeon and Levi had (as we have discussed on pp. 138 f.) settled somewhere in the central territory west of Jordan, and had then, for reasons which are uncertain,[51] migrated and dispersed and thereby made room for the tribes that came later. As we no longer know exactly where they settled to begin with, it is also impossible to describe the exact course of their occupation of the land. It is possible that they had entered the land by roughly the same route as the later tribes of central Palestine. In that case their starting-point will also have been somewhere in the steppes and deserts on the border of the southern land east of Jordan.

Matters were different with the south Palestinian tribes. For them we have, to begin with, a Calebite story which indicates that the tribe of Caleb entered its territory in Palestine from the south, that is, from the region of the so-called Negev. For the tradition on which the story contained in Numbers 13, 14 is based, and which sets out to explain how it came about that Caleb attained possession of the important city of Hebron, undoubtedly originally amounted to the fact that Caleb was assigned the city of Hebron along with its fertile surroundings as a reward for its courageous behavior, without having first to join in the great detour through the southern land east of the Jordan as is suggested by the later insertion of the tradition into the larger narrative complex of the Pentateuch. But the real starting-point of this narrative was the Negev; it was from there that the thrust to the mountains in the north had been made which brought Caleb into possession of Hebron. The situation of the Calebite territory suggests that it is highly probable that this account of the journey of Caleb is historically accurate. By and large the most obvious assumption is that the tribes that had settled in the southernmost part of the west Jordan mountains had come from the adjoining semi-nomadic area to the south. In the case of Caleb there is the additional connection with a tribal association which was also represented among the Edomites.[52] The home of this tribal association of the Kenezites can only have been in the Negev, whence individual components had reached Edom over the *wādi el-'araba* and others had come into the west Jordan mountains. The same applies to Othniel, whose relationship with Caleb and whose one-time membership of the tribal confederation we have just mentioned also suggest that it originally came from the Negev. The Kenites had also apparently come from the south, so far as they settled at all in the vicinity of Caleb and Othniel; since, according to I Samuel 15:6, they had once belonged to the same tribal confederation as the Amalekites, whose territory was somewhere in the northern part of the Sinai Peninsula.

How much one has to reckon on unusual and unexpected tribal migrations is shown by the case of the tribe of Simeon which, although it resided in the extreme south in the region of Beersheba and therefore actually in the Negev itself, had not come from this semi-nomadic area, at any rate not directly, but had migrated from the very heart of Palestine, and, after it had become unable to maintain itself any longer in its original Palestinian settlements, had found a place on the extreme border of Israelite territory, like the tribe of Dan in the extreme north. It is permissible to assume that the southern part of the mountains west of Jordan was already occupied when the remnants of Simeon had to seek for new homes, so that it was only in the Negev that they found a district in some degree suitable for permanent settlement.

It is also very difficult to establish anything for certain about how the tribe of Judah came into occupation of the land. From the south the cities of Hebron, and possibly Debir too, obstructed the access to its territory, and city-states in the region of Jerusalem also made access difficult from the north. The tribe of Judah established itself between these two regions. The situation of its territory suggests that it may either have moved in from the Negev from a southerly direction or from the most southerly end of the Jordan Valley, and therefore, ultimately, from the east. The fact that, in the traditional enumeration of the twelve tribes of Israel, Judah appears in the leading group with Reuben, Simeon and Levi, suggests that it gained a footing in Palestine in the opening phase of the occupation; and as this oldest group of tribes appears to have settled predominantly in the central land west of the Jordan, we are probably entitled to assume that they came in over the lower Jordan from an easterly direction, and this may well have been true of Judah too. There is, however, a complete lack of concrete evidence to make even a moderately firm decision possible.

The course of events is least certain of all in the case of the Galilean tribes and the traditions that have come down to us about them are far and away the scantiest of all. It is highly probable that the ways by which the individual tribes in this group came into possession of their land in Palestine varied considerably. The only case about which we have more detailed information shows how complicated the prehistory of the occupation could be. We refer to the tribe of Dan, which ultimately found a place for itself in the far north near the sources of the Jordan after a vain attempt to gain a footing in quite a different place in Palestine. The situation was, again, quite different in the case of the tribes of Zebulun and Issachar. After the organization of the traditional twelve-tribe system, which we have still to discuss, these two tribes formed a special group on their own, with Reuben, Simeon, Levi and Judah, that is, with the tribes that had settled in the central land west of the Jordan in a very early stage of the occupation, and it is therefore probable that they had entered the land about the same time and in a similar fashion, and had been in more or less close touch with them. Of the Galilean tribes, their homes were nearest to the central part of the west Jordan mountains, only separated from it by the plain of Jezreel or the valley plain of *nahr jālūd* with its city-state territories. It cannot be proved with any

F

certainty, and need not necessarily be assumed, that the tribe itself had once resided there with those other tribes and had only subsequently been forced, for reasons unknown to us, to migrate from there to near-by southern Galilee.[53] But it may be considered probable that they had moved into their later dwelling-places from a southerly or south-easterly direction. The tribe of Naphtali, on the other hand, must have come through the northern land east of the Jordan from an easterly direction, particularly if it may be assumed to have first gained a footing on the "Naphtali" mountains in the region of Kedesh. It is almost impossible to say anything for sure as to how the tribe of Asher reached its territory.

In the Old Testament we have one or two striking statements from which we are able to gather something about the special conditions in which various of the Galilean tribes came into possession of their land in Palestine. In Jacob's blessing the tribe of Issachar is criticized and mocked because—as "a strong ass couching down between two burdens"—it "bowed its shoulder to bear" and "became a servant unto tribute" for the sake of peace and quiet and a pleasant land (Gen. 49:14–15), and the name Issachar (hired labourer) is undoubtedly due to the same cause. If this statement was true, Issachar had acquired its territorial possessions at the price of its independence. What actually happened may be inferred from a few statements in the Amarna tablets, according to which the Canaanite city of Shunem (the modern *sōlem*) which was situated in the later Issacharite territory, was destroyed in the Amarna period and its soil had to be cultivated ("tilled") by forced labour on behalf of, and in the interests of, the then Egyptian sovereign and under the supervision and at the suggestion of the Canaanite city governors.[54] The land-seeking clans apparently offered their services and were settled on the territory of the former city of Shunem and formed themselves into the tribe of "Issachar" and from Shunem they finally occupied the adjoining mountain country to the east. Several other striking statements in the Old Testament about Israelite tribes can probably best be understood in the light of this fairly concrete situation. In the same blessing of Jacob it is said of Zebulun that it "shall dwell at the haven of the sea" and "shall be for an haven of ships"[55] (Gen. 49:13). Now the dwelling-places of this tribe that are known to us did not lie on the coast at all or even anywhere near it; and there is no reason to assume that Zebulun had lived by the sea at some previous time, since all the inhabitable places on the coast had been occupied long before the tribes of Israel appeared. It is more likely that this reference to Zebulun, which was probably intended as a criticism, means that the Zebulunites had to perform certain compulsory tasks, above all in the harbors of the northern coastal plain. And it is not difficult to surmise that the acceptance of this permanent obligation was the price the clans which made up Zebulun had to pay in return for permission from the neighboring Canaanite cities to settle in the lower Galilean mountains in the hinterland of the coastal plain. This supposition is confirmed by the fact that in Judges 5:17b Asher is also said to have "continued on the sea shore," although in fact Asher no more lived on the coast than its neighbor Zebulun, but in the mountainous hinterland of the northern coastal plain. The remark may therefore be assumed to mean the same as the reference to Zebulun. Owing to their dependence on the neighboring Canaanite cities much of the latter's wealth flowed into these tribes on the edge of the northern coastal plain and the plain of Jezreel. There are allusions to the good life in Asher in the blessing of Jacob and in that of Moses too (Gen. 49:20; Deut. 33:24); and in Deuteronomy 33:19, Zebulun and Issachar are even said to "suck of the abundance of the seas," which can only mean that they too gained indirectly from the commercial profits of the Canaanites. In Lower Galilee, therefore, the situation of the tribes was determined in a special way by the direct vicinity of the plains with their cities, and here the occupation of the land seems to have taken place under special conditions.

It is very curious that in Judges 5:17a the tribe of Dan is also said to have "remained in ships" although its dwelling-place lay far away from the sea by the sources of the Jordan, a fact which is obviously taken for granted in the Song of Deborah, and in Judges 18:28 the city of Laish is explicitly stated to have been "far from Zidon." But perhaps the latter remark is significant in so far as it does establish some connection between the territory of Dan and the city of Sidon (*cf.* also Judg. 18:7) and the Mediterranean coast; and it looks as if at the time Zidon had sovereign rights in the uppermost reaches of the valley of the Jordan. The reference to Dan in Judges 5:17a can therefore probably be taken to mean that this tribe also had to buy its settlement by accepting a certain amount of compulsory labour service in South Phoenician seaports. Of all the Galilean tribes Naphtali is the only one which we do not find mentioned in this connection and that is probably no accident, since Naphtali occupied the territory in the mountains west of the Lake Huleh (*bahret el-ḥüleh*) and the Sea of Tiberias which was least favored by nature. The Naphtalite clans probably contented themselves with these modest dwelling-places and thereby preserved their independence.

Since the occupation of the land by the Israelite tribes was therefore a process which covered a long period of time and consisted of various, geographically distinct movements, it is impossible to assign an exact date to the occupation as a whole. All one can do is to give an approximate *terminus a quo* and a *terminus ad quem*. Later on, the Old Testament tradition greatly simplified the process and concentrated it all into a single brief episode, so that as a source of direct information about the temporal duration and sequence of these movements it is quite unreliable; and we neither have nor can expect to have any historical information about these matters outside the Old Testament since, on the whole, the occupation took place more or less unobtrusively, away from the main scenes of the earlier history of Palestine, with no particularly striking events which might be expected to have attracted the attention of the ancient Oriental powers of the time and occasioned some kind of written record. The Amarna period may be considered the *terminus a quo*, but not because otherwise the process of the occupation of the land would be bound to have been mentioned in the political correspondence of the Amarna tablets;[56] the city-states of Palestine, from whose domains the Amarna tablets derive, in so far as they are concerned with Palestine at all, were hardly affected to any degree by the Israelite occupation to begin with. But there are two points which suggest that in the Amarna period the Israelite tribes had not yet settled in the land. At that time Bethlehem was still "a city of the land of Jerusalem"[57] and only later became the center of the tribe of Judah as it was being constituted; and only at that period did the destruction of the city of Shunem produce that gap in the Canaanite system of city-states in the vicinity of the Jezreel plain which was later occupied by the tribe of Issachar.[58] Judah and probably Issachar as well were part of the older group of Israelite tribes which were the first to settle in the land. On the other hand, in the case of Issachar, the actual sequence of events suggests that this tribe moved into its territory not long after the end of the Amarna period. We must therefore place the beginnings of the Israelite occupation in the second half of the 14th century B.C. The final conclusion of the process will probably have taken place at least a hundred years before the accession of Saul. It is true that we have no reliable information at all regarding the temporal duration and sequence of the events recorded as having occurred on the soil of Palestine before the formation of the Kingdom of Israel. But the list of the "Judges of Israel" in Judges 10:1–5; 12:7–15,[59] which belongs to this period, alone embraces sixty-eight years and it is not certain that the series is complete at either end. Judging from this, the occupation had ended at the latest *circa* 1100 B.C.

These dates, especially the last, merely represent the extreme possibilities and they must not be assumed to mean that the occupation took two hundred years all told. That is unlikely. But the tradition being what it is, all we can do is cautiously to mark out the extreme limits of probability. Presumably the occupation took place within a considerably shorter period of time, in the course of a few decades; and the conditions prevailing in the tribe of Issachar, which we have already discussed, suggest that the process took place more in the first than the second half of the period, that is, approximately the 13th century B.C. But it must be remembered that this more precise dating is nothing more than a likely supposition. In recent times attempts have been made to date the process or its individual elements more exactly on the basis of archaeological data. It is now possible to assign related strata of settlements on ancient sites which have been excavated, to a period of only a few decades, even without the aid of epigraphic discoveries, simply on the basis of the evidence of the material remains. The idea inevitably suggests itself of relating the destruction of Palestinian cities, for which there is clear evidence within the period in question, to the appearance of the Israelites in Palestine and dating that appearance accordingly.[60] But so far there has been no absolutely certain evidence of this kind, and such evidence is in fact hardly likely to be found. For the Israelite tribes did not acquire their territories by warlike conquest and the destruction of Canaanite cities,[61] but usually settled in hitherto unoccupied parts of the country. These destructions were more probably due to the continual conflicts of the city governments among themselves, which are known to have occurred in the Amarna period, and, *circa* 1200 B.C., to the warlike emergence of the "Sea Peoples" in the regions of the city-states of Palestine. The Israelites established themselves chiefly in settlements newly founded by themselves. If the beginnings of these settlements could be dated with archaeological accuracy, that would help to ascertain the date of the occupation. But that is scarcely possible. It is true that these new foundations at the beginning of the Iron Age had an enclosure erected with stones instead of the strong city walls of the Bronze Age Canaanite cities which have maintained the successive strata of the settlements intact for thousands of years. The old sites which date only from the Iron Age have usually disintegrated and their remains have been scattered in the course of time and have disappeared: all that has survived on the old sites are miscellaneous relics, usually without any ascertainable stratification. It must also be remembered that the civilization of the Early Iron Age was very much more poverty-stricken and less sharply defined in stages than that of the preceding Bronze Age, and this fact makes it impossible to date the, for the most part scanty, remains at all accurately. It follows that the beginning of the Israelite settlement cannot be dated any more exactly and definitely from an archaeological point of view than from the evidence of the literary tradition. Hence the matter must be left at a cautious defining of the period of the Israelite occupation.

This occupation of the land was, however, part of a wider historical movement. At the same period land-seeking elements appeared everywhere on the borders of Syria and Palestine and, even beyond, in Mesopotamia between the upper reaches of the Euphrates and the Tigris and in the middle of the Euphrates. They settled in large numbers especially in the Syrian interior and in the adjacent area on both sides of the upper Euphrates, and then established more or less permanent and, according to local conditions, more or less comprehensive political organizations. In the immediate vicinity of the Israelite tribes, numerous clans settled, as part of the same movement, in the southern part of the land east of the Jordan, which had hardly been inhabited at all for centuries, southwards towards the Gulf of *el-'aḳaba*, and here they formed themselves into the peoples of the Ammonites, Moabites and Edomites[62] and apparently very early founded kingdoms. In Syria and Mesopotamia these elements were known by the collective name of Aramaeans, a term which occasionally occurs among the neighboring Assyrians in Middle Assyrian royal inscriptions and then is also frequently mentioned in the Old Testament.[63] This great movement, of which the settlement of the Israelite tribes was part and which consisted of many different elements, took place during the transition from the Bronze to the Iron Age, proceeding from the Syrian–Arabian desert into the bordering agricultural lands. It is therefore natural to call the movement the "Aramaic migration" and it is perfectly in order to do so provided one remembers that it was not in fact a uniform and deliberately planned process. In the Old Testament itself the ancestor of Israel is described as an "Aramaean" in a solemn, cultic profession of faith (Deut. 26:5); and the Israelites once spoke an ancient Aramaic dialect before in Palestine they adopted the Canaanite language native there, literally "the language of Canaan" (Isa. 19:18), which was admittedly closely akin to their own ancient Aramaic. The Hebrew of the Old Testament still shows traces of the mixture of various dialects.

To take this view involves the rejection of a theory which is very old and has been revived in various forms and on different grounds right up to the most recent times: the theory that the prehistory of the Israelite tribes was bound up with the Hyksos movement.[64] Since it has been established that the Israelites cannot be simply identified with the conquering ruling class of the Hyksos, it has been thought that they came with the Hyksos migration, namely from Mesopotamia, whence the Hyksos appear to have come and where, according to an Old Testament tradition, the forefathers of Israel had lived.[65] The numerous texts from the 15th century B.C. in which there are references to legal and social institutions such as are familiar from the Old Testament stories of the "Patriarchs,"[66] which have been found in the ancient city of Nuzu east of the Tigris (near the modern *kerkūk*), appear to support this theory. At that time Nuzu was a Hurrian city and still had connections with the Hurrian elements of the former Hyksos movement, and so the Israelites would have become familiar with these Hurrian institutions through their connection with the Hyksos, and so introduced them into Palestine. But the arguments on which these suppositions are based are unsound. These institutions, if there is a real link of the kind supposed, could have been introduced into Syria–Palestine by the Hyksos themselves and could have become known to the Israelites when they entered Palestine. But the tracing of Israel's ancestors to Mesopotamia is based on the accurate tradition of the Aramaic relationship,[67] which was then specifically applied later on to the main Aramaic center on both sides of the upper Euphrates. Against linking the Israelite occupation and the "Aramaic migration" with the Hyksos movement there is the fact that, to the best of our knowledge, the occupation took place much later than the appearance of the Hyksos and that the Aramaeans did not emerge as a migrant stratum until long after the period of the Hyksos; but above all, there is the fact that the Israelite occupation took place in the very regions of Palestine which played no part at all in the Hyksos period and were not directly affected by the Hyksos rule at all, and it proceeded from directions which had nothing in common with the direction of the Hyksos movement. The Hyksos rule in Palestine extended to the city-state regions of the land; but it is clear that originally the Israelite tribes had no connection of any kind with that system of government, but only established a connection sooner or later according to local conditions.

NOTES

1. *Cf.* above all A. Alt, "Das System der Stammesgrenzen im Buche Josua," Sellin-Festschrift (1927), pp. 13–24 = *Kleine Schriften zur Geschichte des Volkes Israel*, I (1953), pp. 193–202, and also M. Noth, *ZDPV*, 58 (1935), pp. 185 ff.

2. It is found in a conglomeration of supplements to the Deuteronomistic work and it is uncertain how it got there. In its present form it presupposes the later incorporation of these city-state territories in the Kingdom of David and Solomon.

3. This list was subsequently used to compile a later and apocryphal list of the numerical strengths of the single Israelite tribes as applicable at the time of the Exodus from Egypt; and so it was assumed that Moses undertook a census of the people, and the whole episode was inserted as an afterthought into the Pentateuch narrative which had already been compiled; *cf.* M. Noth, *Das System der zwölf Stämme Israels* (1930), pp. 122 ff.

4. Noth, *History of Israel*, p. 32.

5. This may be seen, above all, from Genesis 38 where incidents from tribal history appear with other narrative elements in a complex section now not analyzable with any certainty (*cf.* M. Noth, *Überlieferungsgeschichte des Pentateuch,*

pp. 162 f.) and also from the geographical list of the settlements which is contained in I Chronicles 2:4 (*cf.* M. Noth, *ZDPV*, 55 [1932], pp. 97–124). On the incident itself *cf.* M. Noth, *PJB*, 30 (1934), pp. 31–47.

6. From the Old Testament we know the city names *ygbhh* and *yr'lh*; on the other hand, the place-name *yhwd* (Josh. 19:45) is difficult to separate etymologically from the name *yhwdh*.

7. *Cf.* Joshua 11:21 and especially Joshua 20:7; 21:11, where Hebron, which was not inhabited by Judaeans at all, is described as situated on the *har-yᵉhūdā*; *cf.* further II Chronicles 27:4.

8. Judges 1:16; Psalm 63:1.

9. In Numbers 32:12; Joshua 14:6, 14 Caleb is called a "Kenezite"; *cf.* also Joshua 15:17; Judges 1:13; 3:9.

10. *Cf.* Genesis 36:11, 42.

11. *Cf.* Noth, *History of Israel*, p. 33, note 1.

12. Thus, according to the Septuagint.

13. The fairly late information contained in I Samuel 15:6 might originate in the fact of the juxtaposition of nomadic *and* established Kenites. According to Judges 1:16 (text emended) it was especially the Kenite clan of *bᵉnē-hebab* that settled in Palestine.

14. The name of the tribe might indicate that it was an association of desert smiths (*cf.* Arabic *ḳain* = "smith"); but the Kenites who had settled were certainly farmers like the other inhabitants.

15. Of the names of these tribes Othniel and especially Jerahmeel are evidently personal names, that is, names of real or fictitious ancestors of these tribes. On the name of the Kenites *cf.* the previous note. There is still some doubt about the name Caleb, which apparently means "dog" (in an archaic form of the word) and may be a personal name with this meaning; on the other hand, animal names might also be originally tribal names, if not on the basis of an old system of totemism, at any rate in connection with certain tribal tokens or the like.

16. It occurs in fairly old contexts in Joshua 17:17; Judges 1:23, 35; II Samuel 19:21; I Kings 11:28 and also in Joshua 18:5; Amos 5:6; Obadiah 18; Zechariah 10:6.

17. *Cf.* above all, II Samuel 2:4, 7, 10, 11, also I Kings 12:21, 23. The expression "house of Israel" was probably modelled on the expression "house of Judah" as a result of the juxtaposition of the kingdoms of Israel and Judah; thus II Samuel 12:8; I Kings 12:21, and elsewhere (not yet II Samuel 2:10 and 5:3 *cf.* with 2:4). "Israel" was from the very outset not a tribal name at all, but a comprehensive total description.

18. *Cf.* Joshua 17:18.

19. *Cf.* Noth, *History of Israel*, p. 32.

20. It was originally the custom to name the two names in this order and it was only later that the habit arose of putting Ephraim first because of its importance; *cf.* Genesis 48:1–20.

21. This is clear above all in I Kings 4:8; Joshua 20:7; 21:21. Other old references to the expression "Mount Ephraim" will be found in Joshua 17:15; Judges 7:24; I Samuel 1:1.

22. On the striking use of the preposition *'im cf.* Genesis 34:4.

23. This place Ephraim may have been situated on the ruined site of *khirbet el merjame* near *sāmye*; *cf.* W. F. Albright, *JPOS*, 3 (1923), pp. 36 ff. and *AASOR*, 4 (1924), pp. 127 ff. and also A. Alt, *PJB*, 24 (1928), pp. 35 ff.

24. The change of meaning of this name may be compared with that of the name Gilead; on the latter *cf.* M. Noth, *PJB*, 37 (1941), pp. 59 ff.

25. *Cf.* Joshua 17:14–18.

26. More details on this in M. Noth, *PJB*, 37 (1941), pp. 59 ff.

27. *Cf.* also M. Noth, *Das Buch Josua* (² 1953).

28. The tribe of *Banū-yamina* which is known from the Mari-texts (*cf.* W. v. Soden, *WO*, I, 3 [1948]), is only connected with our Benjamin in name (it has the same meaning) but not in fact.

29. Details in M. Noth, *ZAW*, N.F. 19 (1944), pp. 30 ff.

30. The name Gad is difficult to interpret; it may probably be regarded as originally a personal name (*cf.* M. Noth, *Geschichte und Altes Testament = Alt-Festschrift* [1953], pp. 145 f.).

31. There is no reference to the land east of the Jordan until the following verse 17.

32. The meaning of the name Reuben is obscure.

33. It would then be the male counterpart of the name of the female deity *ashērāh*.

34. *Cf.* the personal name Zebul in Judges 9:28 ff. as well as the Ugaritic *zbl*, which appears to be a particular honorary title.

35. *Cf.* pp. 146 f.

36. According to this passage the place Kedesh (modern *kedes*) was specifically situated on the "Mount Naphtali," which may therefore be sought north-west of the uppermost end of the Sea of Jordan, the lake that is now called *hule*. The Naphtalites will therefore have first gained a footing in this district. The same geographical connotation resides in the expression "Kedesh-naphtali" (Judg. 4:6), in which "Naphtali" may be the genitive of the region added to the place-name, as is certainly the case in the similarly compounded expression "Jabesh-gilead" (I Samuel 11:1 and elsewhere) and probably in the expression "Bethlehem-judah" (Judg. 17:7 and elsewhere), in which "Judah" also appears to have retained its original meaning as the name of a region.

37. *Cf.* M. Noth, *Geschichte und Altes Testament = Alt-Festschrift* (1953), p. 146.

38. In Judges 1:34, 35 they are called "Amorites," the general name for the pre-Israelite population. According to the stories of the Danite Samson which are set in the same district (Judg. 13–16) the hostile neighbors were the Philistines, who had set up their dominion over the "Amorites" in the southern coastal plain.

39. *Cf.*, in addition to A. Alt, *Die Landnahme der Israeliten in Palästina* (1925), especially pp. 31 ff., above all, A. Alt, "Erwägungen über die Landnahme der Israeliten in Palästina," *PJB*, 35 (1939), pp. 8–63 = *Kleine Schriften zur Geschichte des Volkes Israel*, I (1953), pp. 89–125 (especially pp. 121 ff.) and pp. 126–175.

40. It is clear from the fact that it is mentioned in the list of the other tribes and also from Genesis 49:5–7 that the tribe of Levi was a "secular" tribe like the

other tribes. In what relation the later Levitical priesthood stood to it is a question on its own, which need not affect the above statement.

41. The equating of the *heros eponymus* "Israel" with the "patriarch" Jacob occurs very early on in the Old Testament but is a secondary process in the historical tradition.

42. Thus Judah, Ephraim, Benjamin and probably Naphtali too; *cf.* pp. 124, 127 f., 130, 134 f.

43. This is true of Issachar; *cf.* p. 146.

44. Manasseh may be considered an example of this—the name is undoubtedly a personal name. Manasseh was presumably a Machirite clan, which did not join in the migration into the land east of the Jordan, and gave its name to all the parts of Machir that remained behind in the land west of the Jordan, and finally included under this name even the East Jordanites who had migrated (*cf.* pp. 129).

45. More details in M. Noth, *Das Buch Josua* (² 1953), pp. 20 ff.

46. It is no longer possible to say to what extent special tribal traditions lurk behind the narrative fragments in Judges 1:1 ff. In quite a different context we have a special tribal tradition in the traditional basis of Numbers 13, 14; *cf.* pp. 143 f.

47. The question as to when Canaanite Jericho came to an end has not yet been completely elucidated archaeologically. Probably Benjamin did not find Jericho an established and fully inhabited city; *cf.* M. Noth, *op. cit.*, p. 21.

48. It is wrong to conclude from Genesis 35:16–20 that Benjamin only subsequently branched off from the "house of Joseph" in Palestine and constituted itself as an independent tribe alongside Joseph. The conversion of narrative details of the "patriarch" stories into tribal history (Genesis 35:16–20 draws attention to Rachel's grave) is inadmissible. Benjamin originated in the first place on the soil of Palestine no more and no less than the other tribes; and we have a specific tradition concerning the manner of Benjamin's occupation of the land.

49. *Cf.* p. 60.

50. The matter is described thus in Numbers 32:1 ff.

51. According to Genesis 34, military conflicts with the Canaanite city of Shechem appear to have been the cause for Simeon and Levi.

52. *Cf.* p. 124.

53. Since we do not know what special circumstances prevailed in this particular case, it is impossible to draw any positive conclusion regarding the earlier dwelling-places of Issachar from the fact that, according to Judges 10:1, 2, the Issacharite Tola lived and was buried in "Shamir in Mount Ephraim" (exact position unknown).

54. The references and their precise explanation will be found in A. Alt, *PJB*, 20 (1924), pp. 34 ff.

55. In the passage about the "ships" the text is not quite in order and impossible to reconstruct with certainty. The final remark, that Zebulun's border "shall be unto Zidon," appears to be a postscript.

56. The Habiru-Hebrews of the Amarna tablets are not to be identified with the Israelites. *Cf.* Noth, *History of Israel*, pp. 33 f.

57. *Cf.* Noth, *History of Israel*, p. 32.

58. *Cf.* p. 146.

59. More details on this traditional element will be found in Noth, *History of Israel*, pp. 101 f.

60. W. F. Albright has repeatedly attempted this in numerous articles.

61. The conquest narratives in the first half of the Book of Joshua (*cf.* especially Joshua 6; 8; 10:28ff.; 11:10ff.) originate in aetiological traditions which proceeded from the later devastated condition of the sites in question (*cf.* M. Noth, *Das Buch Josua* [² 1953]).

62. Further details on these peoples in *WAT*, pp. 68 ff.

63. On the prehistory of the name Aramaean, *cf.* A. Dupont-Sommer, Supplements to *VT*, I (1953), pp. 40 ff.

64. Thus first of all Josephus, *Contra Apionem*, I, 14, § 75 ff. In modern times the opinion has been shared particularly by egyptologists.

65. *Cf.* especially Genesis 24:10 ff.; 27:43 ff.; also Genesis 11:10–32; 12:5.

66. *Cf.* most recently C. H. Gordon, *BASOR*, 66 (1937), pp. 25 ff.; M. Burrows, *JAOS*, 57 (1937), pp. 259 ff.; R. de Vaux, *RB*, 56 (1949), pp. 22 ff.

67. In its original form the tradition exists in the story of the relationship between Jacob and "the Aramaean Laban" (*cf.* especially Genesis 31:19 ff.).

7

THE SCHOOL OF ALT AND NOTH

A Critical Evaluation

John Bright

LET US PROCEED, then, to an evaluation of the methods of the Alt-Noth school, particularly as these have been systematically developed and applied in the work of Noth. In doing so, it would be well if we were to avoid a piecemeal criticism, the endless debating of points of detail, and were rather to attempt to weigh the approach as a whole. We shall be concerned with the questions: Is this approach methodologically sound? Docs it produce satisfying results? And if not, wherein lie its weaknesses? Particular points will be discussed only as they seem symptomatic of the underlying method.

1

If one begins—as one certainly should—by seeking for points of merit upon which to lay the finger, one has no difficulty at all. Indeed, so many are these, and so massive is the learning and so relentless the logic with which the whole structure is supported, that one is moved in the first instance to admiration.

1. The approach is sound, first of all, in that it takes its start from, and is firmly based in, the methods and assured results of literary criticism. This is both evident and expressly developed in the opening pages of Noth's great methodological work [on tradi-

tion-history], (*UG,* 1–44). The closely reasoned analysis of the sources offered there makes it clear that Noth begins his work with his feet firmly planted on the documentary criticism of the past. True, he has elsewhere[1] struck new paths in criticism, especially as regards the relationship of the Tetrateuch to the Deuteronomic corpus, the structure of the Deuteronomic corpus itself, and the problem of the documents in Joshua. But much of this seems very sound, and none of it represents a retreat from literary criticism as such. Alt and Noth are thus, in this respect, heirs of the classic Wellhausen tradition; they share with that tradition the merit that their approach to history begins with a critical scrutiny of the documents.

And it might be submitted at this point that all sound history writing must begin so. It ought to be a first principle that history writing cannot begin until the documents of history have been isolated, placed in their proper historical setting, examined for whatever bias or tendency they may have: in short, evaluated as sources of history. To be sure, the day has passed for such overclever analysis as older scholars were often guilty of, the splitting of a verse between two or three sources and a couple of redactors—a *reductio ad absurdum* of critical method. Yet, if Noth on occasion exhibits more precision in this regard than one can follow, surely he is right in holding to the methods and assured results of literary criticism. Ezekiel Kaufmann, it must be said, is an illustration of what happens when this is not done.

2. Again, the Alt-Noth school is surely correct in its understanding that documentary criticism is only the beginning, that one must seek to press behind the documents into their prehistory. Here Alt and Noth have gone far beyond the Wellhausen school, which too often imagined that to date a document determined the age and value of its contents. This school knows well that such is not the case. On the contrary, even the latest documents contain material of the greatest antiquity. The historian, therefore, cannot stop with the finished document, but must ask after the origin of its material.

We must therefore make it quite plain at the outset that we have no quarrel with the term *Überlieferungsgeschichte* (tradition-history) as such, nor with the task involved in tracing it. For, if we may put it so, the *Überlieferung* (tradition) assuredly had a *Geschichte* (history)! Between the original *Sitz im Leben* (historical setting) of the individual traditions, and the finished form of those traditions in the Pentateuch documents, there was certainly a long and complex history of transmission, oral or written, or both. Anything that can be done to elucidate that history is clear gain. It is only as the original *Sitz im Leben* of a tradition is understood that that tradition can be constructively evaluated. Whatever one may say of Noth's results, there can be no quarrel with the effort to trace the history of tradition as such. And, properly controlled, such results can be most constructive, indeed.[2]

Nor have we a quarrel *per se* with the *method* by which Noth seeks to trace tradition history. Its first step is modest, not new, and indeed no more than an extension of literary criticism. We refer to the manner in which Noth (*UG,* 40–44), from a comparison of J and E, comes to the conclusion that E does not depend on J, nor J on E, but that both go back to a common *Grundlage* (basic source) (G). G may be assumed to underlie wherever J and E run parallel, although the fragmentary state of E prevents the full reconstruction of it. If J is to be dated approximately in the tenth century, this would mean that G must be placed before the rise of the monarchy. Thus, by a deduction from documentary criticism, the horizons of the history of tradition are pushed a step farther back. This, however, is not new; others had already based themselves on a similar deduction.[3]

Noth, to be sure, is at times too hasty in his deductions regarding G. For example (*UG,* 120–4), he reasons that the Hebron-Mamre traditions were no original part of the Abraham cycle because, lacking in E, they were not a part of G, but represent a later addition by J. But if, as Noth has agreed (*UG,* 42), E is too incomplete to allow a full reconstruction of G, this is to exceed the evidence. If J and E are parallel, we may affirm the presence of G behind them; but if they are not, it is risky to assume its absence.

But if we cannot be dogmatic about the extent of G, to establish the fact of it is clear gain. Noth is thus able to go beyond von

Rad's position and to trace all of the major themes of the Penta-teuch, plus the "all Israel" orientation of the tradition, back to G—hence to the period of the Judges. Thus an important step in the history of tradition is made.

Beyond this modest beginning, however, the Alt-Noth school seeks to attack the history of tradition by the methods of form criticism. And, once again, we must make it clear that we have no quarrel with those methods *as such*.

The methods of form criticism were first applied to Old Testa-ment studies by H. Gunkel and his school. No one who is aware of the epoch-making importance of Gunkel's work can doubt the constructive value of the method, if properly controlled.[4] The methods of Gunkel have been further sharpened by Alt and Noth and applied with *éclat,* particularly to the early traditions of Israel. And the results have by no means been barren. One has only to think of Alt's fundamental work on the law to realize that this method, at its best, can be constructive in the extreme.[5] Let us, then, make it quite clear that whatever quarrel we may have with Noth, it does not revolve about the task of *Überlieferungs-geschichte* or its method *per se*.

3. Finally, let it be said that the work of Noth is intrinsically of such great importance that it cannot be brushed aside. Disagree with it, perhaps; scoff at it, no! One is required to take it very seriously.

By this it is not meant merely that one may learn a great deal from Noth. Of course one may! His works exhibit tremendous learning; they are, indeed, triumphs of a logical, orderly mind. That there are insights of penetration and value in them to the right and to the left is no more than one would expect of a scholar of Noth's stature, trained in the school of Alt. But we do not refer to points of detail, but rather to something of an over-all nature: a caution, a corrective, if you will. Noth's whole treatment of early Israel's traditions, much as one may disagree in general and in detail, is at least a timely warning that certainly needs to be heard against a too uncritical use of these tradi-tions. His over-scepticism is a warning against overmuch credu-lity, his remorseless method against slovenly method. One is enjoined against the making of rash combinations, downright statements on the basis of flimsy evidence, elaborate reconstructions of the events that are supported by hypothesis only. One may—and for my part, I do—recoil from Noth's nihilistic treatment of Moses and the Sinai events, but one may not draw a more positive picture merely because one wishes it to be so. It must ever be remembered that much about early Israel is, and will remain, unknown.

The traditions are, as Noth insists, the traditions of the Twelve-Clan League. Nor may we doubt that they reached their normative form after the settlement in Palestine. The historian must use them with the full understanding that this is so. This means that, in writing early Israel's history, he must never oversimplify. He has continually to look behind the traditions, with their schematized "all Israel" frame of reference, to events that were vastly more complex than the Bible narrative indicates. While it would be rash to deny (especially in view of the Ras Shamra texts) that long sagas, or epics, might have been developed even in the patriachal age, it would be equally rash to insist that a connected epic of the Hebrew ancestors existed so early. Still less can the historian, on the basis of this material, engage to reconstruct the actual, chronological sequence of events. More than that, although he may not share Noth's nihilism *re* archaeological evidence, he would do well to remember that not one single event in the story of patriarchs, exodus and conquest can be proved from that quarter to have happened "just so."

In other words, all that we know of Israel before the settlement comes to us from the normative tradition of the later Twelve-Clan League. One need not discount the historicity of those traditions as Noth does, but one must realize that they are not historical documents like, for example, those in the book of Kings. The historian must remember the type of material he is dealing with, and be cautious. In reconstructing the origins of Israel and her faith a great deal must be left open. If this means that the historian must use the words "perhaps," "it is possible," "it seems probable," more lavishly than he would like to do, there is no help for it.

2

So much, then, for the *plus*. What of the *minus*? Let us begin with the question: Has Noth succeeded in presenting a satisfying picture of the origins and early history of Israel? The answer must be: no. On the contrary, his presentation leaves one distinctly dissatisfied. Is this really all that an objective historian can say?

1. As we have seen, Noth is able to derive from the Bible very little of a positive nature regarding the story of Israel's beginnings. The reason for this is that his method forbids him to find any appreciable nucleus of historical fact in the biblical traditions in the form in which they have come down to us.

To be sure, he agrees that the patriarchs were people who actually lived, and their religion an historical phenomenon. But although many of the Genesis traditions reflect historical circumstances, scarcely a single one of them can be said in any strict sense to be "historical." The actual migrations of the Hebrew ancestors cannot be elucidated from them. The ancestors did not come from Mesopotamia at all; the patriarchs themselves belong not in Canaan, but on the desert fringe. The exodus and Sinai traditions rest in history. But these events happened to different groups at different times, and, in any case, nothing can be said of their details. Moses, too, is an historical figure in the sense that he lived—or rather "died"—but he was not the great founder of Israel's faith. He had nothing to do either with exodus or with Sinai; he arose out of a grave tradition at home in the steppes of Transjordan. The Israelite settlement in Palestine happened, yes, and in so far is historical. But it was a vastly different process from that portrayed in Joshua, the narratives of which are largely unhistorical.

It is thus clear that Noth's method, whatever else may be said of it, issues in a very negative evaluation of the traditions. This does not, of course, prove that it is wrong. But it does at least allow us this negative criticism: it leaves many questions unanswered. Most serious of these is, in my opinion, *that the origin of Israel and its faith is left quite without adequate explanation.*

(a) That the Israelite amphictyony with its Yahwistic faith was a going concern in the period of the Judges is, of course, beyond question. Now Noth says that neither the amphictyony nor its twelve clans existed prior to the settlement. What, then, possessed these clans, almost as soon as they came into being, to bond themselves together and to adopt a common faith? In one sense, perhaps, one may justly decline to answer the question. Similar amphictyonies, as Noth has shown,[6] were widely instanced and no special explanation can be required of their origin. But that the question is a fair one, and demands an answer, is tacitly admitted by Noth himself, who asks (*History of Israel*, 137): "how it happened that, directly after the settlement, 'Israel' felt itself to be so much of a unity that a structure of traditions arose which had as its subject a common pre-history of this 'Israel.' "

Why indeed? Noth goes on to say (*ibid.*) that the question cannot be answered with any assurance "since the tradition does not reckon with this happening, and therefore says nothing about it." True—yet not strictly accurate! The traditions *do* reckon with the origins of the Israelite covenant and faith, and Noth does not credit those traditions, namely: that the entity "Israel" existed (albeit, we may agree, not in its later, normative form) and found its distinctive faith *prior to the settlement*. Noth's explanation of the origin of "Israel" and its faith is in any event a very lame one: that both developed gradually on the soil of Palestine, first as participants of the Sinai events introduced the worship of Yahweh, to be followed by others who had experienced the exodus and who gave witness to the mighty acts of the God who had delivered them. As the God of the exodus was identified with Yahweh of Sinai, and as the clans united in covenant league about this God, "Israel" came into being (*History of Israel*, 137 f.).

Now none would deny that Israel's organization and faith underwent development in Palestine. But to posit a development is not to explain it. I should object that Noth has given no adequate explanation of why these scattered clans of diverse origin came together under a common faith in the first place—and did so so strongly that they at once began to posit that they had always had a common history—nor of the extreme suddenness with which, under his theory, this must have been done. It is scarcely 200 years from the final settlement of the clans in the thirteenth century to the rise of the monarchy under Saul in the eleventh. Yet the "all Israel" orientation of the traditions (it is common to J and E and therefore, in Noth's view, goes back to G) was already official before the end of that period. The amphictyony with its Yahwistic faith is clearly in operation by the time of Deborah (twelfth century). Could the various clans have settled, taken shape themselves, gradually developed and adopted a normative Yahwism, bonded themselves in covenant league around it, *and have developed a unanimous tradition that things had always been so* in so short a time? For my part, I find it incredible. It is far easier to believe in the existence of, and a connection between, at least certain of the clans prior to the settlement, and the adoption by them of the Yahwistic faith in the wilderness period.[7]

(b) Equally incredible is the explanation of Moses. How is his stature in normative Israelite tradition to be explained under Noth's view? The fact, which Noth and others have based themselves on, that the figure of Moses does not loom large in the early biblical traditions outside the Pentateuch is not really very impressive. Perhaps it no more than illustrates the fact that Israel's faith was not in Moses, but in Yahweh. How seldom, indeed, are any of Israel's heroes mentioned outside the literature that immediately concerns them![8] On the other hand, the figure of Moses as leader of the exodus, founder of faith and lawgiver, is absolutely central in both J and E (and therefore to G), and thus may be assumed to have been so at least back to the period of the Judges. But if Moses was none of these things—if he was only some Transjordanian *sheikh* whose memory was enshrined in a grave tradition—how can it be explained that he so quickly came to be looked upon not only as the leader of all Israel, but positively as its founder?

Noth's explanation (*UG,* 190 f.) is peculiarly lame. The figure of Moses was drawn quite naturally from the grave tradition into the theme "Entrance into the Promised Land," and thus into the tradition circle of central Palestine, where Jacob was also at home. He thus became, save for Jacob, the oldest individual figure in the Pentateuch tradition, with the result that tales about him grew and grew. But to explain Moses so asks of me a degree of credulity that I cannot manage. The assumption that Israel's faith grew, as it were, out of the ground, without founder, but then straightway felt so keenly the need for a founder that it was obliged to blow up the figure of the colorless Moses to gigantic proportions in order to accord him that status—is really past believing. No literal acceptance of rods turned to serpents or manna from heaven would require a more heroic *sacrificium intellecti* than this. It is far more soberly objective to look upon Moses—with full recognition of the problems entailed—as actu-̣ ally the lawgiver and founder. If to do so contravenes the thesis of the five separate tradition themes of the Pentateuch, it is to be regretted.

Now one could argue that it is unfair to ask the historian to explain everything. Some things we. lack the knowledge to explain. Where this is so, the honest historian can only admit that he has no explanation. True! But it must be remembered that in this case the problem is in good part of Noth's own making. He has followed a method that reduces Israel's traditions—which *had* their explanation of origin—to a *nil,* and then is confronted by the *fact* of Israel, a fact for which he can provide no adequate explanation. Be that as it may, it certainly leaves us with the question if any history of Israel can be called satisfactory that leaves the major factor in that history, Israel's faith, so poorly accounted for. Granted that the traditions of early Israel were normalized in the Twelve-Clan League, and thus have a national frame of reference which we may be sure was not original in all of them, does this force us to a complete mistrust of those traditions? May we not ask, at least, if the picture there given is not more credible in its broad outlines than the construction of Noth? May we not ask further if, when a method of criticism discards so completely the united witness of tradition and ends in a nihilism of its own making, it may not be the method itself that is at fault?

2. This brings us to a second observation of a negative sort regarding Noth's work. Not only is Noth unable to rely on the Hexateuch traditions for the writing of Israel's early history, *he is unable to fill the void thus created by an appeal to archaeological evidence*. Indeed, he exhibits a nihilism regarding archaeology that virtually denies it the right to speak to the point at all. And surely this is unsound.

We have had occasion to refer to this before.[9] The numerous parallels that archaeology has discovered between the Genesis narratives and second-millenium Mesopotamia neither impress Noth nor convince him that Israel's ancestors indeed migrated thence: all this is susceptible of other explanations. The heavy incidence of Egyptian names in the family of Moses and Aaron is no proof that these people were ever in Egypt: this too can be explained in another way. Again, archaeology proves that certain Palestinian towns, a number of them mentioned in Joshua and Judges as taken by Israel, were destroyed in the thirteenth century B.C. But this is no proof of the biblical tradition. After all, we have no reliable biblical tradition of these events in the first place—only etiological tales. Indeed, there is not even any proof that the known destruction was made by Israel at all. It could, for all we know, be the work of the Philistines, or of some forgotten city king in some forgotten war.

Now before we counter that Noth is being wilful, let us grant the point: this is indeed not "proof," if by "proof" is meant irrefragable evidence that the Bible story happened "just so." The fact that the Laban-Jacob stories fit the *milieu* of second-millenium Mesopotamia does not prove one item of these stories to be true, but only that they were told by a people who were familiar with that, or a similar, environment. In spite of all the amazing evidence that archaeology has brought, not one single item in the entire Hexateuch tradition has been proved true in the strict sense of that word. Archaelogy cannot bring that sort of proof. We are warned, therefore, against downright affirmations of an "archaeology-proves-the-Bible" sort, such as are all too common in certain circles. But if dogmatic affirmation is not in order, neither is dogmatic denial!

The question is not, does archaeology "prove" the biblical tradition? but: *where is the balance of probability in the matter?* That is, indeed, the area in which the historian usually labors. He weighs the evidence, *and does not brush aside the more probable for the less probable.*

This is not the place to marshal the archaeological evidence relating to the patriarchal narratives. Suffice it to say that it is massive. To mention but one thing, the nomenclature of Upper Mesopotamia. as it is known from Mari and elsewhere certainly proves that a population akin to the Hebrews was to be found there in the patriarchal age. The Nuzi texts at least prove that the customary law of the patriarchs had its home in the same general area in approximately the same age. And much more. Put all this alongside the unanimous tradition of the Hebrews that their ancestors migrated thence, and the objective historian ought to give in to the overwhelming balance of probability. As for evidence of the Israelite conquest, is archaeology really as helpless as Noth would have it? Can it not tell a Philistine occupation from an early Israelite one? Or a late Bronze Age Canaanite one from an early Iron Age one? Can it not tell if there has been an appreciable gap between destruction and re-occupation? Is archaeology, then, unable to distinguish a destruction of the Amarna Age from one at the hands of the Philistines, and both from one occasioned by Israel (*cf. History of Israel,* 82 f.)? The fact is that archaeology shows that a row of towns, some mentioned in the Bible as taken by Israel, seem to have fallen to Israel in the thirteenth century. Admittedly this is not "proof" of the Joshua narrative, but the probability of a connection between the two is overwhelming.

What, after all, is "proof"? If one were to see the print of a horse's hoof in the mud, one might rashly conclude that this is "proof" that a horse had been there. Not so! However convincing it may be, it is no more than circumstantial evidence. It could have been the work of someone playing a prank! Proof, to stand up in court, must have eye witnesses: someone must have seen the horse. Now the evidence of archaeology, at least in the area with which we are concerned, is of necessity largely circumstantial; "eye-witness proof"—in this case contemporary inscriptions—is seldom forthcoming. If the historian waits for it, as Noth seems to do (*History of Israel*, 46 ff.), he will wait long. But the historian does not work in the law court, and cannot demand that kind of "proof." He is happy when he gets it, but most of the time he must be content with less direct evidence. And from that evidence he seeks the *balance of probability*. No history of Israel could ever be written—Noth's included —did the historian wait at every point for irrefragable "proof" of the sort North demands.

I am convinced that at the bottom of Noth's scepticism *re* archaeology there lies precisely his method. Because of it, he tags the traditions "etiological tales" or whatnot, and so depreciates them that he can affirm that we have no reliable tradition of the capture, say, of Bethel or Lachish. At the same time, a wholly different theory of the conquest is advanced: first a peaceful search of seasonal pasture, then gradual settlement in open areas. Armed conflict, if such there was, represented only the last phase of occupation; but it was, in any event, rare (*cf. History of Israel*, 68 f.). Then scepticism *vis-à-vis* tradition— itself the result of method—plus a preconditioned hypothesis of how the settlement actually took place, "gang up" on archaeology and deny it all relevance. *We have no archaeological evidence bearing upon the conquest narratives of Joshua because, ex hypothesi, there can none.*[10]

3

We see, then, that Noth is driven by his method to a drastic devaluation of the biblical traditions. And this, plus certain preconceived theories regarding the actual course of events, leads him to an equal depreciation of the value of archaeological evidence. Since the real issue lies in the method itself, it is necessary that we proceed to a more detailed discussion of it.

W. F. Albright has already made a searching, if admittedly provisional, criticism of Noth on this score.[11] He points out that Alt and Noth stress three guiding principles in their studies in the field of Hebrew origins: a rigid application of the methods of form criticism; constant emphasis on the factor of etiology in explaining the origin of tradition; emphasis on the *Ortsgebundenheit* of tradition (i.e., the tenacity with which names and tales are supposed to adhere to geographical locations).

1. As for the first of these, there is little that can be added to what Albright has said. Albright freely recognizes the tremendously important contribution that form-critical studies have made, from Gunkel down to Alt himself. But he argues that there is a tendency in the Alt school to make form criticism carry more than its weight, even to the point of imagining that the historicity of a given tradition—or its lack of it—can be established by an examination of the literary form in which it is cast. Ancient bards and scribes had to conform, for lack of alternatives, to "fixed patterns of oral delivery and formal styles of writing" (*ibid.*, 12). Since this is so, form itself can never be the final arbiter of historicity: there must be external evidence. With this one can only agree.

Certainly form criticism is a necessary tool of the historian. Awareness of the form and type of a tradition will inevitably to some degree control its evaluation and interpretation. If the historian knows he has to do with saga, he will not evaluate it as if it were the "David Biography" or the annals of the kings of Judah. If he is dealing with epic material he will treat it like epic. He will, for example, look out for formalized motifs, the subsuming of a whole group migration under the movements of the individual hero, and so on. Form criticism is indeed a control over exegesis and interpretation. But it cannot pass final judgment on historicity. The historian would do well to remember the sober words of Kittel (which I read after I had finished Noth and found like a breath of fresh air): "A dilemma like the following: the patriarchal narrative is either history or saga, or as it might be put: the patriarchal narrative is not history but saga, is therefore entirely wrong. That narrative can be saga as well as history."[12]

One might add that literary form does not, where the facts can be tested, furnish a final test of historicity. Certainly it does not do so today. A novel may be pure fiction or well-nigh autobiography; a newspaper dispatch may be a model of objective accuracy or the most vicious propaganda. Was it fundamentally otherwise in ancient times? The ancient had far fewer literary types to choose from than do we; he was, therefore, under even greater necessity of formalizing what he had to say. Is there any evidence that there were no degrees of historical veracity within a given form? On the contrary, we know that there were. Myths, for example, may contain a greater or lesser degree of historical content.[13] The same is true of epic poems. Some royal annals seem to be conscientiously accurate; others are formalized boasting. By the same token, to class a tradition as a cult legend says nothing *per se* regarding its veracity: the legend might just possibly be correct! To be sure, this is not to say anything very positive. But since historical value can be shown in certain known cases to vary within a given form, it does warn us not to imagine that classification of form automatically renders verdict on historicity. Objective, external evidence is always required.

2. Next, to the second guiding principle of the Alt-Noth school: *stress upon etiology as a creative factor in the formation of tradition.* Here I wish again to second the arguments of Albright and perhaps to reinforce them a bit. I am, indeed, prepared to go quite far in this connection, even to the point of "jumping off the deep end," for it seems to me that nothing is more fundamentally wrong in the method of Alt and Noth than this. I would not wish to deny that the etiological factor is present, and may have given rise to many details in the tradition. But I would like to submit that, *where historical tradition is concerned*, not only can it be proved that the etiological factor is often secondary in the formation of these traditions, *it cannot be proved that it was ever primary.*

We have already noted the stress laid upon this factor by the Alt school. Alt's own treatment of Joshua,[14] where practically everything in Joshua 1–9 is subsumed under this rubric is a classical example. But it is to be found everywhere. For example, the tale of Jacob's purchase of land at Schechem (Gen. 33:19) grew out of the fact that the later amphictyony owned land there (*UG*, 89 f); Jacob's pilgrimage from Schechem to Bethel (Gen. 35:1–5) is the etiology of a later cultic rite *(UG,* 87)[15] Abraham's near sacrifice of Isaac (Gen. 22:1–9) provides the etiology of a local cultic custom originally unconnected with Abraham (*UG,* 121 n. 317, 126); the tradition of the double burial of Abraham and Sarah at Mamre (Gen. 23; 25:7–10) was suggested by the name of the cave Machpelah ("Double Cave"; *UG,* 125; and so on.

The gravity of all this lies in the fact that, in the minds of Alt and Noth, when the etiological factor is present in a tradition, that tradition is automatically suspect. It could hardly be historical, for the etiological factor created it: an existing custom or landmark is explained by telling a story about it. Etiological tales arise to give answer to the "eternal child's question, 'Why?' "[16] I feel strongly that no single feature in the entire method of this school has been more productive of nihilism regarding the traditions than this.

The debate does not revolve about the presence of the etiological factor (it is obviously and frequently present), but about the *priority of that factor in the formation of tradition.* Do tales with etiological features *arise* out of the desire to answer the eternal *Kinderfrage* "Why?" If it can be proved that such is the case, then the etiological factor is primary, and we must simply give in to Alt and Noth and accord such traditions little or no historical value. But if it can be proven that, at least sometimes, this is *not* the case—that sometimes the etiological factor is purely secondary—then it is an extremely subjective procedure to discount the historical value of these traditions *short of objective proof.*

Now the etiological factor is frequently the creative and determinative element in fable and fairy tale: Why is the ocean salty? How did the camel get his hump? Where did the donkey get his loud, discordant bray? How did the crest of yon hill come to be cleft in twain? What giant's hand flung those islands far out to sea? Here is a *genre* of stories told precisely to answer the *Kinderfrage* "Why?" But in such cases there is no question of historicity: the teller does not believe his own tale, and it is a question if the child to whom it is told believes it literally. As for myth, the case is less clear. Myth does deal with the origins of things, and so gives the answer to the question "Why?" But these are scarcely "child's questions." And, although the myth was re-enacted in the ritual, it can hardly be said that the myth was concocted as an etiology of the ritual. The myth of Marduk's conflict with the Chaos Monster was scarcely composed to explain what the Babylonians were already doing on New Year's Day— but quite the other way around. One might as well say that the narrative of the Last Supper was invented to explain why Christians practice such a rite! If any do so say—well, it is going a bit too far!

Be that as it may, stores of etiological flavor do exist in the Bible, which seem to have as their primary function the answering of the question "Why?" One thinks of the story of the Tower of Babel, which explains the multiplicity of languages on earth, and which is made secondarily into an etymology of Babylon: or the story of the fall (Gen. 3) which explains why man must labour for his bread, why women suffer in childbirth—and why snakes crawl on the ground. But even in these cases it is more than a probability that the stories had had a long history before the etiological feature was drawn in. One thinks, too, of certain stories that explain how certain heroes got their names: e.g., that of the birth of Jacob (Gen. 25:21–26) which is a play on the similarity in Hebrew of the words "Jacob" and "heel"; or that of the baby Moses (Exod. 2:1–10) where there is a pun on "Moses" and the verb "draw out" (māšāh). But, here again, it is probable that the etiological factor is responsible only for a single detail of the story, and that we must reckon with the likelihood that the stories develop conventional motifs far older than the etiology they are used to provide. In the case of Moses, if one remembers the stories of the birth and childhood of Sargon of Akkad, this would seem to be certain. The etiology is, therefore, secondary.

In any event, our problem is not primarily with this *genre*, but with the factor of etiology as it is to be observed throughout the traditions of the great Hebrew historical saga. The question is: Can it be proved in the case of these national traditions that, where the etiological factor is present, that factor is always—or even sometimes—primary and determinative in the formation of the tradition? We ought to recall in this connection the sound observation of Kaufmann[17] that one ought not to speak of an "etiological tale" unless it can be shown that that tale *came into being* through the etiological factor.

Now it seems to me that the assumption that such was actually the case can be tested *only in the full light of history*. We shall get nowhere if we confine ourselves to Israel's early traditions, for we do not in truth know how these traditions arose. We should only end up contradicting one another. Nor can we appeal to the traditions of other ancient peoples to settle the matter. In the first place, no other ancient people had traditions of origins comparable to those of the Hebrews. In the second place, we are in no better position to control the origins of such traditions as exist. We can only, in the clear light of history, examine traditions that do have an etiological element, *the origins of which we can trace*, in order to see if in such cases, etiology is necessarily, usually, or ever, the primary or controlling element. I stress this lest the examples shortly to be adduced should seem to some either frivolous or irrelevant.

That this is the correct procedure has been sensed by Albright, who brings forth a number of parallels from the traditions of the modern Arabs. That is, of course, the best place to look for parallels. The Arabs are a Semitic people who live in the land once occupied by Israel; and furthermore their traditions can to a degree be controlled. I regret that I am not competent to add further evidence from this quarter. But it would seem to me that, unless one is going to plead that its operation in ancient Israel was a special phenomenon, oral tradition might be expected to develop according to similar principles wherever it is to be found. In any event, an abundance of popular traditions can be found with a clear etiological factor (i.e. the explanation of some known custom or landmark) where that factor is *demonstrably secondary*. This should at least warn us against a doctrinaire evaluation of the same factor in Israel's traditions.

In Plymouth, Massachusetts, one may see on the beach a

stone with a cupola erected over it; it will be pointed out as the very rock where the Pilgrim Fathers first stepped ashore. And "there it is until this day!" Now it is not much of a rock, but it is at least as notable as that stone pile at Ai (Josh. 8:29) or that cave with five trees about it at Makkedah (Josh. 10:26 f.). It demonstrates in any case that there is an etiological element in the tradition of the Pilgrim. If Alt's and Noth's application of the principle of etiology be correct, we should be obliged to assume that the story of the Pilgrims, at least of their landing at Plymouth, is a tale concocted to answer the *Kinderfrage*: Why is this notable rock here on our beach? But the facts are quite otherwise: the tradition was primary, the etiology secondary. It is a question if the rock had anything to do with the landing of the Pilgrims. It seems to have been brought into the tradition about the time of American Independence; the structure that protects it dates only from 1920. The truth is that, if the story of the Pilgrims *had not already been normative*, no one would have given that rock a second thought.

Again: Americans have the peculiar custom on the last Thursday of November of celebrating Thanksgiving Day by going to church, and then returning home to a bountiful turkey dinner. And many a child has asked his father, "Why?" Corresponding to custom is, as one would expect, legend to explain it: our Pilgrim Fathers shot wild turkeys, harvested the pumpkins and the corn, and then observed this custom in gratitude to God for his mercies—and we thus remember God and them. A practitioner of tradition-history, however, can easily see that the custom created the legend: the legend is, therefore, unhistorical. Actually, of course, Thanksgiving is the survival of an ancient harvest festival the origin of which is unknown. But since it is observed both as a national and as a religious occasion, it is easy to see why the Pilgrims were drawn into it, for they are held to be the fathers of the nation (Virginia resents that! The legend has its focus in Boston!) and men of exemplary faith. Such a religious-national custom would naturally be explained by telling a story about them. But again, the facts are inconvenient. The story of the Pilgrim Thanksgiving, though no doubt dressed up in the telling, is historical (October 1621); the custom did not become normalized as a national holiday until the middle of the nineteenth century, though practiced sporadically and locally before then. Legend thus demonstrably precedes custom. Indeed, had not the legend existed it is doubtful if the custom would have ever arisen.

Again: the legend that George Washington once threw a dollar over the Rappahannock River at Fredericksburg, Virginia. The origin of this legend is obscure. It is enshrined in Parson Weems' edifying book[18] but whether or not it originated in the fertile mind of the author I do not know. In any event it is very old; I had it first—from oral tradition—as a boy. Now any one who has followed the local newspapers (or those of Richmond or Washington, D.C.) in recent years might have read an account of how, in Fredericksburg as a part of the celebration of George Washington's birthday, there is an annual contest to see if any boy of the town can throw a dollar over the Rappahannock. Several, I understand, have succeeded, for the river is not over ninety yards wide just below the town at Ferry Farm, Washington's boyhood home, where the contest is held.

Here we have, then, a custom that requires explanation, and an etiological legend to supply it. Let us trace the history of that tradition according to the principles of the Alt-Noth school. George Washington was, of course, revered in the Thirteen-Colony League, and in its successor, the U.S.A., as the father of his country. He is, thus, the sort of historical figure to whom legends attach themselves. His birthday was early celebrated throughout the Thirteen-State League as a national cultic festival and, of course, nowhere more ardently than in Fredericksburg, for here—tradition has it—was his boyhood home ("See, there is the spot until this day!"). Now such occasions are usually observed by means of sports, contests and picnics with patriotic speeches in which the normative traditions are frequently alluded to—and tend to expand! So at Fredericksburg. In the course of such a picnic long ago, we may imagine, one boy bet another a dollar that he couldn't heave a rock across the river. And there it began. The thing became a traditional event. Soon for the rock there was substituted a ball, and then for the ball a silver dollar; the boy who could toss it to the opposite bank would win a prize. Then the inevitable *Kinderfrage*: "Papa, why do they do that every Washington's birthday?" And what answer could Papa give save that of etiology: "Our father, George Washington, once did the same thing at this very spot; we are celebrating his memory." Then, as pilgrims in great numbers began to come to Fredericksburg to view the holy sites of the national founder, the legend was carried by them to the farthest parts of the country. Thus we see how a local etiological legend takes its place in the normative tradition of the Thirteen-State League!

The trouble about all this is that it is pure moonshine! Whether the legend rests on fact or not I do not know. Washington was a large and powerful man and could easily have done it— though hardly at the age of eleven, as Parson Weems would have us believe. But that is not the point. The point is that, while an etiological connection between custom and legend is explicitly affirmed, *the legend is demonstrably prior to the custom*. The custom, in fact, began in 1936 for purposes, it is feared, of publicity—and on the basis of the legend.[19] Indeed, had it not been for the legend no one would ever have thought of the custom. Of course in demonstrating its priority, the *historicity of the legend is neither affirmed nor denied*.

I am sure that Noth would object that these examples are irrelevant. The traditions of early America were developed in the full light of history, in an age of literacy, and are therefore in no sense parallel to the traditions of early Israel. I fear too, that he might feel that I have been speaking flippantly. I can only reply that I have not offered the above examples in a frivolous spirit, nor do I feel them to be irrelevant. I do not wish to press them too far, for America and Israel are indeed far apart in time and space. But the only possible test of Noth's theories *re* etiology must be made precisely where the facts are in our control. I should like to add, too, that the differences may not be as great as they seem. On the one hand, writing was known throughout the entire period of Israel's origins; on the other hand, in Colonial America schools and books were few and illiteracy high. Oral tradition operated in both cases and, unless it be assumed that it operated in a special way in the ancient Orient, according to similar principles. Yet here, where we can keep check on the etiological factor, it emphatically does not operate as Noth would have it. Therefore when I am told, for example, that the story of the circumcision of Israel at Gilgal (Josh. 5:2–9) is an etiological legend to explain the later practice of the rite of circumcision at that shrine,[20] I am much less than convinced. Far more likely that the custom became popular at Gilgal precisely because of the tradition that great Joshua had once circumcised all Israel there. To say this, of course, neither asserts nor denies the historicity of that tradition; external evidence is required.

May I be pardoned another illustration? It offers (a) a remarkable landmark, (b) a battle, and (c) a hero, as these have been enshrined in oral tradition. It was suggested to me by the arguments of Noth, Elliger and others[21] that the tale of the hanging of the five kings at Makkedah (Josh. 10:16–27) is an etiological legend which grew up to explain a cave with its mouth blocked by stones and with five notable trees nearby.

I spent my childhood on the top of Lookout Mountain, a steep and lofty eminence which towers above Chattanooga, Tennessee. There there was fought in the course of "the recent unpleasantness between the States" (as the Civil War used sometimes to be called), the famous "Battle above the Clouds." Our home was scarcely a mile from the battlefield, and I wandered there often. The battleground itself consisted of a narrow triangle at the "point" of the mountain. Since the mountain's crest is rimmed everywhere with sheer cliffs some 50 or 60 feet in height, the land on two sides of this triangle falls precipitately away to the valley below; only on the side that opens along the ridge of the mountain is it more or less level. Now one of these cliffs in the mountain rim, the tallest and most precipitous of all, was known as "Roper's Rock." And thereby hangs a story.

Let me tell that story as I had it from oral tradition. For not until many years later did I even know that there was a written tradition. Confederate troops under Braxon Bragg—so the legend

G

in oral form—had seized the height of Lookout Mountain, and from it were pouring a murderous cannon fire into the city of Chattanooga below, much to the distress of U. S. Grant's Union forces who occupied it. Clearly Grant could not tolerate an enemy on this commanding height above him. So the decision was made to attack. Selecting a morning when a hanging mist rendered the valley invisible to the Confederates on the summit, Joe Hooker's Corps of Grant's Army deployed and began the assault. Halfway up, their presence was detected as they skirmished with Confederate pickets on the slope. Then the cannonade began. Shot and shell were poured on the assaulting Boys in Blue, but bravely they came on, scrambling up the sixty-degree slope under fire. Finally, they reached the ring of cliffs at the top and could go no farther. All seemed lost; the Blue line wavered. But just then, there leaped to the fore the brave Sergeant Roper, color bearer of the NNth Pennsylvania (?) (or Ohio, or Illinois: oral tradition has forgotten the identity of his unit). Seizing the colors, he scrambled up a crevasse in the sheer rock, shouting the appropriate encouragements to his men as he did so. Bullets whined around him but, miraculously, none took effect. Finally to the top! Planting the colors in a crack, the sergeant grappled in mortal combat with the defending Boys in Grey (or butternut and old rags), while his comrades, thus heartened, swarmed up the cliff behind him.

At this point, the oral tradition splits into two recensions. According to one, the brave sergeant, in the shock of the initial combat, was hurled backward from the cliff and killed. According to the other, he survived the battle unscathed and was decorated for his valor. In any event, Union troops forced the summit. The Boys in Grey did not retreat (that they never did!) but they did advance rapidly to the rear along the spine of the mountain, resisting stubbornly. So the principle of Union and the honor of the Lost Cause were both vindicated. And the name of the gallant Sergeant Roper was given to the rock where he did his deed of derring-do, "and there it is until this day!" So the oral tradition that I knew when I was a little boy.

But how could such a story possibly be true? The etiology

obtrudes like Roper's Rock itself, and this should be enough, if what we are told is correct, to render the whole thing suspect. Sergeant Roper's deed is pure fancy, the Battle above the Clouds itself of dubious historicity. True, it is easy enough to see how such a legend could have developed. There is Roper's Rock, and it is a striking cliff; and people asked the natives why it was so called. And the natives, loath to be caught short by Yankee tourists, came up with the tale. Nor was it sheer, willful fabrication. Traditions of the Civil War hover like ghosts on the ridges about Chattanooga. It was natural for people honestly to suppose that the height of Lookout Mountain, most commanding of all, had a part in the events. But the whole tale is fantastic. No competent general—and U. S. Grant, as even a Confederate might admit, was a competent general—would ever have ordered a frontal assault on so strong a position and, had he done so, would never have succeeded. Such a battle, therefore, never took place. As for Roper's Rock, we may suppose that its name derived from some pioneer family which once had settled nearby, but which had since removed and dropped from memory.

But what are the facts? First, that oral tradition has indeed vastly magnified the Battle above the Clouds. It was actually a skirmish, no more. The Confederates had scarcely more than 2,000 men, plus a few batteries of 12-pounders, on the summit. At most they could lob shells over in the direction of the railway station and scare the horses; they did the troops in the city no harm. But because their guns commanded the Tennessee River and could interdict Federal supplies moving on it, they had to be cleared off. But there was no frontal assault, no wild charge up the slope. Instead, Federal troops, covered by rain and fog, executed a sweeping movement that cleared Confederate outposts from the slope, leaving the troops on the summit invested on three sides. Nor was there any violent connonade. The Confederate guns could not be depressed enough to be brought into play, for when this was done, the roundshot would roll out of the muzzles. Nor was there an assault on the cliffs. The Confederates, nearly cut off and virtually out of supplies, withdrew in the night. The next morning, a Federal patrol reached the summit to find it vacant. Oral tradition has indeed exaggerated the events.

As for Sergeant Roper, the tale of his gallant rush up the cliff cannot be historical: there was no assault on the cliff. Whether there was such a person as Sergeant Roper, and whether he was the first of the patrol to reach the summit and plant the Union Flag there on the morrow of the battle, I do not know. Even if so, he performed no feat of heroism—except in so far as to climb such a crag requires a bit of nerve. Thus we see that we are entitled to look with a critical eye at the details of an oral tradition, particularly at any etiological feature that it may present. But the mere presence of such a feature does not *per se* impeach the essential historicity of the events described. The etiology of Roper's Rock is a secondary embellishment; the Battle above the Clouds, grievously exaggerated as it has been, certainly took place.

Noth, I am sure, would say that this is irrelevant. I do not think so. It is an example of the way in which folk tradition develops in oral transmission—for, I give assurance, I have known of Sergeant Roper through no other source. True, this tradition comes from an age fully lighted by history. But that gives it an added advantage. It lets us see how oral tradition operates close to the source, within less than a century of the events, *and in spite of the fact that there has been a written tradition to control it since the very day of the battle.* Not even this last has prevented etiological features from intruding. But these are seen clearly to be secondary. And the very fact that, where one can pin it down, the etiological feature is, at least often, purely secondary, lays the burden of proof on him who asserts its invariable primacy in the traditions of Israel. This burden of proof, so far as I know, Noth has never accepted. He has asserted it to be so without a single scrap of evidence that it ever was so, and in the face of the fact that, where it can be tested, it can often be shown not to be so. For my part, I remain more than dubious that "etiological tales" ever at any time developed as the Alt-Noth school posits.

3. But to the third guiding principle of the Alt-Noth school:

the stress on the *Ortsgebundenheit* (fixation in place) of tradition. Here again Albright has marshalled a quantity of evidence to the contrary from modern Arab sources. I can add nothing to it. May I be permitted, however, to inject one or two other thoughts which he does not discuss?

The importance of *Ortsgebundenheit* in the method of Alt and Noth can hardly be exaggerated. All traditions have their *Haftpunkt*, some geographical locale to which they adhere, some cult center at which they are handed down. This *Haftpunkt* can usually be inferred from places mentioned in the tradition, in so far as these cannot be shown to be secondary. This last can be a tricky business, to be sure. Thus, the Jacob traditions are originally to be localized at Shechem (*UG*, 60, 86–95), and secondarily at Bethel, although it must be observed that this is achieved by separating the "Transjordanian Jacob" from the patriarch and by regarding the links that connect Jacob to the Negev as secondary (*UG*, 109, n. 289). Abraham and Isaac are localized in the Negev (*UG*, 116 f.)—though again this is managed by ruling that the links that bind Abraham to Hebron, to central Palestine and to Mesopotamia, are secondary. Lot is localized in a cave near Zoar (*UG*, 168), Moses at a grave near Baal Peor (*UG*, 186 ff.). The conquest traditions of Joshua 1–9 are specifically Benjaminite (all the events happen in the area of that tribe) and had their *Haftpunkt* at the great shrine of Gilgal.[22] That is to say, they are the property of the tribe to whose soil they relate—an hypothesis that rules out the possibility that any of them could refer to united action by more than one of the clans.

For my part, the very word *Ortsgebunden* has an almost mystical connotation that I quite fail to understand. True, place names in tradition are extremely tenacious. True, there *are* local traditions, in the sense that some traditions are developed locally, concern only local affairs and do not tend to be of interest to a wider circle. But the very notion of a tradition being attached to a *place* is to me an incongruous one—a sort of mixed metaphor, if you will—while the doctrinaire consistency with which Alt and Noth apply the principle seems to be one-sided and unrealistic in the extreme. A number of objections can be raised.

First, aside from the fact noted above, that the *Haftpunkt* of a tradition is often arrived at by eliminating evidence, it must be insisted that to establish the geographical locale of a tradition does not establish its *Haftpunkt*, but only its "theatre of operation." *All events happen somewhere*; and the fact that an event happened in a given area does not make the tradition of it the property of the people of that area nor fix the site of its transmission there. Is the surrender of the British at Yorktown a Virginia tradition because it has a Virginia locale? Or is the Declaration of Independence a Pennsylvania tradition because it took place in Philadelphia? The great theatre of the Civil War was Virginia. But is the Civil War a Virginia tradition? Of course traditions tend to be more cherished in the locale to which they refer (the Civil War is hard to forget in Richmond), *but they do not belong to, or inhere in, the locale; they belong to the people who participated in their making.* So the mere fact that the bulk of the conquest narrative refers to Benjaminite soil does not say one thing about to whom the tradition belongs. It must be proven by other means that Benjamin, and Benjamin alone, was concerned in these events, before it can be asserted that the tradition is a Benjaminite tribal one. But Alt and Noth merely assert it; they do not prove it.

Second, it is a demonstrable fact that traditions can shift locations. Albright has given several examples from present-day Palestine, as well as one from the Bible: a tradition of Rachel's tomb both in the area of Benjamin and at Bethlehem (*cf.* Gen. 35:16–20; Jer. 31:15), no doubt because of confusion over the place name Ephrath. Alt and Noth themselves allow for this sort of thing: e.g. the removal of certain Jacob traditions from Schechem to Bethel (*UG*, 86 ff.). On the other hand, it is possible for a tradition to be perpetuated far from its original geographic location, by a people who have no living contact with that locale.[23] It seems to me that here again we are dealing with principles which, if true at all, should be true of oral tradition anywhere, and which, therefore, may be discussed in the light of history on the basis of traditions whose development we can control. I therefore suggest the following examples.

We have already mentioned the legend of Washington's throwing the dollar over the Rappahannock. This tradition has long ago, like that of Rachel's grave, shifted locations. One often hears it said that Washington threw the dollar over the Potomac, and recently I saw this in print.[24] The reason for the shift is obvious. Washington is popularly more associated with Mt. Vernon, on the Potomac near Washington, D.C., than with Fredericksburg on the Rappahannock. The tradition has followed the man. The fact that the Potomac at Mt. Vernon is a tidal estuary over a mile wide, and that no man living or dead could throw a dollar or anything else over it, does not 'trouble oral tradition. The tradition is not *Ortsgebunden*: not only did it transfer its location, *it is not handed down at either place*, but by the American people in general. Tradition moves with the people it concerns, and is transmitted by the people who feel participation in it.

Again: many of the folk ballads of the southern Appalachians have demonstrably been handed down in oral transmission from early settlers, whose forebears brought them ultimately from Elizabethan England, and that with a remarkable tenacity of content. But frequently the tendency may be noted to substitute local names for the original English ones, with the result that English lords and ladies wander and plight their troth somewhere by the Forks of Big Sandy. Traditions can move, touch down anywhere and begin to assimilate the locale of the new environment. This again points up the fact that traditions belong not to places, but to the people who feel participation in them.

All this leads to the conclusion that, while place names do indeed have amazing tenacity, *Ortsgebundenheit* is a misnomer that ought to be given up. Traditions are not, and never have been, in any strict sense *Ortsgebunden* (tied to places); they are *Volksgebunden* (tied to people), if we may coin the term. They move through as wide an area as the people that transmit them move; their *Haftpunkt* is not a geographical location (admitting that traditions tend to be more cherished at the place where they originated) but the entire circle of people who feel personal concern in them.

It seems to me that, especially in the case of the patriarchal traditions, this stress on *Ortsgebundenheit* is dangerously wrong. Traditions adhere to people, and the people in this case were semi-nomads who, in the very search of seasonal pasture that Alt and Noth posit, must have roamed from one end of the land to the other. Therefore to localize the Jacob traditions in Shechem, the Abraham and Isaac traditions in the Negev and so forth, *is to localize people who, by their manner of life were not localized at all.* For my part, I see no *a priori* reason why traditions of Abraham, for example, that link him to Mesopotamia, Shechem, Bethel, Hebron, the Negev, Egypt, might not all of them be primary (though to say this does not, of course, in itself pass verdict on their historicity).

The mobility of the nomad must not be underestimated. True, the patriarchs were ass-nomads, not camel-nomads, and their wanderings were thus somewhat restricted. But even semi-nomads can get about amazingly. One might well think of the North American Indian in this connection. These were for the most part semi-nomads and that without benefit of beast at all (the horse was introduced relatively late and then only on the Western Plains); they were canoe-nomads or foot-nomads. Yet if one reflects on their wide rangings, one will not be tempted to tie the ancient semi-nomad down too tightly. For example, Indians from Lake Superior and beyond traded furs regularly with the French in Montreal; in the "French and Indian War," Indians from as far as the Mississippi and beyond fought in New York State under Montcalm. The range of the Hebrew nomads in the Pentateuch narrative, from Mesopotamia to Palestine, to the Negev and to Egypt, is vastly more restricted. And we may assume that their traditions moved with them. In the light of all this, a doctrinaire localizing of early Israel's traditions at fixed *Haftpunkt* is most unrealistic.

4. Might one now venture, with all diffidence, a final and far more sweeping criticism of the method of Noth? Let it be put in the form of a question, namely: *Even if this method be used*

with caution, is it in any event possible on the basis of present knowledge to write a "History of Tradition" on the scale and with the exactitude that Noth attempts? And if not, has a firm basis been found thereby for reconstructing the early history of Israel?

Noth begins his study of tradition-history with the isolating of five major themes in the Pentateuch. Each of these he holds to have had separate origin and development from the others. *This is the pillar of the whole thesis.* Should it fall, the entire structure would have to be altered radically, if not demolished. But I should like to question precisely if the themes can so be isolated with the finality that Noth posits.

I do not wish to be dogmatic. The great unifying structure of Pentateuch history and theology was certainly imposed on the traditions relatively late (in G, but defiinitely in J); before that time, we may believe that individual traditions and blocks of traditions had their separate existence. Indeed, if one cares to press it, each individual tradition had its own separate origin and its own history of transmission before it entered larger cycles of tradition and, ultimately, the Pentateuch documents. One should not rashly deny the possibility that blocks of tradition—such as the Sinai traditions—may actually have had separate existence until a relatively late time. Furthermore, the five themes that Noth isolates are *there,* and one may certainly set them apart for the sake of convenience, if one wishes, much as one might isolate the major themes of a novel or a play, the better to grasp the whole. But do these themes have the real separation that Noth posits? For my part, I am not convinced.

Now four of these themes are already present in the ancient Cultic Credo of Deuteronomy 26:5–9 and in Joshua 24.[25] That means that these themes were associated with one another back to a time, we may guess, soon after the conquest. That is to say, as far back as we have evidence, they are *already together.* Notably absent, however, as both von Rad and Noth have pointed out, is the theme "Revelation on Sinai"; the Credo does not mention it. From this it is argued that this block of tradition was linked to the others only later. Noth, as we have seen, further deduces that exodus and Sinai events happened to different groups at different times.

The possibility that all this was so cannot be ruled out of court. But at least three observations may be made. First: failure to mention a tradition does not prove ignorance of it. For example, does the fact that so many of the Royal Psalms mention David and David alone, argue that the Psalmist knew nothing of the other traditions of his people? Or does the fact that the primitive *kerygma* of the New Testament includes no reference to the Last Supper prove that the earliest church knew nothing of that event? Or does the fact that on Thanksgiving Day we mention the devotion of the Pilgrim Fathers prove that we have never heard of Sir John Smith and the Jamestown colony? Second: it is likely that the Credo had its *Sitz im Leben* precisely in a regular ceremony of covenant renewal (*cf. History of Israel,* 128). Note how the narrative of Joshua 24 leads straight to covenant; the mighty acts of God are recited that the people might respond in reaffirming the covenant. Now it is in this ceremony, according to Noth himself, that the Sinai tradition was at home. There would be, then, no place in the Credo for a recitation of the Sinai events; on the contrary, the people were expected to recreate those events, and participate in them, by their own act of covenant renewal. Finally: in the Decalogue itself (Exod. 20:2; Deut. 5:6) exodus and Sinai law *are* brought together.[26] Noth, of course, like many others, would deny that the Decalogue goes back to Mosaic days (*History of Israel,* 128), but I must strongly side with those who take the contrary view.[27] But if the Decalogue represents the basic covenant law, then exodus and Sinai tradition are mated from the beginning. For these reasons one may doubt that the Sinai tradition was ever the separate entity it has been made out to be.[28]

No part of Noth's treatment is more prejudiced by the thesis of five separate themes than is his analysis of the Moses tradition. The figure of Moses runs through four of these themes, but it cannot be allowed that he was original in all, and thus the *grosse Klammer* (great clamp) that binds all together, else as Noth tacitly agrees (*UG,* 177), the whole thesis would fall to the ground: a real independence of the themes could not be maintained. So the job is to find in which of them Moses is original. Nothing in Noth's work is more subjective than his procedure here. May I facetiously, but with dead seriousness, apply Noth's method to the figure of George Washington? I have no desire to try to reduce serious work to an absurdity, still less to make Moses and Washington identical figures. But it seems to me that any such hypothesis—and this is no more than a hypothesis— ought to be amenable to testing in the case of other historical figures who have been magnified in tradition, and who have extended themselves into many traditionary themes.

We may, then, isolate in the traditions of the Thirteen-Colony League six themes. (1) "Settlement of the Wilderness": this theme has its nucleus in Massachusetts in the area of the Plymouth colony, but like the theme "Patriarchs" has been expanded with similar material from elsewhere. Indeed, each of the thirteen colonies had its local tradition of migration, but most of these have been suppressed by the normative tradition. (2) "The Brewing Storm": this has to do with the troubles leading up to the Revolutionary War. It has its original *Haftpunkt* in the shrine of Boston, where the "Tea Party" is celebrated, but it too has been expanded with traditions from elsewhere, notably from Virginia. (3) "The Shot Heard Round the World": this tells of the outbreak of the struggle and has to do with such things as Paul Revere's ride and the fight at Concord Bridge. Its *Haftpunkt* is again the great shrine at Boston. (4) "A Nation Is Born": this centers around the formation of the Continental Congress, and the Declaration of Independence of 1776. It is a Pennsylvania tradition, its locale the shrine of Philadelphia. (5) "Through the Night of Defeat": this is a middle-American tradition and has to do with the dark days of 1776–8; its nucleus adheres to the pilgrim shrine at Valley Forge. (6) "Final Victory": basically a Virginia tradition at home in the shrine of Yorktown, but supplemented with other material, particularly of Carolina origin.

Now Washington runs through all these themes save, of course, the first. But this cannot be original, else the thesis of separate themes falls. After all, it must be remembered that we are dealing with the traditions of the Thirteen-State League in normative form. It is quite natural, therefore, that Washington, being revered in all the states, has been drawn into all the traditionary themes. The task of the historian is to discover in which of them he is original. Let us proceed by elimination, as Noth has done.

Clearly Washington is not original in "The Brewing Storm." Indeed, he hardly appears here at all save as a militia officer under Braddock in the fighting around Pittsburgh. This, of course, is secondary: the effort of western Pennsylvania to have a part in the father of his country. The original figures in this theme are men like John Hancock and Sam Adams in Massachusetts, Patrick Henry in Virginia. "The Shot Heard Round the World"? Hardly! Here again he is secondarily drawn in: indeed, his whole link to it is "rather weak" (*verhältnismässig schwach*). He appears only at the very end to take command (July 1775) of the forces besieging Boston. But this is not historical; it represents the natural desire of the "Hub of the Universe" to annex a bit of the national hero. Washington here has overlaid (as Moses at Sinai the elders of Israel) the humble and nameless heroes of Concord Bridge and Bunker Hill. "A Nation Is Born," then? Again, no! Indeed, Washington is weakest of all in this theme. He is introduced, to be sure; but one would expect that. The original figures were men like Thomas Jefferson and Ben Franklin. They were, alas, not military heroes, and so had to give place for the great leader. "Through the Night of Defeat"? Washington is stronger here, but the explanation is simple. Since tradition had him to be the commander of the army in its final victory, it was naturally supposed that he was also the creator of the army. Of course the original figure here is the crusty von Steuben. But he was a foreigner and the national hero overshadowed him. Then, too, because the fighting in the Middle Colonies was led for the most part by men who were grossly incompetent (Horatio Gates, Charles Lee), if not downright traitors (Benedict Arnold), these leaders tended to sink behind the immaculate and able figure of the hero.

But when we come to the last theme, "Final Victory," it is

clear that our search is nearing its end. For this is a Virginia
tradition, and the figure of Washington is of Virginia origin. Even
here, however, Washington is not original. The original heroes
of Yorktown were lesser men: "Mad Anthony" Wayne, perhaps,
or Rochambeau or de Grasse, or the debonair Lafayette. Washington has simply overlaid them. This, too, is easy to understand,
for none of these men were Virginians; and local traditions tend
to gather around a local hero. Actually the *Haftpunkt* of the
Washington tradition is a grave at Mt. Vernon ("see, there it is
until this day"). For, as Noth says (*UG,* 186), "A grave tradition
elsewhere usually gives the surest index of where a given figure
of tradtion is originally at home." From this grave tradition the
figure of Washington grew, as did that of Moses.

We may reconstruct the matter thus: Washington was an
important squire in Northern Virginia, and no doubt a leader
of the struggle for independence there. But of his exploits we
know next to nothing. He may have participated—though this
is not certain—in some minor capacity in the fighting at Yorktown. But, since he was the ranking military leader of Virginia,
Virginia tradition gradually exalted him above the others, until
he became the Commander of the Army and the architect of
victory. Then, since Virginia early assumed a dominant position
in the Thirteen-State League, the infant U.S.A., Virginia tradition
naturally tended to become normative throughout the entire land.
Thus Washington became the Father of his Country and, as such,
his figure found its way into all the traditionary themes.

But the reader has no doubt become impatient and has cried
out, "But this is preposterous! Furthermore, it is frivolous and is
not to be taken seriously!" One can only reply: "Precisely!" Certainly it is not to be taken seriously, nor should any sweeping
conclusions be drawn from it. Washington is not Moses: he
stands, and has always stood, in the full light of history. The
traditions about him are not of the sort of the early traditions of
Israel, nor was exodus and conquest a united action like the
American Revolution. The point, however, is this: if what we
have done with the figure of Washington is arbitrary, is what
Noth has done with the figure of Moses any less arbitrary? Is

the removal of Moses from the exodus theme, for example, anything but arbitrary? Could Noth's method of dealing with Moses be applied to any other figure of history without absurdity? And if to fragment the traditions of early America into separate themes represents a procedure patently absurd, what assurance is there that such an hypothesis has validity in the case of the traditions of early Israel? Noth assumes its validity as the basis of his whole tradition-history, but he can scarcely be said to have proved it. Yet if this assumption be not granted, the whole structure of his argument collapses. For my part, I find that structure so speculative that nothing can be based on it.

The trouble is that one cannot by direct argument prove Noth wrong. That is why arguments such as the above have been resorted to. But neither can Noth prove himself right. We move in a realm where we can no longer lay hold of objective evidence; we can only contradict one another. But the burden of proof is definitely on Noth. The entire structure of tradition-history rests upon certain assumptions, and deductions from those assumptions —no more. It is a very formidable structure, indeed—until someone timidly pipes, "But did it actually happen so?" In truth, there is no assurance that it did anything of the sort. There is no reason to assume that oral tradition followed such hard and fast rules, or that it developed at all in a manner so amenable to logic. Indeed, the amazing and incongruous thing about it all is that Noth is able, with but little objective evidence to go on, to give us the most elaborate and closely reasoned *Überlieferungsgeschichte* telling us to the last detail how Israel's traditions developed— but he can give us no history of how Israel itself developed, for of this we have no information! It would seem that if the one can be reconstructed by hypothesis, so could the other. And if there is no data for writing the prehistory of Israel before the settlement—what shall we say of this *Überlieferungsgeschichte?*

It seems to me that objective evidence allows us to separate with some confidence the various Pentateuch documents. It allows us also, from a comparison of J and E, to posit a common *Grundlage*—though of its full contents we cannot be sure. The evidence further requires us to assume that behind this there lay a long and complex history of oral transmission, leading from individual tradition to larger cycles of tradition, to great traditionary sagas. In some cases, too, the evidence allows us to follow a particular tradition back to its original *Sitz im Leben*. But no more! It does not extend to a complete history of tradition. The attempt to write one represents, in my opinion, an extrapolation from the known data of a sort that sober method cannot consider permissible. I say all this, I repeat, with great diffidence and with unabated admiration and respect for the scholarship of Alt and Noth, from whose work I have learned far more than I can begin to indicate here.

NOTES

1. Especially *Überlieferungsgeschichtliche Studien I* (Halle, M. Niemeyer, 1943).

2. The schools of Alt himself and of Albright have been especially fruitful in this regard, but a full bibliography of what we have in mind would take pages. As examples of what we have in mind, *cf*. Alt, *Das System der Stammesgrenzen im Buche Josua* (*Sellin-Festschrift*, Leipzig, A. Deichert, 1927, 13–24; reprinted in *KS* I, 193–202); Albright, "The List of Levitic Cities" (*Louis Ginzberg Jubilee Volume*, New York, American Academy for Jewish Research, 1945, 49–73).

3. E.g., R. Kittel, *GVI*, I, 249 ff.

4. Especially Gunkel-Begrich, *Einleitung in die Psalmen* (Göttingen, Vandenhoeck & Ruprecht, 1933).

5. Alt, *Die Ursprünge des Israelitischen Rechts* (Leipzig, S. Hirzel, 1934; reprinted in *KS* I, 278–332). A recent, splendid example of form-critical method is G. E. Mendelhall, "Covenant Forms in Israelite Tradition," *BA*, XVII–3 (1945), 50–76; *cf. idem*, *BA*, XVII–2, 26–46. (Both reprinted as *Law and Covenant in Israel and the Ancient Near East*, Pittsburgh, The Bible Colloquium, 1955.)

6. Noth, *Das System der zwölf Stämme Israels* (Stuttgart, W. Kohlhammer, 1930).

7. Many of the older Wellhausen school who, like Noth, discounted the tradition of unified onslaught as found in Joshua were driven by that very fact to find the beginnings of Israelite unity in the wilderness: e.g., A. Lods, *Israel*, 309 f.

8. For example, judging from the infrequency with which they are mentioned, one could similarly reason that neither Isaiah nor Jeremiah were known widely in Israel until the post-biblical period.

9. See *Early Israel in Recent History Writing*, pp. 54 f. and references there.

192 OLD TESTAMENT ISSUES

10. "But so far there has been no absolutely certain evidence of this kind, and such evidence is in fact hardly likely to be found. For the Israelite tribes did not acquire their territory by warlike conquest and the destruction of Canaanite cities . . ." (*History of Israel*, p. 82).

11. Albright, "The Israelite Conquest of Canaan in the light of Archaeology," *BASOR*, 74 (1939), 11–23. Reference to Albright in this section is to this article.

12. R. Kittel, *GVI*, I, 270.

13. *Cf.* F. M. T. deLiagre Böhl, "Mythos und Geschichte in der altbabylonischen Dichtung" (*Opera Minora* [Groningen, J. B. Wolters, 1953], 217–233). He compares the figures of Gilgamesh, Adapa, Sargon of Akkad and Semiramis. All these figures are cloaked in myth; but while the last two are clearly historical individuals, the first two, Böhl thinks, probably are not. For my part, I should hesitate to declare even Gilgamesh entirely unhistorical. But Böhl's point is certainly sound. Again, among the Ras Shamra texts, the epics of Kerit and Dan'el are much less purely mythological than is the Baal epic, and may contain a kernel of legendary history (*cf.* Albright, *Archaeology and the Religion of Israel*, Baltimore, Johns Hopkins Press, 3rd. ed. 1953, 90).

14. Alt, *Josua* (*BZAW*, 66 [1936], 13–29; reprinted in *KS*, I, 176–192).

15. *Cf.* Alt, "Die Wallfahrt von Sichem nach Bethel," reprinted in *KS*, I, 79–88.

16. Alt, *op. cit.*, 182 f: "Antworten auf die grosse Kinderfragealler Zeiten 'Warum?' "

17. *BAC*, 71, etc.

18. The Rev. Mason L. Weems, *The Life and Memorable Actions of George Washington*, ca. 1800.

19. On the origin of the custom see "Big Train vs. Big Myth," *Sports Illustrated*, Feb. 21, 1955, 61. "Big Train," it should be explained, refers to Walter Johnson, one-time star pitcher of the Washington Senators, and possessor of one of the most powerful throwing arms in the history of baseball. He was brought down to initiate the custom and, apparently, to make sure that the first test would succeed. It did!

20. E.g. Noth, *Das Buch Josua* (*Handbuch zum AT;* Tübingen, J. C. B. Mohr, 1938) 5 f.

21. See references in Bright, *op. cit.*, p. 64, n. 1.

22. *Cf.* especially Alt, *Josua*, 183.

23. For example, some of the poems of Ras Shamra, notably the Keret Legend, though perpetuated in Ugarit far to the north, seem to have their original setting in southern Phoenicia and the adjoining area. *Cf.* the cautious remarks of R. de Langhe, *Les textes de Ras Shamra-Ugarit et leurs rapports avec le milieu biblique de l'Ancien Testament* (Paris, Desclée de Brouwer, 2 vols., 1945), II, 97–174, 245 f.

24. In the syndicated newspaper magazine, *This Week* (Sunday, Dec. 13, 1953).

25. The theme "Wandering in the Wilderness" is not explicit in the former, but it is in the latter (Josh. 24:7b). In any case, this theme has, I think, least right of all to separate existence.

26. See the able study of G. E. Mendenhall, "Covenant Forms in Israelite Tradition," *BA*, XVII-3 (1954), 50–76.

27. *Cf.* H. H. Rowley, "Moses and the Decalogue," *BJRL*, 34 (1951), 81–118 for a defense of this view and full bibliography.

28. A. Weiser, *Einleitung in das Alte Testament* (Göttingen, Vandenhoeck & Ruprecht, 2nd ed., 1949), 66 f., has also argued against separating Sinai and exodus traditions.

8

INTRODUCTION TO PSALMS

Mitchell Dahood

Father Dahood describes his new work on the Psalms as "a prolegomenon," that is, an elaborate preface, rather than the usual form of commentary. He chose to concentrate primarily on the new light thrown on the Psalms by the Ugaritic literature and language, which he describes.

In the general introduction (p. 4), mention was made of the view at the turn of the century that the Psalms, all of them, are very late. Father Dahood's commentary reflects a disposition among present-day scholars to ascribe an early date to many, perhaps most, of the Psalms. Since his chief tool is the new linguistic knowledge derived from the Ugaritic, Father Dahood concentrates on some technical linguistic matters which may well be beyond the student, without some words of guidance. Accordingly, it is to be noticed that earlier scholarship thought that the Hebrew text of the Psalms was very corrupt, that is, full of mistakes, the result of faulty copying. Father Dahood represents the trend of scholars which now asserts that the traditional text (called the Masoretic, after the early Jewish students of the text, the Masoretes) has come down in relatively good condition. It may help the student to understand Father Dahood's continuing argument by reminding him that written Semitic languages are consonantal; the vowels found in modern printed Hebrew Bibles were added only in the middle ages. Significantly, a greater range of possible ways of interpreting the consonantal text now exists than the possibly over-hasty tendency of the older scholarship to

regard a Scriptural text as corrupt, especially if an ancient transla-
tion, such as the Greek LXX, seemed to be based on a differing
Hebrew. Father Dahood discusses the justice of emending the
Hebrew because of readings in the ancient translations. Further-
more, Hebrew uses certain consonants as prefixes and suffixes;
prior to modern learning the prefixes were rather rigidly inter-
preted. Such is the case with the letter lamedh; *but Ugaritic*
demonstrates a much higher flexibility to the lamedh *than was*
previously known.

That student who does not know Hebrew will, of course, not
be able to follow Father Dahood's argument in all its details. I
have omitted some of his examples which seemed too difficult
for students. By bracketed additions and by the use of italics
superimposed on Father Dahood's text, I have tried to make the
argument at least a little comprehensible to one who knows little
or no Hebrew. Yet even such a student should be able to see the
two main reversals of scholarship represented here, namely, the
vindication of the traditional Hebrew text, and the vindication of
the great antiquity of much of the Psalter. He can see also the
argument that the Palestinian Ras Shamra texts are more likely
to have influenced Scripture than materials in Akkadian from
Mesopotamia, which older scholars emphasized, simply because
the Ras Shamra materials had not yet been found.

Only the first of Father Dahood's intended two volumes has
been published; it contains the first fifty of the one hundred
and fifty psalms.

AN INTRODUCTION should more properly be written when the
study of all one hundred and fifty Psalms has been completed. A
number of conclusions, however, have already emerged with
sufficient clarity to warrant at this time a brief, preliminary
formulation.

What with the recent spate of Psalms' translations and commentaries, a new work on the Psalter would appear almost as
difficult to justify at this juncture as another book on the Scrolls
of Qumran. But the translation offered here differs from earlier
efforts in that it is not the fruit of a confrontation of the Hebrew

text with the ancient versions, from which the least objectionable reading is plucked. Much less does it follow the method of the recent *Psalterii secundum Vulgatam Bibliorum Versionem Nova Recensio,* edited by Robert Weber (Clervaux, Luxembourg, 1961), *pro manuscripto,* which presents a Latin version based on a comparison of the Hebrew original with Jerome's Vulgate, the *Juxta Hebraeos,* and the *Psalterium Novum* of the Pontifical Biblical Institute. What is attempted here is a fresh translation, accompanied by a philological commentary, that lays heavy stress on the Ras Shamra-Ugarit texts and other epigraphic discoveries made along the Phoenician littoral. Though some thirty-five years have passed since the discovery and decipherment of the Ras Shamra-Ugarit texts, no subsequent translation of the Psalms[1] has yet availed itself of these clay tablets. In 1941, when reviewing C. H. Gordon's *Ugaritic Grammar* (the fourth edition under the title *Ugaritic Textbook* [abbr. *UT*] appeared in 1965 [Analecta Orientalia 38; Rome]),[2] W. F. Albright wrote that:

the tremendous significance of the North Canaanite religious literature of Ugarit for biblical research is becoming clearer every day. It is not too much to say that all future investigations of the Book of Psalms must deal intensively with the Ugaritic texts. . . . Thorough knowledge of Ugaritic grammar, vocabulary and style is an absolute prerequisite for comparative research on the part of biblical scholars. Moreover, the significance of Ugaritic for historical Hebrew grammar, on which will increasingly rest our reconstruction of the literary history of Israel, cannot be overestimated. Ugaritic was only dialectically different from ancestral Hebrew in the generations immediately preceding the Israelite occupation of Canaan. Ugarit and Canaanite Palestine shared a common literary tradition, which profoundly influenced Israel. For these reasons Gordon's *Ugaritic Grammar* is of greater lasting importance for OT research than any dozen assorted recent commentaries taken together.[3]

Nearly a quarter of a century has passed since Albright stressed the relevance of Ugaritic for Psalms research, but most translators and commentators have continued to treat the Ras Shamra texts as, at best, only peripherally significant. To be sure, Sigmund Mowinckel, in his studies on the Psalms, has displayed a familiarity with the Ugaritic myths, but his failure to exploit the rich linguistic material at his disposition makes some of his conclusions philologically vulnerable.[4] H. J. Kraus, in his two-volume commentary on the Psalms that first began to appear in fascicles in 1957, does cite a few articles which seek to apply the new Ugaritic data to problems in the Psalter, but he is not convinced that Ugaritic is terribly important for a better understanding of the Psalms. His remarks in the *Einleitung* to the first volume of the 1961 revised edition are symptomatic: "Difficult or rare Hebrew words can sometimes be explained from Ugaritic poetry (cf., above all, Ps. 68). . . . With great prudence one must check to see if individual words and expressions are open to new possible definitions because of Ugaritic."[5]

One may, however, legitimately ask whether Kraus is exercising *Vorsicht* (prudence) vis-à-vis the new material, or an excess of caution with regard to the new canons of Hebrew philology being imposed by the Ras Shamra discoveries and by progress in Northwest Semitic philology. An example to illustrate. There are two textual difficulties in the second colon of Psalm 4:7, *nᵉsāh 'alēnū 'ōr pānekā yhwh* (translated usually, Lift up upon us the light of thy contenance, o Lord"). Kraus accepts G. R. Driver's proposal that *'ālēnū* here denotes *"from* us," as in Phoenician and probably also in Ugaritic, but fails to appreciate that consonant *nsh* (from *nūs*) is the verb "to flee," a synonym of *brḥ*, "to flee," precisely the verb with which *'l*, "from," is employed in Phoenician. Though his translation reflects the sense of the line, "The light of your face has departed from us," Kraus introduces the gratuitous emendation of consonantal *nsh* (to be pointed *nāsāh,* with archaic third-person masculine ending) to *nāsᵉ'āh*. In other terms, he resorts to the method of emendation instead of fully availing himself of the Phoenician parallel which offers a smooth exit from the textual impasse and permits the clear and literal rendering, "The light of your face *has fled from us,* O Yahweh."[6]

The present work is not a commentary on the Psalms in the traditional sense of the word; a better term would perhaps be a prolegomenon to a commentary. The topics usually treated in a standard commentary, such as the name "Psalms," the title of the Psalms, their arrangement and use, the origin and authorship of the Psalms, etc., have been waived in the interest of the primary scope of this study, namely, a translation and philological commentary which utilizes the linguistic information offered by the Ras Shamra tablets. Psalms as such have not yet been unearthed at Ras Shamra so that the Ugaritic texts do not directly bear on such questions as literary classification or *Sitz im Leben* (historical setting); the treatment of these problems therefore will also be cursory and incidental to the main purpose at hand. Numerous recent works examine such problems fully and competently, so there is no pressing need to rehearse them in the following pages. To judge from reviewers' comments, nothing is more depressing than having to read the long introductions which merely rehash issues that have already been well aired. However, a more ample discussion of the more important issues of literary criticism is foreseen for the second volume of Psalms in this series, covering Psalms 51–150.

DISCOVERIES AT RAS SHAMRA-UGARIT

The history of the discovery and subsequent excavations of Ras Shamra has been well summarized. The entry on "Ugarit" in *The Interpreter's Dictionary of the Bible* (abbr. *IDB*) (New York, 1962) runs to fifteen columns. Ugaritic has taken its place as a major language (or more properly, a dialect of Canaanite) in the Semitic family of languages.

About seven miles north of Latakia (ancient Laodicea ad Mare) on the north Syrian coast stands an artificial mound about sixty feet high and covering some seventy acres. Today called Ras Shamra (Fennel Promontory), this mound concealed the ancient city of Ugarit, known from Babylonian, Hittite, and Egyptian records. In the spring of 1928, a north Syrian peasant was plowing his field when the plow jammed against a stone slab which happened to form part of the ceiling of a corbelled tomb. Informed of this strike, the archaeological authorities commissioned C. F. A. Schaeffer of Strasbourg, who began excavations at the site in 1929 and has continued in that capacity to the present day. He has thus far conducted twenty-seven archaeo-logical campaigns at Ras Shamra. The discoveries seem unlimited —each season's dig seems to yield a rich harvest. The discoveries include enormous quantities of pottery, weights, bronzes, jewelry, statuary, stelae, tombs, constructions such as temples, palaces, private homes, sanitation systems, and above all, texts.

Since the initial discoveries in 1929, thousands of tablets in at least eight different languages have come to light. Our present interest focuses on those in a previously unknown cuneiform alphabet of twenty-nine or thirty signs. Many of the copies date to the reign of a certain King Niqmad of Ugarit, a contemporary of the Hittite king Shuppiluliuma (*ca.* 1375–1340 B.C.). Though copied in this period, the myths and legends recorded on the tablets are doubtless much older, the Baal Cycle reaching back, in all likelihood, to the third millennium B.C. The decipherment was worked out in less than a year's time by three scholars working independently: Hans Bauer in Germany, Édouard Dhorme in Jerusalem, and Charles Virolleaud in Paris.

The longest and most important composition is the Baal Cycle, a collection of episodes about the Canaanite gods, preserved in eight tablets and in a number of fragments; it numbers more than two thousand lines. Next in importance is the *Legend of King Keret,* a semi-historical poem, recorded on three tablets and sev-eral fragments which total some five hundred lines, while the Epic of Aqhat runs to about four hundred legible lines on four tablets. Two other mythological poems have been published, both of which seem to be complete. One is named after its invocation, *The Beautiful and Gracious Gods,* and describes the birth of the twin deities Dawn and Dusk. The other is a hymn celebrating the marriage of the goddess Nikkal to the Moon-god. Finally, there are tablets which list offerings to the gods, sacred and secular professions, rituals; some contain private letters, economic and juridical texts, and even medicinal formulas for curing ailing horses. In recent years a series of lexicographical tablets has been found, one of them a quadrilingual vocabulary containing some two hundred words, as well as a perfectly preserved incanta-tion of seventy-five lines. The very variety of subjects treated in these texts makes them an inexhaustible source of information for the biblical philologist and exegete.

One need not be surprised, therefore, to encounter among the plates accompanying the text of C. F. A. Schaeffer's *The Cuneiform Texts of Ras Shamra-Ugarit* (London, 1939) a figure, taken from a fresco in the Church of Santa Maria Antica in the Roman Forum, which shows Hezekiah, king of Judah, sick in bed with his face turned toward the wall, while the prophet Isaiah, standing at the foot of the bed, talks to him. On page 41 [of Schaeffer's volume] the reader is informed that the biblical name of the remedy made of boiled figs that Isaiah recommended is identical with the name of a remedy used by the veterinary surgeons at Ugarit in the fifteenth and fourteenth centuries B.C.!

Since the decipherment of the texts in 1930, the linguistic classification of Ugaritic (as the language came to be called) has been a matter of dispute. The widely held view that Ugaritic is a Canaanite dialect whose closest affinity is to biblical Hebrew, especially in the poetic books, has been winning the day. The publication of new texts by Virolleaud in 1957 and 1965, and recent comparative studies disclosing added points of contact in the areas of phraseology, imagery, prosody, and thought, have corroborated the Canaanite classification of Ugaritic. The numerous equations and comparisons proposed in this volume point to the same classification, and though many of them are admittedly banal, their inclusion will enable the comparative Semitist to make a more accurate assessment.

COMPARATIVE STUDIES

The nineteenth century witnessed the rise and progress of Egyptian and Babylonian studies, a rise which was to exert a tremendous impact upon Old Testament research. In time, however, the legacy left by these two disciplines for a clearer understanding of the biblical text turned out to be much less than was imagined, say, thirty years ago.[7] History, then, cautions scholars to moderate their claims on behalf of a new discipline and its bearing on Old Testament inquiry. The *raison d'être* of the following study is precisely to set forth the relevance of the Ugaritic texts for

Psalms research; that considerable risk is involved in such an ostensibly restricted approach to the Psalter and its problems does not, in the light of recent history, escape the present writer. But the positive results flowing from an application of Ugaritic grammatical and stylistic principles to the Hebrew text of Psalms appear to be sufficiently numerous and significant to merit detailed presentation. Not all the proposals submitted here will stand the test of present criticism or future discoveries, but if the present effort succeeds in showing what possibilities are open to the modern student of the Bible, the effort will have proved worth while. The evidence is registered throughout the notes accompanying the translation, but for the sake of general orientation, some observations on the areas of Psalms research affected by Ugaritic and Northwest Semitic philology may not be out of place.

THE CONSONANTAL TEXT

Biblical poetry teems with textual cruxes, and the Hebrew text of Psalms is no exception. In fact, if one were to base his opinion of the consonantal text upon those Psalms, such as 14 and 18, which are preserved in doublets, he would conclude that the text is corrupt and stands in need of constant emendation. But happily these doublets prove not to be typical, and the consonantal text of the first fifty Psalms is remarkably well preserved; in my opinion, resort to emendation can be justified in fewer than half a dozen instances. This does not mean that all the textual difficulties have been solved; it merely suggests that the rich thesaurus of forms and constructions in the Ugaritic and Phoenician texts severely restricts the freedom of the textual critic to emend the text. For example, in Psalm 24:4, *napšī* [*my* soul] is customarily emended to *napšō* [*his* soul] since, as Kraus (*Psalmen*, I, p. 193) writes, "The context requires this correction," but now it turns out that Hebrew, like Phoenician and probably Ugaritic, also possessed a third-person singular suffix (masculine and feminine) in *-ī;* more than ninety examples, listed under Psalm 2:6, have thus far been identified in the poetic books of the Bible. Biblical morphology has thus been enriched with a new morpheme and both the consonantal and punctualized texts have been vindicated in over eighty cases. The Masoretes almost certainly did not understand the morpheme, but they nonetheless preserved it. Or again, in a number of texts the presence of a *lamedh* has proved embarrassing and, to many, deletion was the only viable expedient. But the well-documented existence in Ugaritic of both *lamedh emphaticum* and *lamedh vocativum* considerably widens the choice a philologist can make when faced with such a problem. Consider, for instance, Psalm 140:7, *'āmartī lᵉyahweh 'ēlī 'attāh ha'ᵃzīnāh yhwh qōl taḥᵃnūnay;* the Tetragrammaton [*lᵉyahweh; to the Lord*] in the second colon is, on the strength of the Syriac reading, deleted. When, however, the *lamedh* preceding *yhwh* in the first colon is parsed as vocative, the presence of *yhwh* in the second colon is rendered necessary by both parallelism and meter. Hence I translate, "I said, O Yahweh, you are my God; hear, O Yahweh, my plea for mercy." A similar situation obtains in Psalm 73:1, *'ak ṭōb lᵉyiśrā'ēl 'ᵉlōhīm lᵉbārē lēbāb,* where *lᵉyiśrā'ēl* [to Israel] is often labeled the product of faulty word division and critics widely adopted the emendation first proposed by H. Graetz in the last century, *layyāšār 'el* [God is good to the upright]. But the analysis if *lᵉ* in *lᵉyiśrā'ēl* as *lamedh vocativum* produces this version, "Truly good, O Israel, is God to the pure of heart," a fine example of smoothly flowing enjambment. The fact that in Ugaritic the vocative *lamedh* is particularly frequent with personal names, enhances the likelihood that this is the particle preceding personified Israel.

Often enough, of two nouns in parallelism, one has a pronominal suffix and the other has none. Critics have generally supplied the lack, but the principle of double-duty suffix, employed by Canaanite poets for metrical or other reasons, shows that the inventiveness of textual critics has in this instance been misplaced. In brief, the textual critic is today obliged to familiarize himself with Northwest Semitic philology before venturing to set the biblical text to rights. Otherwise he may find himself writing in a vein similar to that of a well-known biblical scholar who confesses, "Indeed, this particular example serves the present writer as a stern warning against hasty textual 'emendation'; for, when he began his researches into the Psalter along the lines indicated by 'The Role of the King in the Jerusalem Cultus,' he followed the usual practice of attempting to improve the reading, and only discovered later, as his work developed, that in so doing he was destroying a valuable piece of evidence and an important link in his argument."[8] A. E. Housman has written of Richard Bentley that "the best prize that Bentley missed, and the richest province left for his successors, is the correction of those verses of Manilius which he precipitately and despotically expelled." (quoted from *A. E. Housman: Selected Prose,* ed. John Carter [Cambridge University Press, 1961], p. 30).

THE MASORETIC TEXT

The reverence of the Masoretes for the consonantal text outstripped their knowledge of archaic Hebrew poetry: the result is that their vocalization, and even their word division, must sometimes be disregarded if one is to find the way back to the original sense. The *crux interpretum* in Psalm 45:5, *w^e 'anwāh ṣedeq* [meekness of righteousness] is a Masoretic creation; divide and point the same consonants in the light of Psalm 82:3, *'ānī wārāš ḥaṣdīqū,* and the result is *w^e'ānāw ḥaṣdēq,* "and defend the poor," an unimpeachable sequence to "ride on in behalf of truth." The meaning of many substantives has been lost, with the inevitable consequence of false vocalization. A probable illustration presents itself in Psalm 2:8, *mimmennī* [ask *of me* and I will make the nations your heritage], which is preferably pointed *m^{e}mōnī,* "my wealth" [ask *my wealth* and I will give it]; while Psalm 33:7, *kannēd* [like a heap] gives pellucid sense when pointed *kened,* "pitcher," a substantive known from Akkadian and Ugaritic. The resultant image is completely changed. Where KJV translates, "He gathereth the waters of the sea together as an heap," which evokes the imagery of Exodus 15:8, "the floods stood upright as an heap" (KJV), we would read, "He gathers into a jar the waters of the sea."

The practice of using plural forms of names of dwellings, though with a singular meaning, seems to have escaped the Masoretes. In Psalm 15:1, MT (Masoretic, the traditional Hebrew) reads singular *b^e'oh^{o}lekā* [in your tent], but some manuscripts more correctly read the plural form *b^e'ōh^{o}lekā* [in your tents]. . . .

An imperfect knowledge of archaic divine appellatives will explain the repeated confusion between [in the identical consonantal words] 'el, 'ēlī, "the Most High," and the prepositions 'al [on] and 'ālay [upon], respectively; cf. Psalms 7:9, 11; 16:6; 62:3; 68:30, 35; 106:7. From this imperfect knowledge stems the erroneous division of consonants in Psalm 75:10, where MT reads grammatically incongruent 'aggīd leᵉ 'ōlām [I will declare forever] for ᵃgaddēl 'ōlām, "I shall extol the Eternal," parallel to "I shall sing to the God of Jacob." In other words, the real parallelism intended by the Psalmist is between the God of Abraham, who in Genesis 21:33 is called 'ēlōām, "El the Eternal," and the God of Jacob. The Masoretes missed the historical allusion. The LXX [translators] experienced difficulty with the consonantal division and read 'āgīl, "I shall rejoice forever"; many modern versions have opted, ill-advisedly in my judgment, for the LXX emendation.

These observations should not, however, be construed as a warrant for setting the MT at nought whenever the text proves recalcitrant. In the temple and later in the synagogue, there must have been a strong tradition of prayer and singing which secured the pronunciation of the Psalms even when the grammatical parsing of forms was not immediately evident. This living tradition was never interrupted for Judaism in its totality. . . . Critics have found it necessary in scores of verses to change the pronominal suffix -ī to -ō, since the context desiderates the third person. If one admits, as now it seems one must, that Hebrew, like Phoenician, possessed a third-person singular suffix -ī,[9] one will see that the Masoretes, who probably did not understand the morpheme, nonetheless safeguarded the correct tradition. This explanation may sound much like "you name it, we have it," but the plain fact is that the Northwest Semitic morphological and lexical treasure-trove offers the biblical philologist choices unthinkable three decades ago.

THE ANCIENT VERSIONS

In the present study the ancient versions are cited infrequently, not because they have not been consulted, but because they have relatively little to offer toward a better understanding of the difficult texts. For such texts, the critic who seeks succor from the ancient translations will usually be disappointed. A significant corollary of Ugaritic studies will be the devaluation of the ancient versions. My consistent experience in studying Psalms (as well as Job and Proverbs) has been that Ugaritic embarrassingly exposes—at least in the poetic books—the shortcomings of the versions and seriously undermines their authority as witnesses to the original text. The *Bible de Jérusalem* can be taxed with a serious error in method when, in the poetic books in particular, it detours to the LXX when ever the Hebrew text throws up an obstacle. The numberless details of grammar which Phoenician and Ugaritic place at the disposal of the Hebraist allow him to ask anew: "How much grammar did the translators in antiquity understand? Were they familiar with the poetic vocabulary of the second millennium, the language often used by the biblical poets? How many mythological allusions did they seize?"

In response to the first query, Psalm 49:16 may serve as an object lesson: *'ak ᵉlōhīm yipdeh napšī miyyad šᵉ'ōl kī yiqqāḥēnī*, is rendered by the LXX, "But God will redeem my soul from the power of that mansion *when* it receives me," and by the Vulgate, *"Verumtamen Deus redimet animam meam de manu inferi, cum acceperit me"* ("But God will redeem my soul from the hand of hell, *when* he shall receive me"), while the *Psalterii Nova Recensio* of 1961 adopts the Vulgate reading except for the substitution of *acceperit* by *abstulerit*. Even the most casual reader will notice an imbalance that's uncharacteristic of biblical verse-structure. Four clear Ugaritic examples of an emphatic *kī*, which effects the post-position of the verb at the end of its colon, suggest the following translation and verse division: "But God will ransom me, from the hand of Sheol will he *surely* snatch me." The first colon thus ends with *napšī* and the second with *yiqqāḥēnī;* the rhyme was doubtless intended by the poet. In fact, none of the ancient versions grasped the nature of the construction in any of the passages where it is admittedly employed: Genesis 18:20; II Samuel 23:5; Isaiah 7:9; 10:13; Psalms 49:16; 118:10–12; 128:2. They were equally strangers to the *waw emphaticum* in such texts as Psalms 4:5; 11:6; 25:11; 49:11; 77:2, etc.

Their knowledge of poetic vocabulary leaves much to be desired. The psalmists frequently used *'ereṣ,* "earth," in the poetic sense of "nether world," as in Akkadian and Ugaritic, but this nuance was lost on the ancient translators. Psalm 75 abounds in divine appellatives, but this could never be gathered from a perusal of the version. Ttitles such as *'ōlām,* "the Eternal," *lē',* "the Victor," *mārōm,* "the Exalted One," *hammēbīn,* "the Observer," were simply not reproduced in antiquity and now must slowly be recovered with the aid of Northwest Semitic texts.

A poetic practice, notably clarified by recent discoveries, is the use of plural forms of nouns signifying "home, habitation," which, however, are to be translated as singular. Thus the ancient versions render *miškānōt* as plural in Psalms 48:3; 84:2; and 132:5, 7, where the singular would appear more correct.

Many of the biblical images and metaphors do not come through in the ancient versions. A probable instance is the Psalm 78:26, *yassa' qādīm baššāmāyim wayᵉnahēg bᵉ'uzzō tēmān,* poorly reflected in LXX, "He removed the southeast wind out of heaven, and *by his power* brought on the southwest wind." This rendition can scarcely be correct since it fails to preserve the synonymous parallelism which characterizes the preceding and following verses. The more plausible reading would be, "He let loose the east wind from heaven, and led forth the south wind *from his stronghold.*"

The ancient versions do, however, make a positive contribution to textual criticism in their flexible attitude toward prepositions, an attitude which modern translators might well adopt. They often translated according to the needs of context, rendering *bᵉ* "from" when the context required this meaning. Contrast the translation of Deuteronomy 1:44, *bᵉśē'īr 'ad ḥormāh,* "from Seir to Hormah," as rendered by LXX, Vulgate, and Syriac, with the less felicitous efforts of CCD and RSV (CCD: "in Seir as far as Horma"; RSV: "in Seir as far as Hormah"). Notice their handling of *baššāmāyim* in Psalm 78:26, cited above. This sense has amply been confirmed by Ugaritic where *b* and *l* denote precisely this in many cases; in Canaanite poetry *min* was unknown and its function was filled by *b* and *l*. The introduction of *min* into biblical Hebrew did not completely deprive *b* and *l* of their older function. Here the testimony of the LXX, Vulgate, and Syriac can be extremely valuable. But the overall judgment that the ancient versions invite in view of the new testimony is that they are not always reliable witnesses to what the biblical poets intended.

COMPARATIVE LITERATURE

Just as Canaanite literary documents of the second millennium cast some doubt on the authority of the ancient versions, so do they also reduce the immediate relevance of Egyptian and Mesopotamian literature for the direct elucidation of biblical poetry. While the literatures of Egypt and Babylonia will continue to retain their value *ad complementum doctrinae,* they must, in the area of comparative studies, yield pride of place to the clay tablets of Ras Shamra. James A. Montgomery has written:

The Assyro-Babylonian and Egyptian literatures have for long been easily accessible to all students. But here is a literature far more closely related, geographically, linguistically, and culturally, to the Hebrew Scriptures, and even its gross polytheistic contents present a thesaurus of theological terminology which became the traditional inheritance of the thought and language of Israel's unique religion. . . . Canaan, i.e., Palestine-Syria, now no longer appears as a land backward in culture and literature, but is revealed as making its contribution to high literature in poetry and drama, during the age before Moses.[10]

On the level of lexicography, a reassessment of the conclusions set forth in Heinrich Zimmern's *Akkadische Fremdwörter als Beweis für babylonischen Kultereinfluss,* 2d ed. (Leipzig, 1917), on the basis of the available Canaanite glossary (more than twenty-seven hundred roots are listed in the Glossary of C. H. Gordon's *UT)* would produce some highly interesting results which might serve as a gauge for measuring the other relationships between Babylonian and Hebrew cultures. How many Hebrew words described as *Akkadische Lehnwörter* in the authoritative *Hand-*

wörterbuch of Gesenius-Buhl, 17th ed. (Leipzig, 1921), retain their authenticity today?[11] Textual studies which try to explain difficult texts in the Bible on the basis of Akkadian words must now show, to be genuinely convincing, that the Akkadian word is also reported in non-biblical West Semitic texts. For example, the correspondence of Psalm 33:7, *kened* (MT *kannēd*), "pitcher," to Akk. *kandu*, "jug, pitcher," takes on new suasive force with the knowledge that *knd* was current in the economic texts of Ras Shamra. In passing it may be noted that Zimmern[12] identified Akk. *kandu* with Heb. *kad*, but the fact that Ugaritic distinguished between *kd* and *knd* indicates that the same distinction must be maintained in Hebrew. As S. Kirst has observed[13] in connection with his discussion of *tᵉhōm* in Hebrew, Ugar. *thmt*, "It is no longer strictly necessary to maintain that the Hebrew word is directly borrowed from Akkadian, even though in Akkadian the primordial flood Tiamat imaginatively stood for the female element of chaos" (*"Damit ist eine direkte Entlehnung des Wortes aus dem akkadischen Sprachbereich fürs Hebräische keine zwingende Notwendigkeit mehr, obwohl auch dort die Tiāmat als die Urflut das weibliche Chaoselement versinnbildlicht"*). How important for the correct interpretation of a text is the just appreciation of the relationships that might be found among the different Semitic languages is illustrated by C. Virolleaud's treatment of the unusual form *lšmn* encountered in the Ugaritic tablets published in 1957.[14] Virolleaud's reasoning goes like this: the Hebrew plural of *lāšōn*, "tongue," is feminine *lᵉ'sānōt*, while Akkadian preserves two plural forms, feminine *lišanāti* and masculine *lišānū*; accordingly, Ugaritic *lšnm* must be a masculine plural form. His own oft-stated conviction that Ugaritic is a Canaanite dialect closely related to Hebrew should have cautioned him against using Akkadian morphology to account for a newly attested West Semitic form. Hence W. F. Albright,[15] followed by Otto Eissfeldt,[16] had no difficulty in refuting Virolleaud's analysis by showing that *lšmn*, parallel to dual *dnbtm*, "two tails," was a dual form, like Ugaritic *ydm* or *kpm*, denoting a "double or forked tongue"; *cf.* Psalm 60:10.

Hermann Gunkel's identification of numerous mythological

motifs in OT poetry is a major contribution to biblical theology. But even this contribution must be reassessed in the light of the Ugaritic texts. While Gunkel seeks to make the biblical poets directly dependent upon Mesopotamian mythology,[17] the Ugaritic myths and legends show that the biblical exegete need not go so far afield to locate the source of Hebrew mythopoeic thought and expression.[18] Or again, while one cannot quarrel with H. Wheeler Robinson's statement that "The *ultimate* [my italics] origin of the conception of Yahweh's council is doubtless to be found in Babylonia; we hear of the deliberation of the gods in the story of creation,"[19] the existence of such Ugaritic phrases as *'dt ilm,* "the assembly of the gods," which scholars recognize as the equivalent of Psalm 82:1, *'ᵃdat 'ēl,* shows that in the search for the immediate origin of mythological motifs in the Bible a new orientation is needed.

The origin of the theological wordplays registered in such passages as Psalms 47:3, 6; 97:7—often credited to the influence of the Akkadian epics in which this practice is a recognized feature (the puns on many of Marduk's fifty names suggest themselves)—can be more fruitfully sought among the Canaanites, who are known to have indulged in such paronomasia: for example, UT, 77:17–18, *tn nkl yrḫ ytrḫ,* "Give Nikkal that the Moongod might marry."

THE DATING OF THE PSALMS

The work of Sigmund Mowinckel in stressing the cultic background of most of the Psalms makes it impossible today to write a commentary along the lines of Moses Buttenwieser's *The Psalms Chronologically Treated with a New Translation. . . .* Buttenwieser sought to arrange the Psalms in chronological order, using several criteria, principally the purported historical allusions and the literary dependence of the Psalmists upon historically debatable writings, especially the prophets. By showing that many of the supposed historical phrases are cultic expressions whose origins cannot be dated with any meaningful precision, Mowinckel has seriously undermined Buttenwieser's primary presupposition. The Ugaritic texts now conspire to drain the method

H

of literary dependence of much of its plausibility by introducing the possibility that both the Psalmist and, say, the prophet were indebted to a literary tradition long resident in Canaan. For instance, Buttenwieser, on the basis of their literary resemblances to Isaiah 63:1–6, would date Psalms 2 and 110 to the post-Exilic period, while at the 1964 annual meeting of the Catholic Biblical Association of America one speaker proposed that Psalm 110 is a product of the period of the Chronicler or Qoheleth (400–200 B.C.). An examination of the vocabulary of these Psalms reveals that virtually every word, image, and parallelism are now reported in Bronze-Age Canaanite texts; the present writer would tentatively date Psalms 2 and 110 to the tenth century B.C. If they are poems composed shortly prior to the LXX, why is it that the Alexandrian Jewish translators understood them so imperfectly? Roughly contemporary works should fare better than they did in translation.

Pursuing the method of literary affiliation, Pierre Bonnard, *Le Psautier selon Jérémie* (Paris, 1960), p. 39, concludes that the Psalms containing the phrase *bōḥēn libbōt ūkᵉlāyōt*, "he who tests minds and hearts," are dependent upon Jeremiah, where the phrase appears characteristic. But the occurrence of part of the phrase, *klyth wlbh*, in a Ugaritic text of incantatory type strongly suggests that both Psalmist and prophet drew from a common source. The appearance of part of the clause in an incantatory text hints that the entire expression *bōḥēn libbōt ūkᵉlāyōt* [literally, "he tests hearts, that is minds and livers, that is, intelligence"] may have been used in incantations; the discovery of inscribed liver models during a recent campaign at Ras Shamra may resolve the problem. One may proceed further and submit that Psalm 7, where the phrase in question occurs, appears to be linguistically too archaic and too difficult to have been composed in the Exilic or post-Exilic period, that is, after Jeremiah.

The tendency in recent years to assign earlier rather than later dates to the composition of the Psalms comports with the evidence of the Ras Shamra texts. These show that much of the phraseology in the Psalter was current in Palestine long before the writing prophets, so the criterion of literary dependence becomes much too delicate to be serviceable. On the other hand, the inadequate knowledge of biblical poetic idiom and, more importantly, of biblical images and metaphors displayed by the third-century B.C. translators of the LXX, bespeaks a long chronological gap between the original composition of the Psalms and their translation into Greek. Even the admittedly later poems in the Psalter are considerably older than the Hodayot (hymns of praise) from Qumran, which freely borrowed the phraseology, the imagery, and the central ideas of the Book of Psalms. These considerations thus point to a pre-Exilic date for most of the Psalms, and not a few of them (e.g., Psalms 2; 16; 18; 29; 60; 68; 82; 108; 110) may well have been composed in the Davidic period.

NOTES

1. One monograph and numerous short articles have examined the Psalms in relation to the literary corpus from Ras Shamra; some of these will be referred to in the course of this study. The positive results of such studies have not as yet found their way into any better-known translations.

2. In citing the Ugaritic texts, I follow the numbering and transliteration of *UT*.

3. In *JBL* 60 (1941), 438 f.

4. To cite but one instance, Mowinckel, *The Psalms in Israel's Worship,* I, pp. 77 ff., has placed considerable emphasis upon Psalm 45:7, which he renders, "Thy throne, O God, is for ever and ever," as explicit evidence for the existence in Israel of a form of divine kingship. However, the translation and philological commentary proposed below remove this verse from among his proof-texts for divine kingship in Israel.

5. *Psalmen,* 2d ed., I, p. xii.

6. Similar criticism of Kraus's handling of this text has been made by J. H. Eaton in *Theology Today* 67 (1964), 356.

7. This point has been more fully developed by the present writer in *Gregorianum* 43 (1962), 55–57.

8. Aubrey R. Johnson, *Sacral Kingship in Ancient Israel* (Cardiff, 1955), p. 81, n. 1.

9. See above, p. 203.

10. In his review of J. H. Patton, *Canaanite Parallels in the Book of Psalms* (Johns Hopkins Press, 1944), in *JBL* 63 (1944), 418 f.

212   OLD TESTAMENT ISSUES

11. No less interesting would be a restudy of the data in E. Kautzsch, *Die Aramäismen in Alten Testament* (Halle, 1902), in light of the Northwest Semitic thesaurus that is available today.

12. *Akkadische Fremdwörter als Beweis für babylonischen Kultureinfluss*, p. 33.

13. In *FuF* 32 (1958), 218.

14. *Palais royal d'Ugarit*, II (Paris, 1957), p. 12.

15. In *BASOR 150* (1958), 36, n. 5.

16. In *JSS* 5 (1960), 34.

17. See his *Schöpfung und Chaos in Urzeit und Endzeit* (Göttingen, 1895), pp. 106 ff.

18. *Cf.* the sound observations of Kraus, *Psalmen*, II, p. 649.

19. See his article, "The Council of Yahweh," in *JTS* 45, 1944), 152, n. 1.

9

WISDOM AND JOB

Robert Gordis

Three books, Proverbs, Ecclesiastes, and Job, are frequently classed together as biblical representatives of Wisdom Literature, a category which is considerably increased when there are added to it some surviving ancient books which did not make their way into Scripture. Occasionally a voice is raised against including Job within Wisdom Literature. Certainly the praise of Wisdom in Job 28 would suggest such inclusion, but a very large number of scholars have believed that this chapter is not an original part of Job, but was a free floating document which somehow was copied into Job. The excerpt from Professor Gordis' book is not directly a defense of classifying Job as Wisdom Literature; however, it reflects in rounded form the importance of the Wisdom tration in Israelite history.

As we have seen, the Law, which was the province of the priest and later of the scribe, and the Vision, which was the experience of the prophet and later of the apocalyptist, did not exhaust the range of spiritual activity in ancient Israel. A third strand was supplied by *Hokmah* (Wisdom), which was cultivated by the sage *(hakam)* or the elder *(zaken)*. This discipline was more inclusive and more concrete than is suggested by the honorific and rather abstract term "Wisdom."

Hokmah may be defined as a realistic approach to the problems of life, including all the practical skills and technical arts of civilization. The term *hakam*, "sage" or "wise man," is accordingly applied in the Bible to all practitioners of the arts. Bezalel, the skilled craftsman who built the Tabernacle and its appointments in the wilderness, and all his associates, are called "wise of heart" (Exod. 28:3; 35:31; 36:1). Weavers (Exod. 35:25), goldsmiths (Jer. 10:9), and sailors (Ezek. 27:8; Ps. 107:27) are described as *hakamim* [wise men].

Rabbinic Hebrew undoubtedly preserves an ancient usage when it applies the term *hakamah* [wise woman] to the "midwife," upon whose skill life and death depend. The women skilled in lamentation (Jer. 9:16) and the magicians and soothsayers with their occult arts were similarly described as "wise" (Gen. 41:8; I Kings 5:10–12; Isa. 44:25; Jer. 9:16). Skill in the conduct of war and in the administration of the state (Isa. 10:13; 29:14; Jer. 49:7) are integral aspects of Wisdom, for the successful management of affairs—in war and in peace, at the royal court and in the confines of the individual family—requires a realistic understanding of human nature, the exercise of practical virtues, and the avoidance of at least the major vices.

Above all, *Hokmah* refers to the arts of poetry and music, both vocal and instrumental. Song in ancient Israel was coextensive with life itself. Harvest and vintage, the royal coronation, the conqueror's return, courtship and marriage, all were accompanied by song and dance.

This relationship between song and Wisdom was so close that often no distinction was made between the two. Thus in I Kings (5:10–12 Hebrew, 4:29–32 Christian versions) we read: "Solomon's wisdom excelled the wisdom of all the children of the east, and all the wisdom of Egypt. For he was wiser than all men, than Ethan the Ezrahite, and Heman, and Chalcol, and Darda, the sons of Mahol; and his fame was in all the nations round about. And he spoke three thousand proverbs; and his songs were a thousand and five."[1] Ethan and Heman are the eponymous heads of the musical guilds mentioned in I Chronicles, 15:19, to whom Psalms 88 and 89 are attributed. First Chronicles ascribes these guilds of singers to the Davidic age and traces their genealogy back to Korah, the contemporary of Moses.[2] Today the tradition is no longer dismissed as an unhistorical, artificial "throwback" of a later institution to an earlier age. There is growing evidence in Ugaritic sources of musical and other guilds connected with the temple cult.[3]

Since improvisation was often the rule, no line was drawn between the composer and the poet, the instrumentalist and the singer: all were part of Wisdom. Thus, in Psalm 49:4–5 we read:

> My mouth shall speak Wisdom,
> My heart shall meditate[4] understanding
> I shall turn my instrument[5] to a parable,
> I shall begin my riddle with the lyre.

All the material aspects of *Hokmah*, as embodied in art, architecture, and the manual crafts, disappeared with the destruction of the physical substratum of ancient Hebrew life. All that has remained of Wisdom is its incarnation in literature, which has survived, only in part, in the pages of the Bible. The Wisdom writings are concerned not only with the practical arts of living, but also with the development of a sane, workable attitude toward life as a whole, without which proficiency in the technical skills will avail men little. To convey the truths of Wisdom, a specific literary genre came into being, the *mashal*, or (less frequently) the *hidah*.[6]

The term *mashal*, derived from the Hebrew root meaning, "represent, resemble, be similar," develops a variety of related senses. Its most common meaning is "proverb," a short, pithy utterance expressing some observation on life and human nature. Reasoning from the known to the unknown, the *mashal* frequently depends on analogy to make its point:

> As a door turns on its hinges,
> So does a sluggard on his bed (Prov. 26:14).

The term is also applied to somewhat lengthy literary compositions such as the allegory, parable, or fable. It also refers to more extensive collections of proverbs[7] or poetic utterances,[8] in which poetic comparisons or philosophical reflections are common.

The *hidah*, or "riddle," is a term which appears much less frequently and is more restricted in meaning.[9] In several passages where it occurs it is defined by some scholars as "an enigmatic, perplexing saying."[10] A more satisfactory rendering would be "an utterance on a mysterious theme." This would explain its application to oracles or psalms dealing with such ultimate issues as the fate of the cruel Chaldean foe, the suffering of the righteous, or God's ways with His people.[11]

These literary techniques were not ends in themselves. Basically, Wisdom was an intellectual discipline, concerned with the education of upper-class youth in Israel. It is highly probable that the *hakam* was a professional teacher[12] whose function was to inculcate in his pupils the virtues of hard work, zeal, prudence, sexual moderation, sobriety, loyalty to authority, and religious conformity—all the elements of a morality aimed at achieving worldly success. When necessary, *Hokmah* did not hesitate to urge less positive virtues on its youthful charges, such as holding one's tongue and distributing largesse as aids in making one's way. In brief, this practical Wisdom literature represented a hard-headed, matter-of-fact, "safe and sane" approach to the problems of living.

The discovery and elucidation of ancient oriental literature has made it clear that Hebrew Wisdom was not an isolated creation in Israel. On the contrary, it was part of a vast intellectual activity that had been cultivated for centuries throughout the lands of the Fertile Crescent—Egypt, Palestine, Syria, and Babylonia. Everywhere its basic purpose was to prepare youth for success in government, agriculture, commerce, and personal life. These branches of oriental Wisdom were older than biblical *Hokmah*, the Fertile Crescent countries having attained political and cultural maturity long before Israel. Naturally there are many adumbrations of biblical Wisdom in oriental literature, as well as many illuminating parallels. These similarities have been noted by scholars who, flushed with the natural excitement of discovery, have sometimes displayed more enthusiasm than caution in postulating borrowings. While the extant remains of Babylonian and Egyptian Wisdom rarely reach the level of Hebrew *Hokmah*, they are invaluable in supplying a general background and in shedding light on particular details.

The *Hokmah* of the biblical sages, unlike the Torah of the priests or the Vision of the prophets, usually made no claim to being divine revelation. It was, of course, self-evident that the source of Hebrew *Hokmah*, as of every creative aspect of man's nature, was God. Thus when Isaiah described the ideal Davidic king who would govern in justice and wisdom, he sees "resting upon him the spirit of the Lord," which is defined as "the spirit of wisdom and understanding, the spirit of counsel and might, the spirit of knowledge, and the fear of the Lord" (Isa. 11:2).

Nevertheless, some of Wisdom's most fervent disciples went even further. They sought to win for Wisdom a status almost equal to that of Torah and Prophecy by endowing her with a cosmic role. In composing hymns of praise to Wisdom, the Hebrew sages were able to draw upon motifs found in Semitic mythology.[13] Thus a Mesopotamian text of the late second millenium B.C.E. describes the goddess Siduri Sabito as "goddess of wisdom, genius of life." Albright, in calling attention to this reference, suggests that she was a prototype of a Canaanite goddess of Wisdom. In the Aramaic *Proverbs of Akiqar*, emanating from the sixth century B.C.E., a passage reads:

> Wisdom is from the gods,
> And to the gods she is precious,
> Forever her kingdom is fixed in heaven,
> For the lord of the holy ones has raised her up.[14]

Passages such as these inevitably suggest comparison with Hebrew poems. In the Book of Proverbs, Wisdom is pictured as dwelling in a temple with seven pillars (9:1) and as declaring,

> Ages ago I was poured out, at the first,
> Before the beginning of the earth (Prov. 8:23).

The present Book of Job contains a magnificent "Hymn to Wisdom" (chap. 28), in which *Hokmah* is endowed with cosmic significance and is virtually personified. Ben Sira (Ecclesiasticus), in the first half of the second century B.C.E., also personifies Wisdom:

> I have come forth from the mouth of the highest,
> And like the vapor I have covered the earth;
> I have made my abode in the heights
> And my throne on a pillar of cloud (Eccsul. 24:3–4).

The Book of Enoch pictures Wisdom as homeless among men and therefore returning to the abode of the angels (42:1–2).

But the similarity in language, interesting as it is, is far less significant than the fundamental difference between the Hebrew poets and sages, on the one hand, and the pagan writers, on the other. For the biblical and post-biblical authors the personification and glorification of Wisdom is mythology, not religion; it is poetry, not truth. To heighten the vividness and power of their compositions they utilize the resources of their Semitic inheritance, as Dante, Shakespeare, and Milton invoke the gods of Greece and Rome; but like the later writers, they do not believe in these echoes of a dead past.

In their most lavish paeans of praise to Wisdom, the Hebrew sages do not attribute to her any independent existence, let alone the status of a goddess or a divine being. She is indubitably the creation of God, His play thing, His companion, His delight, perhaps even the plan by which He fashioned the world, but nevertheless, completely God's handiwork, as is the entire cosmos:

> The Lord created me at the beginning of his work,
> The first of His acts of old.
> Ages ago I was poured out, at the first,
> Before the beginning of the earth.
> When there were no depths I was brought forth,
> When there were no springs abounding with water.
> Before the mountains had been shaped,
> Before the hills, I was brought forth;
> Before He had made the earth with its fields,
> Or the first dust of the world.
> When He established the heavens, I was there,
> When He drew a circle on the face of the deep,
> When He made firm the skies above,
> When He established the fountains of the deep,
> When He assigned to the sea its limit,
> So that the waters might not transgress His command,
> When He marked out the foundations of the earth,
> Then I was beside Him, as His ward.[15]
> I was daily His delight, frolicking before Him always,
> Rejoicing in His inhabited world and delighting in
> the sons of men (Prov. 8:22–31).

All wisdom comes from the Lord
And is with Him for ever.
The sand of the seas, and the drops of rain,
And the days of eternity—who can number them?
And the height of the heaven, and the breadth of the earth
and the deep—who can trace them out?
Before them all was Wisdom created,
And prudent insight from everlasting.
The root of Wisdom, to whom has it been revealed?
And her subtle thoughts, who has known them? . . .
One there is greatly to be feared,
The Lord sitting upon His throne;
He Himself created her, and saw, and numbered her,
And poured her out upon all His works;
Upon all flesh, in measure,
But to those who love Him, without limit.
(Ecclus. 1:1–10)

In Palistinian Judaism, where the study and interpretation of the Torah ultimately produced the Mishnah and the Midrash, Wisdom was equated with the Mosaic Law. This idea is clearly set forth by Ben Sira, who indites another extended "Paean to Wisdom" (chap. 24) and then cites verbatim the verse in Deuteronomy (33:4):

All these are the book of the covenant of the All-High God,
The Torah which Moses commanded to us,
The inheritance of the congregation of Jacob (24:23).

The same identification of Wisdom and the Torah is expressed in the apocryphal Psalm 152, long known in a Syriac version.[16] The Hebrew original has now been discovered at Qumran and may emanate from the same period as Ben Sira.[17] In rabbinic thought the equation became virtually axiomatic and is part of the Jewish liturgy to the present day.[18]

In the Diaspora, outside of Palestine, where Greek ideas were more influential, Wisdom was given a more philosophical interpretation. In the apocryphal Wisdom of Solomon the spirit of the Lord and Wisdom are explicitly identified and are taken to encompass both the creation of the natural world and its moral government (1:6; 7:24).[19]

In some circles, the earlier personifications of Wisdom were taken literally and served as the point of departure for a complex development. Of the various forms which this concept assumed, the most notable was the Philonic doctrine of the *Logos* or the Divine Word, which became the demiurge or instrument by which God creates and governs the universe. It is only a further step to conceive of the Divine Word as the intermediary between God and the world, even as a distinct "person" or "aspect" of the divine nature.

Thus the process has come full circle. The independent god or divine being who first appears in an early though far from primitive mythology, reappears, in vastly transformed guise, in a later, highly sophisticated theology. But for all the writers of the Hebrew Bible, whether priest, prophet, or sage, such doctrines were totally outside their purview. Had they been able to conceive such ideas at all, they would have rejected them as vitiating the Unity of God. In any event, it must be remembered that these later developments took place long after the Book of Job was written.

To revert to biblical Wisdom, it is to be expected that in an ancient society in which religion permeated every aspect of life, the effort would be made to give *Hokmah* a supernal position in the divine plan. Thus it could claim a status not too markedly inferior to God's revelation embodied in the Torah or His communication with the prophets. Basically, however, the claim of biblical *Hokmah* to authority rested on its pragmatic truth. The teachers of Wisdom insisted that the application of human reason and careful observation to all the problems of life "worked," that it brought men success and happiness. Its origin might be in heaven, but its justification was to be sought in the lives of men on earth:

The Lord by wisdom founded the earth;
By understanding He established the heavens;
By His knowledge the deeps broke forth
And the clouds drop down the dew.
My son, keep sound wisdom and discretion;
Let them not escape from your sight,

And they will be life for your soul and adornment for your neck,
Then you will walk on your way securely and your foot will not
  stumble.
If you sit down, you will not be afraid;
When you lie down, your sleep will be sweet.
Do not be afraid of sudden panic
Or of the ruin of the wicked when it comes;
For the Lord will be your confidence and will keep your foot
  from being caught (Prov. 3:19–26).

I have counsel and sound wisdom;
I have insight; I have strength.
By me kings reign
And rulers decree what is just. . . .
I love those who love me,
And those who seek me diligently find me. . . .
Endowing with wealth those who love me
And filling their treasuries. . . .
For he who finds me finds life
And obtains favor from the Lord;
But he who misses me injures himself;
All who hate me love death (8:14–15, 17, 21, 35–36).

The Bible regards King Solomon as the symbol of Wisdom
and attributes to him the books of Proverbs and Ecclesiastes, as
well as the Song of Songs. Though this tradition is not to be taken
literally, neither can it be dismissed as valueless. It reflects the
established fact that King Solomon's reign was marked by wide
international contacts and internal prosperity which contributed
to the flowering of culture in general and to the intensive cultivation of Wisdom in particular.

The roots of *Hokmah*, as the extra-Hebraic parallels make
abundantly clear, are pre-Solomonic. The Bible has preserved
some precious examples of early Wisdom literature. The unfor-
gettable "Parable of Jotham" (Judg. 9:7 ff.), which compares
the would-be king to a sterile thornbush, must go back to the
primitive democracy of the age of the Judges.[20] It could not have
emanated from a later period, when the monarchy was well
established and regarded as legitimate. In I Samuel 24:13, David
quotes "an ancient proverb" *(meshal hakkadmōnī)*, "Out of the

wicked cometh forth wickedness, but let not my hand be upon thee." The prophet Nathan's moving parable of the poor man's lamb (II Sam. 12:1 ff.), with which he indicts his royal master, David, constitutes another valuable remnant of ancient *mashal* literature.

A particularly significant passage for the development of Wisdom is to be found in II Samuel 14. Here we have a "wise woman" (*'ishāh ḥākkāmāh*) whom Joab calls, and probably pays, to present an imaginary case to King David. She possesses dramatic skill as well as literary inventiveness. Thus she prepares herself for the role of a mourner (vs. 2) and then presents her suit for the king's decision. When David pronounces judgment, she confesses that her fictitious case was a *mashal*, a parable of the king's relationship to his son Absalom, the murderer of Ammon. Finally, she climaxes her appeal for the king's forgiveness by a reference to the melancholy brevity of human life, thus going beyond practical Wisdom to its more philosophical aspect: "For we must surely die and be like water poured out on the ground, which is not gathered up and which no one desires" (vs. 14).[21]

The Book of Kings preserves another parable which is post-Solomonic—that of Joash, king of Israel, in which he contemptuously dismisses Amaziah of Judah as a thistle by the side of a cedar (II Kings 14:9).

The various collections in the biblical Book of Proverbs emanate from different periods. Yet it is being increasingly recognized that the individual apothegms, which often cannot be dated, are largely derived from the First Temple period, and in part, at least, may go back to Solomon's reign, as several headings indicate (Prov. 1:1; 10:1).

As we have noted, the Babylonian Exile and the Return witnessed the decline and disappearance of prophecy and ushered in a new phase of oral interpretation of the Torah. It was then, in the early centuries of the Second Commonwealth, that Wisdom reached its golden age, largely because of a basic shift in the primary concern of religious faith and thought.

While the Torah and the prophets were divergent in substance and temper, they were agreed in placing the nation in the center of their thinking. Both were concerned with the weal or woe of the entire people and called for the fulfillment of God's will, which the priest found embodied in the Law, and which the prophets saw expressed in the moral code. To be sure, it was the individual who was adjured to obey, but only as a unit of the larger entity, his destiny being bound up, indeed submerged, in the well-being of the nation. This concern with the group was a fundamental aspect of traditional Semitic and Hebrew thought.

The individual, however, could never be completely disregarded. His personal happiness and success, his fears and hopes, were by no means identical with the status of the nation. The people as a whole might be prosperous and happy while an individual was exposed to misery. On the other hand, even if the nation experienced defeat and subjugation by foreign masters, the individual would still seek to adjust himself to conditions and to extract at least a modicum of happiness and success from his environment. This recognition of the individual plays an enormous role in the Torah. Being a practical code of life it necessarily had to deal with man's problems and conflicts, as its civil and criminal ordinances abundantly attest.[22] Increasingly, too, the prophets, whose basic concern was the ideal future of the nation, became concerned with the happiness of the individual: "Say of the righteous that it shall be well with him; for they shall eat the fruit of their doings. Woe to the wicked! It shall be ill with him; for the work of his hands shall be done to him" (Isa. 3:10–11). With the later prophets, Jeremiah and Ezekiel, the problem of individual suffering becomes a central and agonizing element of their thought.[23] Fundamentally, however, Torah and prophecy remained concerned with the group, its present duties and its future destiny.

It was the decline of faith in the fortunes of the nation, coupled with the growth of interest in the individual and his destiny, that stimulated the development of Wisdom. Wisdom was not concerned with the group, but with the individual, with the realistic present rather than with a longed-for future.

Wisdom's eminently practical goals for success in the here

and now appealed principally to those groups in society which were least dissatisfied with the status quo—the government officials, the rich merchants, the great landowners, whose soil was tilled by tenant farmers. These groups were concerned less with the will of God than with the way of the world. This was true even of the high-priestly families among them, whose prestige and income derived from their position in the hierarchy of the temple. The goal of upper-class education was the training of youth for successful careers. These needs were admirably met by the Wisdom teachers who arose, principally, if not exclusively, in Jerusalem, the capital city.

Nearly two decades ago I called attention to the striking resemblance between the Wisdom teachers and the sophists of classical Greece, who performed a similar function for the upper-class youth of Athenian society, teaching them the practical skills needed for government and business.[24] There were, of course, far-reaching religious and cultural differences between Greece and Israel. These differences dictated different roles for the Greek sophists and the Hebrew *hakamin*. For example, while the art of public speaking was intensively cultivated in Greece, it was not a conscious discipline in Israel, at least so far as extant sources indicate. All the more striking, therefore, are the similarities between the two groups. The semantic development of the Greek *sophia* closely parallels that of the Hebrew *Hokmah*. The basic meaning of the Greek word is "cleverness and skill in handicraft and art"; then, "skill in matters of common life, sound judgment, practical and political wisdom"; and ultimately, "learning, wisdom, and philosophy."[25] The adjective *sophos* bears the same meanings, as descriptive of sculptors, and even of hedgers and ditchers, but "mostly of poets and musicians."[26] The substantive *sophistes*, "master of a craft or art," is used in the extant literature for a diviner, a cook, a statesman, and again for poets and musicians.[27] From Plato's time onward, its common meaning was that of a professional teacher of the arts.[28]

The most illuminating parallel lies in the division of the Wisdom teachers into two numerically unequal groups, a process evident everywhere in Egypt and Babylonia as well as in Israel and Hellas.[29] Most of the exemplars of Wisdom were hard-headed, realistic teachers of a workable morality, intent on helping their youthful charges attain successful careers. Among the oriental Wisdom teachers, however, were some restless spirits who refused to be satisfied with these practical goals.

In the relatively extensive remains of Egyptian Wisdom, which bear the name *sboyet*, "instruction," two literary types are included: "discourses on worldly prudence and wisdom intended merely for schools"; and "writings far exceeding the bounds of school philosophy."[30] Babylonian Wisdom exhibits the same division between "practical maxims" and "meditations on the meaning of life."[31]

In Greece too, a small number of thinkers were unwilling to limit the scope of their thought. Though they derived from the sophists, "the wise," they adopted the less pretentious name of "lovers of wisdom," or "philosophers," with perhaps a touch of Socratic irony. Their contempt for the sophists (with whom, however, they had many affinities) parallels the rejection by the Hebrew literary prophets of any identification with the popular prophets from whom they emanated, as in Amos' scornful denial, "I am no prophet nor a member of the prophetic guild!" (Amos 7:14).

In Israel, both types of Wisdom are clearly marked. From the practical-minded teachers of youth emanated the short maxims of the Book of Proverbs, as well as the longer essays of Ben Sira, who makes explicit reference to the *bet hamidrash*, or "academy," in his call "Turn to me, ye fools, and tarry in my house of study" (Ecclus. 51:23). These two books are the principal Hebrew repositories of the "lower" Wisdom, practical in goal, conventional in scope.

For a few bolder spirits within the schools of Wisdom these practical goals were not enough. They had been trained to apply observation and reasoning to the practical problems of daily life, but the more fundamental issues intrigued them: the purpose of life, man's destiny after death, the basis of morality, the problem of evil. When they weighed the religious and moral ideas of their time by these standards, they found some things they could accept, but much that they felt impelled to reject as either untrue or unproved. Hence the higher or speculative Wisdom books are basically heterodox, skeptical works, at variance with the products of the practical school.

As well as we can judge, no violent antagonism existed between the teachers of practical Wisdom and those who ventured into uncharted waters. In part, at least, the reason lies in the fact that these more original thinkers continued to pursue the calling of professional teachers of practical *Hokmah*. That conditioning would affect their style and thought ever after. In sum, both the conventional and the unconventional teachers of Wisdom spoke the same language, reflected the same environment, and shared a common outlook. The epilogue in Ecclesiastes 12:9 ff. testifies to this conventional activity of the unconventional author of the book.[32]

In seeking to penetrate the great abiding issues of suffering and death, these rare Wisdom teachers were unwilling to rely on tradition and conventional ideas. When they insisted on applying observation and reason to the ultimate questions, they courted tragedy—but achieved greatness.

Like so many rationalists since their day, they found unaided human reason incapable of solving these issues. Some, no doubt, finally made their peace with the traditional religion of their time. But others, tougher-minded, refused to take on faith what reason could not demonstrate. Consequently, their writings reveal various degrees and types of skepticism and heterodoxy. Several of these devotees of the higher speculative Wisdom were able to transmute the frustration and pain of their quest into some of the world's greatest masterpieces, notably Job and Koheleth (Ecclesiastes). Smaller in compass and frequently enigmatic in content is the fragment imbedded in the Book of Proverbs and ascribed to Agur ben Yakeh (Prov. 30).[33]

Koheleth, the skeptical observer of life and man's pretensions, was keenly aware of the problem of injustice in society. He reacted far more strongly than one might have expected in view of his upper-class orientation. Primarily, however, his malaise was intellectual in origin: he was troubled by man's inability to discover ultimate truth—the real meaning of life and the purposes of creation.[34]

The author of Job, on the other hand, though by no means inferior in intellect, possessed a far deeper emotional nature and a greater capacity for involvement in the joy or misery of his fellow men. He was roused to indignation, not by man's intellectual limitations in a world he had not made, but rather by man's suffering in a world into which he had not asked to be born. The result was a work of grand proportions, the writing of which probably spanned his lifetime. He attempted to grapple with the crucial questions with which the psalmist, prophet, and poet alike had wrestled for centuries and which remain the greatest stumbling blocks to religious faith: Why do the wicked prosper and the righteous suffer? Why is there evil in the world created by a just God?

The Book of Job represents the supreme achievement of Hebrew Wisdom. In form and approach, as well as in background and content, its affinities with both conventional and unconventional Wisdom teaching are striking.

When the full scope of biblical Wisdom is kept in mind, it is clear that by virtue of its literary form Job belongs in this category. It obviously qualifies as a branch of *Hokmah*, since it is given over to the discussion of a basic problem in the form of a great debate. All the resources of argument, as they were undoubtedly practiced in the Wisdom academies, are found here. While a detailed analysis of its style will be set forth later, we may note here such forensic features as the *argumentum ad hominem*, the personal attack upon one's opponent (including the citation and refutation of contentions by the other side). The book is marked by the frequent use of the *mashal*, the characteristic literary genre of Wisdom, which appears in metaphoric, proverbial, and other forms.

The recent discovery in Babylonian and Egyptian literature of complaints by individuals about their suffering at the hands of gods or men has injected a new element into the discussion. Some scholars have argued that the Book of Job belongs to the literary genre of elegiac complaints rather than to Wisdom.[35] It is true that Job begins with a lament on his tragic lot (chap. 3) and ends with a soliloquy describing his former prosperity and his high standard of rectitude (chaps. 29–31). Job's pain breaks out time and again during the course of his replies, while the Friends offer him, however woodenly, both comfort and hope. In addition, there are hymns praising the creative power of God imbedded in the speeches of the Friends (e.g., 5:19 ff.) and in the words of Job (9:4 ff.; 12:14 ff.), though given in radically different spirit.

Nonetheless, it is clear that the bulk of the book does not consist of these literary "complaints." Nor are the hymns independent compositions. Both the complaints on man's suffering and the hymns extolling God's power are introduced as means to an end—to illumine the agonizing problem of the suffering of the righteous. This is discussed in accordance with the rational canons of Wisdom thought, here heightened by the passion of the poet.

Moreover, even if the book is atomized into these components, it still testifies to the Wisdom character of Job. For as we have seen, poetry in general, and lamentation in particular, constituted an important segment of the Wisdom activity which was carried on in ancient Israel by the *hakhamim* and the *hakhamot*, "men and women skilled in the arts of composition." Thus the Book of Job, in its constituent parts and in its structure as a whole, belongs to Wisdom by virtue of its form.

The authentic Wisdom character of Job is even more strikingly attested by its approach to the basic theme. All the protagonists in the debate—Job, his friends, Elihu, and the Lord—seek to establish the validity of their respective positions by using the methods of logical argument, the observation of reality, and the evidence of experience. Thus Job calls attention to the manifest inequity in the world, while the Friends counter by invoking the longer experience of the race to demonstrate the triumph of justice and underscore the undeniable fact that all men are imperfect. It is true that in one moving passage (4:12–21) Eliphaz declares that he has been vouchsafed a revelation in a dream from on high. The content of that revelation, however, the idea that all men are sinful when compared with the moral perfection of God, is eminently defensible by the canons of rational thought and indeed is not disputed by Job. When the Lord speaks, following the dialogue of Job and his friends, He does not seek to demonstrate the truth of His position by invoking some supernatural faith beyond the canons of reason. Nor does He offer an escape from evil by flight to a mystical refuge, open only to the elect and denied to the generality of men. The author of Job makes it clear that the question of man's suffering in God's world cannot be fully answered by the application of human reason, experience, and observation, but only because the problem is cosmic in scope and it would be senseless to expect a solution with instruments of lesser compass. As an exponent of Wisdom, the author of Job might well have approved the words of a modern believing skeptic, "It is not wisdom to be only wise." For the poet, faith goes beyond reason, but does not negate it, and to believe the absurd would be the height of absurdity.

Finally, the integral place of Job within Wisdom literature is amply demonstrated by its content and background. By its very nature, Wisdom, assiduously cultivated throughout the ancient Near East, was broadly human rather than rooted in a specific national milieu. This supplied an ideal vantage point for the author, because the mystery with which he was concerned had no root in class or nation. In choosing Job, a non-Jew, as his hero, the author underscored the universal significance of his theme and was, incidentally, able to bypass the problems of the observance of Jewish ritual law, which loomed so large in the religious consciousness of the post-Exilic community. Job is a man of integrity and piety who fears God and eschews evil. No more need be said.

The upper-class orientation of Wisdom literature emerges at many points in Job.[36] Whether the author himself was born a member of these affluent groups or merely identified himself with them is impossible to determine (as is the case with Koheleth). What is significant is the author's choice of an upper-class figure as his hero. In order to exhibit the tragedy of human suffering, the poet has selected a man of great prosperity who is hurled to the lowest depths of misfortune, rather than a member of the lower classes who has suffered a lifetime of poverty and misery. It may, of course, be argued that this contrast between Job's earlier prosperity and his later calamities makes for a more dramatic plot. Nevertheless, the fact remains that the Book of Job poses the problem of evil in the form most likely to confront a member of the upper classes. And the evidence goes much further. We have perhaps the only reference in later biblical writings to a multiplicity of wives in one family in the passage, "his widows will not weep for him" (27:15).[37] Polygamy was always restricted to the rich, who alone could afford the luxury. In Job's moving Confession of Innocence (chap. 31), which represents the code of conduct of a Jewish gentleman, it is obviously a patrician who speaks. He takes pride in the consideration he shows the poor, the widow, and the orphan. Unlike the crasser members of his class he is deeply sensitive to the truth that both he and his slave are fashioned alike by God. Nor has his wealth ever tempted him to arrogance. Job reveals a wholly admirable quality in his insistence:

Have I ever concealed my transgressions like Adam,
Hiding my sin in my bosom
Because I stood in fear of the crowd
And the contempt of the masses terrified me—
So that I kept silence and did not go out of doors? (31:33-34).

Yet in this moral courage and scorn for the mob there is at least an echo of the pride of the wellborn and well-circumstanced.

At every turn, the author himself, and not merely his hero, gives evidence of an upper-class environment. The poet's wide familiarity with various geographical locations—mountain and desert, sea and plain—points to his being widely traveled, an activity possible only for the rich in ancient times. His reference to the papyrus ships (9:26) and his colorful descriptions of the hippopotamus (40:15 ff.) and the crocodile (40:25 ff.) do not prove that the author was an Egyptian,[38] but they do show that he had visited the land of the Nile. Similarly, his vivid description of hail, ice, and snow, suggests a knowledge of the north.[39]

Because of his knowledge of agriculture and medicine, astronomy and anatomy, mining and warfare, Pfeiffer concluded that "the author was the most learned ancient before Plato."[40] This range of knowledge and experience, which recalls that of Shakespeare, is, of course, a tribute to his curiosity and intellectual powers, but it would have been denied him had he been poor.

It is in the area of religious thought that the poet's upper-class orientation is particularly clear. In this regard, the use of divine names is highly instructive.[41] In Egyptian and Babylonian Wisdom the individual names of gods do not totally disappear, but they yield increasingly to general descriptions of "God" or "the Gods." The names of individual deities are generally retained only in traditional apothegms or in contexts concerned with the attributes of a specific god.[42]

The use of divine names in Hebrew Wisdom is similar. In the lower Wisdom books like Proverbs, JHVH, the national name of the God of Israel, occurs exclusively in the oldest collections (10:1–22; 16:25–29), which are probably pre-Exilic. Yet even here, when JHVH does occur it is often in stock phrases like "the fear of JHVH," "the blessing of JHVH," "the abomination of JHVH," "the knowledge of JHVH."[43] The later collections in Proverbs use JHVH much less consistently. In Ben Sira the general term, 'ēl ("God"), is used in half the cases. The use of JHVH here is apparently to be attributed to the author's identification of the God of Israel with the world creator, so that the specific national name has become divested of any particularistic character.

In the higher Wisdom books the name JHVH is avoided ˑwith such consistency that it cannot be accidental. In Koheleth, 'elōhīm is the exclusive designation of the Deity.[44] In the poetic sections of Job, the specific name of JHVH is ˑalmost completely rejected in favor of the general terms, 'ēl, 'elōah, 'elōhīm, Šaddai.[45] Only in the prose narrative, which is a recasting of an ancient folk tale, does the traditional name JHVH occur. In avoiding local or national divine names in favor of the general designations, the higher Wisdom writers were seeking to express their concept of God in the broadest and most universal terms.

The upper-class orientation of Job emerges again in the treatment of the book's basic theme—the problem of suffering. Fuller consideration will be given to this issue later. Here it suffices to note that Wisdom writers could not shut their eyes to the inequities of the present order. At the same time, as representatives of the affluent groups in society, they did not find the status quo intolerable.

The lower classes, ground by poverty and oppression at the hands of domestic and foreign masters, were tormented by the prosperity of the wicked and the suffering of the righteous. Holding resolutely to their faith in God, they were nevertheless unable to see divine justice operating in the world about them. Their solution to this agonizing problem was the espousal of the doctrine of a future world where the inequalities of the present order would be rectified. Thus, the idea of life after death became an integral feature of pharisaic Judaism and of Christianity.[46]

The teachers of Wisdom, on the other hand, felt no need to adopt these new views. The sages of the conventional Wisdom schools continued to maintain the old view of collective retribution here and now, where the sins or virtues of the fathers determine the destinies of the children.[47] The idea of a future life is not so much as mentioned in Proverbs, probably because the material is comparatively early. However, by the time of Ben Sira, in the second century B.C.E., the doctrine of an afterlife had achieved such wide currency that it could no longer be ignored. The sage therefore explicitly negates this belief (Ecclus. 10:11): "When a man dies, he inherits worms, maggots, lice and creeping things."[48] His grandson, who translated the book into Greek, gives the passage a pharisaic interpretation by having it affirm judgment after death: "Humble thy soul greatly, for the punishment of the ungodly is fire and worms."

The unconventional sages, the authors of Job and Koheleth, are too clear sighted and too sensitive to overlook the manifest instances of undeserved suffering and undeserved prosperity in the world. Yet neither of them accepts the pharisaic solution of a life after death, although both are familiar with it.

Koheleth dismisses the idea of an afterlife with a shrug of the shoulders:

Furthermore, I saw under the sun that in the place of judgment there was wickedness, and in the place of righteousness, wrong. I said to myself, "Both the righteous and the wicked, God will judge, for there is a proper time for everything and every deed—over there!" I said to myself concerning men, "Surely God has tested them and shown that they are nothing but beasts." For the fate of men and the fate of beasts are the same. As the one dies, so does the other, for there is one spirit in both, and man's distinction over the beast is nothing, for everything is vanity. All go to one place, all come from the dust and all return to the dust. Who knows whether the spirit of man rises upward and the spirit of the beast goes down to the earth? So I saw that there is nothing better for man than to rejoice in his works, for that is his lot, and no one can permit him to see what shall be afterwards (Eccles. 3:16–22).

What you are able to do, do with all your might, for there is neither action, nor thought, nor knowledge, nor wisdom in the grave towards which you are moving.

Though man does not know his hour, like fish caught in an evil net, like birds seized in a snare, so men are trapped in an hour of misfortune, when it falls upon them suddenly (9:10, 12).

Job lacks the tough-mindedness of Koheleth. He cannot pretend to be indifferent to the hope for an afterlife. He wishes he could accept it as true, but he sorrowfully comes to the conclusion that the renewal of life after death is not given to men.

> For there is hope for a tree—
> If it be cut down, it can sprout again
> And its shoots will not fail.
> If its roots grow old in the earth
> And its stump dies in the ground,
> At the mere scent of water it will bud anew
> And put forth branches like a young plant.
> But man grows faint and dies;
> Man breathes his last, and where is he?
> As water vanishes from a lake,
> And a river is parched and dries up,
> So man lies down and rises not again;
> Till the heavens are no more he will not awake,
> Nor will he be roused from his sleep.

Oh, if You would hide me in Sheol,
Conceal me until Your wrath is spent;
Set a fixed time for me, and then remember me!
If a man die, can he live again?
All the days of my service I would wait,
Till my hour of release should come.
You would call and I would answer You;
You would be longing for the work of Your hands.
For then You would number my steps;
You would not keep watch over my sin.
You would seal up my transgression in a bag,
And You would cover over my iniquity.

But as a mountain falls and crumbles
And a rock is moved from its place,
As waters wear away stones
And a torrent washes away the earth's soil,
So do You destroy man's hope (Job 14:7-19).

It is in their reaction to the problem of evil that the social background of the authors of Job and Koheleth is most clearly revealed. The fact that they did not accept the nascent idea of life after death has usually been attributed to the general conservatism of the Wisdom writers. This explanation is, however, totally inadequate, for we should then have expected to find in Wisdom an adherence to the older doctrines of the "day of JHVH," as expounded by Amos, Isaiah, and Jeremiah, or the conception of the "End-time," as developed by Isaiah, Jeremiah, and Ezekiel. Actually the Wisdom writers, whether conventional or not, accepted neither the older nor the newer views that ran counter to their group associations. Neither the hope for a Messianic era on earth nor the belief in an afterlife is echoed in their writing. Nowhere in the entire literature do we find the prophets' faith in a dynamic world. The Wisdom teachers are preeminently guides to the status quo, in which they anticipate no alteration. Whether they accept contemporary society as fundamentally just, as do the conventional Wisdom writers, or have doubts, as does Koheleth, or are passionately convinced that justice and truth are trampled under foot by God and man, as does Job—they do not contemplate any serious change in the structure of society.

The clear-cut social conservatism of Wisdom literature as a whole sheds light on several hitherto unexplained characteristics of Proverbs, Koheleth, and the Wisdom Psalms.[49] Our present concern is with Job, which reflects the same point of view, indirectly but unmistakably. In the dialogue, the Friends frequently give extended descriptions of God's power (5:9 ff.; 25:2–6; 26:6–14).[50] In response, Job also gives elaborate pictures of divine power, but with a significant difference: while the Friends stress the beneficent and creative functioning of the Almighty as revealed in the gift of rain (5:10), the discomfiture of the wicked (5:12 ff.), the glories of the heavens (26:2–3), and the mysteries of creation (26:5 ff.), Job emphasizes the negative and destructive manifestations of God's power:[51] God moves the mountains, makes the. earth tremble, and shuts up the sun and the stars that they give no light (9:5 ff.).

The same spirit permeates Job's description of God's might in chapter 12: God destroys beyond rebuilding and imprisons men so that they cannot escape; he withholds water to cause drought and pours it forth in flood; nations are exalted only to be destroyed (12:14, 15, 23). The rest of Job's description is to be understood in the same light—as evidence of God's destructive power.

> He leads counselors away stripped,
> And of judges He makes fools,
> He opens the belt of kings
> And removes the girdle from their loins.[52]
> He leads priests away stripped
> And the mighty ones He confuses.
> He deprives counselors of speech
> And removes the discernment of the elders.
> He pours contempt on princes,
> And looses the girdle of the strong.
> He reveals deep secrets from the darkness,
> And brings the blackest gloom to light.
> He makes nations great, and then destroys them.
> He enlarges nations, and forsakes them.
> He removes understanding from the people's leaders
> And leads them in a pathless waste astray.
> They grope in the dark without light,
> And He makes them stagger like a drunkard (12:17–25).

There is a striking contrast in spirit between Job's picture of social transformation and the descriptions found elsewhere in the Bible of God's power to transform conditions so that the proud are abased and the humble exalted.[53] These hymns are intended as paeans of praise:

> Those who were full have hired themselves out for bread,
> And the hungry have ceased (to starve),
> While the barren woman has borne seven,
> And the mother of many has languished. . . .
> The Lord makes poor and makes rich;
> He casts down and raises up (I Sam. 2:5, 7).

> He raises the poor from the dust
> And the needy from the dunghill,
> To seat him among the princes,
> The princes of his people (Ps. 113:7–8).

Job's description has nothing in common with such pictures of social change. The salient difference lies in the fact that the psalmists who praise God's greatness depict both aspects of the change — the fall of the mighty and the rise of the lowly. Similarly Eliphaz, who extols God's power (5:11): "He sets the lowly on high, and the afflicted are raised to safety." Job, however, describes only half of the picture—the decline of the powerful—because he is arraigning his Maker as a destructive force.

Nor is Job's attitude similar to that of the prophets. They saw in the collapse of these elements of society the deserved punishment of a sinful people (e.g., Amos 6:1 ff., 7 ff.; Isa. 3; Mic. 3) and the necessary prelude to a reconstructed social order (Isa. 1:24–28; 5:8–17; and often). But for the author of Job, as for the Wisdom writers in general, a transformation of the social and political status quo meant catastrophe.

In conclusion, we have seen that Hebrew *Hokmah* is one element in the cultural and spiritual activity of the Hebrew genius during its most creative era. The Book of Job represents the highwater mark of biblical Wisdom, embodied in a unique literary genre of extraordinary power and originality. The author's roots lie deep within his people and his class; yet the specific *locus standi* of the poet impugns neither the truth nor the relevance of his insights for every manner and condition of men. For his masterpiece is endowed with two qualities which know no limits of time or space, nation or class—a sensitivity to human suffering and a love of truth.

NOTES

1. Or better, read with Septuagint, "five thousand."
2. *Cf.* I Chronicles 6:7, 16, 22; 15:19; 16:4–5.
3. See W. F. Albright, *Archaeology and the Religion of Israel* (Baltimore, 1942), pp. 125–29, who first called attention to the Canaanite origin of musical guilds. The Ugarite guilds *šrm* and *bn šrm*, "singers" and "members of the singers' guild" (C. H. Gordon, *Ugaritic Manual* [Rome, 1955]), Glossary No. 1385. On the Ugaritic guilds in general and their possible relationship to the biblical guilds associated with the Temple, see B. A. Levine, "The Netinim," *JBL* LXXXII (June, 1963), 211–12.
4. For the noun *v'hagūt* a verb is required by the parallelism. Hence read *v'hāgāh*, or preferable revocalize *vehagāt*, the older form of 3rd person fem, perf.; *cf.* '*asāt* (Lev. 25:21), *hayāt* (II Kings 9:37, *Kethib*); Lev. 26:34; Jer. 13:19; Ezek. 24:12. On *lebh* as fem., *cf.* Prov. 12:25.
5. Interpreting '*ozni* (and perhaps revocalizing it) on the basis of '*azēnekhā* (Deut. 23:14), "your implement, tool," *BDB.*, p. 24b.
6. See the painstaking study of O. Eissfeldt, "Der Maschal im A.T.," (Beihefte, *ZATW,* XXIV [Giessen, 1913], who makes a careful analysis of the etymology and semantics of *māšāl*. He distinguishes six meanings: (1) folk proverb; (2) taunt song; (3) proverb of individual composition; (4) didactic teaching; (5) allegory; (6) oracle. This effort to establish the genetic relationship among the six meanings he assigns to the term is not altogether successful. Thus he explains that the noun developed the meaning of "taunt song" (as e.g., Deut. 28:37; Isa. 14:4; Jer. 24:9; etc.) from "folk proverb," because "people generally prefer to mock their neighbors rather than praise them, hence *māšal* is 'a subject of negative discussion'" (*ibid.* p. 3). Eissfeldt's distinction between a folk proverb and an individual proverb is difficult to establish since even a folk proverb obviously has its beginning with an individual. As for the categories he calls "oracles" (Num. 23:7, 18; 24:3, 15, 20, 21, 23) and "didactic teaching" (Job 27:1; 29:1), we believe that the term *māšal* is best regarded as synonymous with *šir*, "song," or *ḥidah*, "riddle," or both, since it is couched in poetic form and deals with the mysteries of existence.
7. As, e.g., in Proverbs 10:1; 25:1.

8. As, e.g., Numbers 21:27; Psalms 49:5; 78:2; Job 27:1; 29:1. It occurs in parallelism with *māšal* in Psalms 49:5; 78:2.

9. *Cf.* Judges 12:12 ff.; I Kings 10:1; II Chronicles 9:1. See the stimulating study of N. H. Tur-Sinai, "Hidot vegilgulehen besifrut Hamiqra" ("Riddles and Their Transformations in Biblical Literature") in *Halašon Vehasepher, Kerekh Hasefer* (Jerusalem, 5711=1950), pp. 58–73.

10. E.g., *BDB*, p. 295a.

11. *Cf.* for these three uses Habakkah 2:6; Psalm 49:5; and Psalm 78:2, respectively.

12. For the professional status of the *ḥākām*, we may note the parallel phenomenon among the Greek sophists concerning whose high fees we are specifically informed. See Gordis, *Social Background of Wisdom Literature*, pp. 85–86, and the epilogue in Koheleth (Eccles. 12:9–10); see also Gordis *Koheleth—The Man and His World*, pp. 75, 84–85, 340.

13. See the suggestive treatment of W. F. Albright, *From the Stone Age to Christianity* (Baltimore, 1940), pp. 282–85, and his "Canaanite-Phoenician Sources of Hebrew Wisdom," *Supplement to VT*, No. III (1955), pp. 1–15, where he cites the Semitic parallels and relates them to the biblical passages. In this instance, however, I believe he does not give sufficient weight to the fundamental differences in outlook between Semitic paganism and Hebrew monotheistic thought, which was most highly developed among the Wisdom writers. Accordingly, he fails to distinguish between mythological allusions and religious beliefs, a difference which he has repeatedly emphasized elsewhere in his discussions of Hebrew thought. B. Oppenheimer, in "Psalms 152, 153 from Qumran," in the Hebrew journal *Molad*, No. 191–92 (Aug.-Sept. 1964), pp. 328–43, goes further and argues not merely that there is divergence of outlook, but "a clear polemic intent" against paganism in the biblical writers (p. 334). The non-argumentative tone of the various Hebrew paeans to Wisdom does not support so extreme a conclusion, but his critique of Albright seems to me valid.

14. See *AJSL*, Vol. XXXVI, p. 285. While the text has several lacunae, Albright's restoration is highly convincing and the general sense is clear.

15. Rashi, Ibn Ezra, and many moderns, as well as Goodspeed and Moffatt ("as his foster-child"), follow AV, "as one brought up with him," in rendering the enigmatic and crucial *'āmōn*. RSV renders "master workman," which is supported by the reminiscence of the Proverbs passage in the Wisdom of Solomon (7:22): "For she [i.e., Wisdom], the artificer of all things, taught me Wisdom" (S. Holmes in R. H. Charles, *Apocrypha and Pseudepigrapha of the O.T.* [Oxford, 1913], I, 546). On the other hand, Wisdom of Solomon may be embodying later, post-biblical conceptions of *Hokmah.* (See this text). The parallelism strongly favors the first interpretation of *'āmōn*. See also the divergent approach of Oppenheimer, *op. cit.*, p. 335. R. B. Y. Scott, *Proverbs-Ecclesiastes (Anchor Bible* [New York,

1965], pp. 69–72), correctly rejects the attempts to hypostasize Hebrew Wisdom on the basis of alleged parallels from oriental mythology. Less convincing is his suggested vocalization *'ōmēn*, which he renders "uniting, binding together"; see *VT*, X (1960), 213–23.

16. The latest edition, with a Hebrew retroversion, is by M. Noth, "Die fünf syrisch überlieferten apokryphen Psalmen," *ZATW*, XLVIII (1930), 1–23.

17. The texts are published by J. A. Sanders in "Two Non-Canonical Psalms in Q Psᵃ, *ZATW*, LXXVI (1964), 57 ff., which should be supplemented by the suggestive study by Oppenheimer, *op. cit.*

18. In the opening section of *Midrash Berēšit Rabbāh* on Genesis 1:1 we read: *Hatōrāh 'ōmeret 'anī hāyithi kelī ūmānūthō šel kakkādōš ʸʸᵑᵣᵥq hū*, "The Torah says, 'I was the instrument employed by the Holy One blessed be He [at creation].'" Here the identification of *Hokmah* and Torah has undoubtedly been influenced by Philonic ideas of the *Logos*. In the Jewish Prayer Book, the classical repository of rabbinic thought, Wisdom is identified with the Torah. Thus the service at the return of the Torah Scrolls to the Ark includes the verses in Proverbs 4:2; 3:18, 17 (in this sequence), which praise Wisdom.

19. See J. C. Rylaarsdam, *Revelation in Jewish Wisdom Literature* (Chicago, 1946), *passim*, esp. pp. 99–104.

20. On the entire institution, see R. Gordis, "Primitive Democracy in Ancient Israel," in *Alexander Marx Jubilee Volume* (New York, 1950), English Section, pp. 369–88.

21. Reading for the meaningless *velō yissā 'elōhīm nāpleš*, by a slight change, *velō yissā 'alehem nāpheš*. For the variety of interpretations of this verse and the evidence for my proposed emendation, see *Koheleth— The Man and His World*, p. 350, n. 22.

22. See, for example, the Book of the Covenant (Exod. 21–23); the Holiness Code (Lev. 18–21); and in the Book of Leviticus, the laws of sacrifice (1–5; note particularly 5:20–26), of leprosy (13–14), and of ritual impurity (15).

23. *Cf.* Jer. 12:1 ff.; 31:28 ff.; Ezek. 18:1 ff.

24. See *The Social Backgrounds of Wisdom Literature*, pp. 84 ff., and *Koheleth—The Man and His World*, pp. 18 ff.

25. In its first meaning, *sophia* is applied to Hephaestus, the god of fire and the arts, to Athena, to Daedalus, the craftsman and artist, and to the Telchines, a primitive tribe who are represented under three aspects: (1) as cultivators of the soil and ministers of the gods; (2) as sorcerers and envious demons who had the power to bring on hail, rain, and snow, and to destroy animals and plants; and (3) as artists working in brass and iron. (Gen. 4:20–22 offers a suggestive parallel.) *Sophia* is used of such crafts as carpentry, driving a chariot, medicine, and surgery. It is used particularly of singing, music, and poetry (*Homeric Hymn to*

Mercury, II.483, 511; Pindar, *Odes* 1,187; Xenophon, *Anabasis* I, 2, 8). On the usage of all three terms here discussed, see Liddell and Scott, *A Greek-English Lexicon, s.v.*

26. *Cf.* Pindar, *Odes* 1.15; Euripides, *Iphigenia in Tauris* I. 1238; Plato, *Laws* 696c. See Liddell and Scott, *op. cit., s.v.*

27. *Cf.* Pindar, *Odes* 1.5.36; Aeschylus, *Fragmenta* no. 320. See Liddell and Scott, *op. cit., s.v.*

28. *Cf.* Xenophon, *Memorabilia* I.6,13; Thucydides, *History* 3.38; Plato, *Protagoras* 313c.

29. For a conspectus of oriental Wisdom, see J. Fichtner, *Die altorientalische Weisheitsliteratur in ihrer israelitisch-jüdischen Ausprägung* (Giessen, 1933). A briefer survey appears in my *Koheleth—The Man and His World*, pp. 8–13. The principal texts are available in Pritchard, *ANET*.

30. *Cf.* A. Erman *The Literature of the Ancient Egyptians*, trans. A. M. Blackman (New York, 1927).

31. See W. G. Lambert, *Babylonian Wisdom Literature* (Oxford, 1960), p. 1. Lambert's hesitation to apply the term "Wisdom" to the second category is unjustified in view of the parallels we have adduced and the intimate organic relationship between the two types of Wisdom writings.

32. See my *Koheleth—The Man and His World*, pp. 339 ff., for a full discussion of this significant passage, the meaning of which had not previously been fully understood.

33. In addition to the standard commentaries on Proverbs, see the analysis of the document in my *The Social Backgrounds of Wisdom Literature*, pp. 106–7.

34. For a full study of the book, see my *Koheleth—The Man and His World* (2d edi.).

35. This is the contention of P. Volz, *Hiob und Weisheit in den Schriften des alten Testaments* (Göttingen, 1921), and C. Westermann, *Der Aufbau des Buches Hiob* (Tübingen, 1956). The position is subjected to stringent but justifiable criticism by G. Fohrer in *VT*, VII (1957), 107–11.

36. For a complete discussion of the upper-class orientation of oriental and biblical Wisdom, see my *The Social Backgrounds of Wisdom Literature*.

37. The plural "widows" in such passages as Isaiah 9:16; Jeremiah 15:8; 49:11; Ezekial 19:7, refers, of course, to the surviving spouses of many men. The same is true of Psalm 48:64b, where the exact phrase is used in reference to Israel as a collectivity.

38. Against P. Humbert, *Recherches sur les Sources égyptiennes . . .* (Neuchâtel, 1929).

39. See G. Hölscher's (*Commentary*, p. 7) correct conclusion that the author of Job was a Palestinian who had traveled widely, hence his familiarity with Egyptian flora and fauna, the Sinai desert, and the hail, ice, and snow of the north, probably the Lebanon region.

40. R. H. Pfeiffer, *Introduction to the Old Testament* (New York, 1941), p. 687.

41. See my *The Social Backgrounds of Wisdom Literature*, pp. 89 ff., for a fuller discussion.

42. E.g., *Proverbs of Amenemope* (col. XXV, 1.496): "The strength of Ra is to him that is on the road" as an instance of a popular saying.

43. Thus, taking Proverbs 16 at random, we find JHVH used ten times, of which at least four are in stock phrases (vss. 5, 6, 7, 20). On divine names in Wisdom, see Fichtner, *op. cit.*, pp. 103 ff.; O. S. Rankin, *Israel's Wisdom Literature* . . . (Edinburgh, 1936), p. 39, note.

44. Even the Temple in Jerusalem is called *bēt 'elōhīm* not *bēt Adōnai* in Ecclesiastes 4:17!

45. JHVH and *Adōnai* occur in the poetry of Job: (a) in 12:9, which is either an interpolation or, more probably, a reminiscence of Isaiah 41:20c, *yad JHVH* being a stock phrase; (b) in 28:28, in which *yirat 'Adōnai* is again a typical phrase of the Wisdom schools (the entire chapter is an independent poem); and (c) in 38:1 and 40:1, in the superscriptions announcing the appearance of the Lord "from the whirlwind." Here the traditional association of the God of Israel with storm, thunder, and lightning, led to the use of His name. *Cf.* the theophanies in Exodus 19:16; Judges 5:4–5; Isaiah 64:1; Nahum 1:3–4: Habakkuk 3:3 ff.; Psalms 18:8 ff.; 29 *passim* 144:5–6.

46. See W. O. E. Oesterley and T. H. Robinson, *Hebrew Religion* (London, 1930), p. 223 also Rankin, *Israel's Wisdom Literature*, pp. 124–97.

47. *Cf., e.g.,* Proverbs 13:22; 14:26; 20:7; Ecclesiasticus 44:10–11.

48. *Cf.* also Ecclesiasticus 17:27; 14:14.

49. For a fuller treatment of these passages, see my *The Social Backgrounds of Wisdom Literature*, pp. 111–16.

50. While the last passage is attributed to Job in the Masoretic Text, it obviously belongs to one of the Friends, probably Bildad, to whom it is assigned by Reuss, Duhm, Siegfried, Dhorme, and Hölscher. See their commentaries, *ad loc.*

51. This distinction is clearly recognized in ICC *Job*, I, 85–86.

52. On this rendering, which presupposes a minor emendation, reading *vayyāsar* (root *sūr*) instead of *vayye'sōr* (root *'asar*), and interpreting *Beth* in *b'mothneihem* as "from," as in Ugaritic, see the commentaries, *ad loc.*

53. Failure to note this difference in attitude has led some scholars to delete considerable portions of chapter 12. Siegfried and Grill retain only verses 1–3; Jastrow omits verses 4c, 5 in part, 6c, 10, 12, 13, 17–19, 22, and 23. Volz transfers verses 4–10, 13–25, and 13:1 to Zophar in chapter 11. Only Budde argued strongly in favor of the authenticity of the passage a half-century ago. See Commentaries, *ad loc.*

I

IO

A SYMPOSIUM ON
THE CANON OF SCRIPTURE

Samuel Sandmel, Albert Sundberg, Jr., and Roland E. Murphy, O. Carm.

The recovery of lost books from the biblical age, as for example, the Dead Sea Scrolls, serves to renew the attention of scholars to the problem of canon. As is known, the list of books which gained inclusion into the Hebrew Bible is shorter than the list which gained inclusion in the Jewish Greek Bible and thereafter in the traditional Christian Bible. In the 16th century, Protestants regarded the list in the Hebrew Bible as the proper one, and since then the books which had been admitted into the Greek Bible but not the Hebrew have been known among Protestants (and Jews) as Apocrypha. Scholarship knows nothing about the process of the formation of the Jewish Greek canon, and very little about the process of the formation of the Hebrew, though, of course, the end result is evident, as reflected in our printed Bibles. Recurrently scholars address themselves to the question of canon, as do the three papers reproduced here. They were read in sequence at the December, 1965, meeting of the Society of Biblical Literature. Father Murphy's paper summarizes the Roman Catholic attitude to canon; my own paper summarizes the traditional Jewish view, but also raises some questions about the significance of canon from the standpoint of modern scientific scholarship. Professor Sundberg's paper raises the issue of the justice of propriety of ex-

cluding the Apocrypha from Scripture, as has been the Protestant practice for three hundred years.

The discussion of the papers, especially Professor Sundberg's, was quite animated, but, unfortunately, was recorded neither stenographically nor by tape.

1. SAMUEL SANDMEL: "ON CANON"

When the invitation came to participate in this panel, with the mandate to prepare a fifteen-minute talk, my immediate impulse was to define the topic for myself as a renewed inquiry into the question of the history of the formation of the canon. On reverting to the usual standard books, and the newer ones, however, I discovered that a rather good consensus exists among scholars of all viewpoints respecting the Pentateuch and the Prophets, and slightly divergent theories about the Hagiographa, which either accept Jamnia 90 or else suggest some alternative. In sum, however, much as this or that scholar deviates in some particular, the consensus about the history of the canon of the Hebrew OT seemed rather fully established. Since this is an audience of Bible men, it did not seem to me to be reasonable to spend my time and yours in reviewing a matter so extensively agreed upon and so extensively known.

It seemed to me that I might say something relatively useful, if I made some comments, not on the history of the canon, but on canon in the Jewish tradition and if, thereafter, I commented on the significance of canon to someone who is both a loyal adherent of that tradition, but also something of a modern scientific scholar and also a modern religious man. Accordingly, my short paper is divided into three parts.

First, then, from the standpoint of the Jewish tradition, the Jewish inquiry into the *history* of the canon is a reflection of the general trend of biblical scholarship. The great name in the specific Jewish inquiry is that of Elijah Levita who was born near Nuremberg in 1468 and died in Venice in 1549. Under the patronage of Aegidius of Viterbo of the Augustinian Order, he wrote, between 1509 and 1522, a series of books on Hebrew grammar. His work on canon, *Massoret ha-Massoret*, was published in 1538; a year later a second edition appeared, with some parts translated into Latin by Sebastian Münster. The book, influential on Christian Hebraists, underwent frequent reprinting, and frequent translation, as into German in 1772, and into English in 1867.

Subsequent to this book, those Jews who in any way have participated in the trends of Western European biblical scholarship used Levita and his successors, and, of course, the modern scholars.

Second, and turning away, though, from the question of the history of the canon, it may be in order to speak a few words on what I shall call quasi-canonical. What I have in mind is the position of sanctity and authority of the rabbinic literature in Judaism. This literature has served Jews almost as if it were inherently blended into Scripture, and almost equal to it in sanctity and authority. It was through the interpretive norms of the rabbinic literature that Jews derived their understanding of the contents of Scripture; the body of interpretation, to which the name Oral Torah was given, was both authoritative in its influence, and no less than the determining factor in the shaping of subsequent Judaism. While Jews, on developing a historical sense, inquired into the origin of the various aspects of rabbinic literature, and in the 19th century set forth theories about the origin of this or that rabbinic work on a scientific rather than traditional basis, the rabbinic literature was uniformly accepted as co-authoritative with Scripture in a way that calls for a term such as quasi-canonical.

When the sect of Karaites arose in the 8th century, its thrust was in the direction of reverting to Scripture, of asserting the Jewish equivalent of *sola Scriptura,* and of denying the validity of the accrued rabbinic appendixes to Scripture. Because of this biblical "centralism," the sect received its name of Karaites, which we can translate "biblists." One can, indeed, put it this way, that the Karaites rejected the quasi-canonical status of the rabbinic literature. Again in the 19th century when Reform Judaism emerged, an attitude toward rabbinic literature both similar to and yet distinct from that of the Karaites arose. Reform Judaism denied the binding authority of the rabbinic *halacha* as religious requirement, but Reform, as a child of the study of the "history of religions," could not and did not deny that the rabbinic literature and the rabbinic developments had had both ongoing consequence and also a shaping factor in the emergence of its inherited Judaism and its projection for the future. Hence, both Karaism and Reform Judaism denied the quasi-canonical character of the rabbinic literature, though one must say that the Karaites did so out of hostility while the Reformers did so with considerable, but not with unbroken, affection.

Turning now to the third part, let me lead into it by saying that I am simultaneously a loyal adherent of Judaism and also something of a modern scientific scholar. As a loyal adherent, I have no wish to create meaningless upheavals. As this relates to the canon of Scripture, I would never dream of suggesting for divine worship that the scriptural lessons, which form the traditional readings, be altered or amplified so as to include books which did not get into the canon. Elsewhere in the divine service, however, as for example, when Reform Jews read the "praise of great men" from Ben Sira at the memorial service on Yom Kippur, I am quite happy for such random selective insertions. With respect, then, to the ongoing practice in my own tradition, I am quite content to let the ancient canon determine the synagogue practice.

As a student, however, I must persist in regarding canon as a logical development, but also as one determined by fortuitous circumstance. If I may put it in this way, suppose that canon had waited for the 6th Christian century instead of being fixed in the first or early part of the second, a quite different collection would have been made, and if somehow or other canon were to become open in the 20th century, I would be among those who would vote to exclude Esther, and I think that there are a number of suggestions for inclusions that I would make, such as 4 Maccabees. I must confess that I cannot share in those theories which attribute to the generations that formed the canon an insight which was truly divine, nor can I acquiesce in the proposition which I frequently read that the canonical books simply by being canonical possess values which exceed those of the non-canonical. My point here is not that as a student I must give attention to Jubilees as well as to Genesis, for I take that to be self-evident; rather, my point is that in the subjective matter of value, as a modern free student would interpret value, canon is in itself no guarantor of value. Canon only reflects the sanctity which a given era chanced to assign to a given number of books.

The implication of this position is that there is a possible tension between the assessments of authority and sanctity made at a given period by the tradition, and the assessments that a modern, free scholar would make. I would not hesitate to describe this position as untraditional. I would rather be straightforward, though, and suggest this kind of position, rather than to resort, instead, to what seems to me to be a deviousness, or to something perilously close to intellectual dishonesty, such as strained exegesis, especially the allegorical. The recourse to such imported meanings seems to me a device by which to continue to sanctify that which the very adoption of allegory or of strained exegesis implies is not essentially and truly sacred.

I raised this issue in my book, *The Hebrew Scripture,* in a somewhat different way. I said there, "To regard the Tanach (Old Testament) as sacred is reasonable, but its sanctity ought to be impressed on us by study, rather than assumed beforehand." By its very nature, the term canon implies that we are completely assured of the sanctity of a given aggregate of materials, even before we have looked at them.

Canon, moreover, seems to imply that all the books that achieve a place on the approved list are of similar, or comparable, or interchangeable sanctity. Perhaps, in a given tradition, one section may be, as it were, *primus inter pares:* the Pentateuch, I would judge, is among Jews in this situation, in relation to the Prophets and the Hagiographa. There is, however, among Jews a sense of an abiding equality in all the books that got into Scripture. Nevertheless, I wish I could believe that the Book of Joshua is as ethically motivated as the Book of Jonah, but I cannot believe that this is the case. I cannot believe that the Book of Chronicles matches the Books of Amos and Jeremiah. I cannot believe that the Book of Proverbs has the profundity of the Book of Psalms. Whenever I chance to make the gradations for my own comprehension of the values in the canonical books, I find myself encountering comparisons, and then I move on to distinctions which to me are tremendous. It is not that I believe that I am barred from understanding how it was that Ezekiel or Daniel got into the canon; it is that I do not find them speaking to me in the same clarity that 2 Isaiah speaks. I often speculate on the fate of Obadiah, had it appeared in Scripture only in that portion which one might say lies buried in the Book of Jeremiah, and had not reached the accidental eminence of being its own book.

What all this amounts to is the double statement that on the one hand not everything that has come into the canon possesses for someone as subjective as me a full value, and second, there are writings which chanced not to get into the canon, and indeed, some books so late as not to have been eligible for the ancient canon, that do speak to me.

It also seems inescapable to me that just as there was a pre-canonical period, so for the modern religionist there has to be a post-canonical period. Yielding to no one in my love of the Hebrew Scriptures, and also the Greek Jewish Scriptures, canon for me is neither a guarantor nor a security of relevancy, or of relevant sanctity. All the canon, all of it, is illuminating to me and, in a certain sense, to use an old word, a *hodogete,* something which leads one along the way. But canon is neither the sole guide nor the complete guide. Canon is an incident, and no more than that. The books themselves are in part much more important, and in part much less important than the act of canonization.

Lastly, what I here set forth is not something that I advocate for anyone else. It is the place in which I personally stand in my quandaries; it is that and no more than that.

2. ROLAND E. MURPHY:
"THE OLD TESTAMENT CANON IN THE CATHOLIC CHURCH"

The viewpoint of the Catholic Church on the canon of the OT has been substantially expressed in three ecumenical councils: Vatican I, Trent, and Florence. Florence was the first great council to give a list of biblical books: the decree for the Jacobites in 1441 acknowledged that the one and same God was the author of both Testaments "because by the inspiration of the same Holy Spirit the holy men of each Testament spoke," and it listed the books by name.[1] It should be noticed that canonicity is defined in relation to inspiration.

The Council of Trent[2] followed the list of the Council of Florence, and it also named the books, "lest any doubt can arise as to which they are." Not only these books, but "All their parts" are mentioned. The allusion is to portions like the additions to Esther and Daniel. A further specification is added: "as they have been customarily read in the Catholic Church and are found in the old vulgate Latin edition." The thrust of these remarks is to indicate a basis for the decision: The Bible which the Church had been using during previous centuries *did* contain the Word of God, and let no one eliminate any of these books or their parts. It should be noted that these remarks are *not* a canonization of the Latin text, as many often assume. The tenor of the council is the recognition of the fact that the text of the Latin Bible is in need of a critical treatment. In fact, the council legislated toward this end: "that Holy Scripture, especially this old and vulgate edition, be later printed as correctly as possible." It is true that the *Insuper* decree[3] of the Council established the vulgate Latin edition as "authentic" for public readings and theological discussion. But "authentic" did not connote any intrinsic superiority as far as textual criticism is concerned. It merely meant that the longevity of the Latin Bible in the Western Church entitled it to official status as a witness to the Word of God. But it should also be said that this contributed to a hard and fast position that solidified in the post-Tridentine Church: the primacy of the Vulgate. The proper emphasis on the Hebrew text was only applied, in an *official* way, in the encyclical of Pope Pius XII, *Divino afflante Spiritu,* of .1943.

In 1870 Vatican I repeated the Tridentine doctrine on canonicity. However it took into consideration more recent views which it deemed inexact. The biblical books are sacred and canonical. Why? Not because "being written by merely human industry, they were later approved by ecclesiastical authority," or "just because they contain revelation without any error." The basic reason is:

"because, being written under the inspiration of the Holy Spirit, they have God as their author, and as such they were given to the Church."[4]

I have attempted to summarize briefly the essential teaching of the Catholic Church on the canon. Some observations and questions now follow, which hopefully will stimulate the discussion that is the purpose of this symposium.

1. For a Catholic, canonicity is viewed in function of inspiration. Inspiration has to do with God's influence on the composition of the OT; canonicity is the external attestation of the inspiration of a book.

2. To what extent is the problem of the canon merely an historical one? History aims to supply the data relative to the formation of the canon, such as the practice and the theory of the Church Fathers, and of the councils. But on the other hand, ultimately and *pro me,* the adherence to a canon of books, inspired and normative, is a religious commitment, an act of faith. History cannot establish such a motivation.

3. Why did a canon become an historical necessity for both Jews and Christians? I am not asking why collections of writings were made, but why were collections selected out of a wide range of writings as canonical?

Several considerations seem pertinent here: a) The interaction of Judaism and Christianity is a powerful factor in canonization. Thus, Justin's dialogue with Trypho could properly be only on the basis of a given collection (not to mention the text form, a problem to which we shall return). b) As the Synagogue and Church grew, there was an inherent necessity (the necessity of seeking self-understanding) to define the book of the Koranic phrase, "the People of the Book."

4. What is canonical—the book or the text? The answer to this is perhaps not easily given. Recently, D. Barthélemy[5] has argued that the text is inspired, and specifically the text of the LXX, which formed the OT of the early Church up until the middle of the fourth century. Before Pentecost the LXX was the "final actualization of the message of Moses to the nations"—hence it was the "canonical, and therefore, original form of the Old Testa-

ment for the people of Pentecost." This point of view has been urged recently by French scholars in particular, such as P. Benoit, P. Auvray, et al.[6] It implies, of course, the inspiration of the LXX —not merely insofar as being a translation it presumably renders the original faithfully, but in its very composition. Personally, I think canonicity refers to a book, whatever be the form of the text (which can be determined only by textual criticism).

A. Jepsen has also addressed himself to the question of what is canonical, book or text:

The primitive (Christian) community did not yet know the Masoretic text and canon—or at least did not consider itself bound merely to these, as the use of the LXX text and a few extra-Masoretic text readings indicate—what then is today the Old Testament for the Church of the Reformation. A unilateral attachment to the canon and text of the Synagogue seems impossible in view of the situation described in the New Testament. Rather, an answer to our question can be obtained only by clarifying the New Testament judgment on the Writing which came to the primitive community. Because "Old Testament" for an evangelical Church can be nothing else than what the "Writing" was for the primitive community. Writing for the New Testament is the tradition of the Word of God which occurred in Law and Promise—a tradition that was not exactly determined either in its text or in its extent. This "Writing" was heard and acknowledged because and insofar as it directed toward Christ, as Luther formulated this faith. . . . Altes Testament is die Schrift, die auf Christum treibet."[7]

Jepsen's practical conclusion is to support both careful textual analysis and criticism, and also to value variant readings as a "totality of the tradition" which the Church today is free to hear.

As regards this view of Jepsen, which I presume would find supporters here in the United States as well as in Germany, it may be asked: is "was Christian treibet" an adequate principle for determining the extent of the OT? Theologically, is it too vague: what of the book of Esther, for example? Historically, is it merely one factor in many others—such as practical decisions: does the book agree with orthodox doctrine? is it read in the Churches?— which became operative in the historical process of forming the canon (*cf.* the Catecheses of St. Cyril of Jerusalem, c. 4, for example[8])? It is quite true that, relative to the Jewish position on the Law, Prophets, and Writings, Christianity introduced a norm of its own by the fact that it speaks of an *Old* Testament. The norm is Christ, and the apostolic witness to him that is recorded in the New Testament. But can this fact be erected into an adequate principle of canonicity?

5. What is the nature of the Catholic Church's recognition of a book as canonical? It comes down to the practice of the Church, as the Tridentine reference to the "old Latin vulgate edition" indicates. The 1965 Constitution on Revelation from Vatican II puts it this way: "through the same tradition [i.e., a living tradition, which comes from the apostles and develops with the help of the Holy Spirit] the Church's full canon of the sacred works is known, and the sacred writings themselves are more profoundly understood and unceasingly made active in her." At the Council of Trent[9] several of the Conciliar Fathers (e.g., Cardinal Cervino) wanted to go into a theological study of the differences of opinion to be found among many early Fathers of the Church, and thus provide a scholarly basis for decision. This did not occur; the view was taken that the council of Florence had virtually settled the canon. Nevertheless, it should be noted that many of the Conciliar Fathers (e.g., Seripando, the Augustinian General) operated after the fashion of Jerome, distinguishing between what was the Word of God and what was useful "for the edification of the faithful." Many also tried to further a division of biblical books according to their inner meaning (a counterpart to the "was Christum treibet" of Luther?), but this move did not succeed. A particular factor that clouded the whole issue of canonicity was the problem of authenticity, especially for the New Testament writings that were attributed to apostles (e.g., Hebrews).

6. An outstanding Catholic theologian, Karl Rahner, has proposed a view of inspiration that looks more to the ecclesial than to the literary aspect. For him inspiration means the divine will establishing the Scripture as a constitutive element of the primitive Church (*Urkirche*): "the inspiration of Holy Scripture is nothing else than God's founding of the Church, inasmuch as this applies to

precisely that constitutive element of the Apostolic Church which is the Bible."[10] How does the Old Testament fit into this view? "Ultimately God effected the production of the Old Testament books to the extent that they were to have a certain function and authority in the New Testament. The Old Testament is then not merely *de facto* an account of the Church's prehistory and the truths communicated in the course of it; if the completion of the Old Testament could be reached only in the New, then the Old Testament is by its very essence *pre*-history." Rahner rejects as implausible the view that "the tradition concerning the inspiration of a particular book was first handed down only in an individual community," and that it then spread universally. Rather, the revelation of the inspiration of a writing "is given simply enough through the fact that the writing in question is produced as a genuine ingredient of the Apostolic Church's self-realization." Then a history of the process of the canon becomes possible. At a given point in time the Church recognizes by "con-naturality" that a given writing belongs among those that accord with her nature.

Another Catholic theologian, Bernhard Brinkmann, has suggested an important modification to this view.[11] He sees the establishment of the Canon as simply a decision of the Church, a function of her infallible authority. Thus no revelation, which Rahner postulates, is necessary. Thereby one safeguards the *Einmaligkeit* and finality of revelation in Christ (expressed in the terminology of most Catholic theologians as "before the death of the last apostle"), while allowing for the writing of a work like 2 Peter in the second century. For Brinkmann it is also theoretically possible that a lost epistle of an apostle could still be accepted into the canon, although practically the Church regards the canon as closed.

3. ALBERT SUNDBERG, JR.:
"THE PROTESTANT OLD TESTAMENT CANON:
SHOULD IT BE RE-EXAMINED?"

Some years ago I preached a Labor Day Sunday sermon from the handsome text on the laborers in Ecclesiasticus 38. After describing the work of the plowman, the cutter of signets, the smith, the potter, the passage concludes,

> Without them a city cannot be established,
> and men can neither sojourn nor live there. . . .
> . . . they keep stable the fabric of the world,
> and their prayer is in the practice of their trade.

The service was a summer union service with Baptists, Methodists, and Congregationalists participating. It was held in the Baptish church where the pulpit Bible was a fine old book with wooden binding fitted with wrought-iron hinges and an iron clasp for pad-locking the book. It was, of course, a Protestant Bible, but old enough to contain, also, the books Protestants call the Apocrypha. So the text was handy to come by and there was no need to bootleg it. When the service was concluded and the congregation had gone, I discovered that three Baptist deacons remained and wanted to speak with me. After perfunctory comments on the sermon they came to the point. "Where did you get that text?" they asked. I swallowed hard, and heard my mouth say, "Well, from your Bible." And with that my brush with a Baptist inquisition ended.

In ways that I did not then know, this episode sets the problem or, at least, part of the problem of the OT canon in Protestant Christendom, because what those Baptist deacons were asking was not the source of my text but whether it was canonical, taken, as it was, from the Apocrypha.

As everyone knows, the books of the Apocrypha have been on the losing side of discussions about the OT canon among Protestants since Luther.[1] It was during discussion of the second subject, the doctrine of purgatory, in his debates with Johann Maier of Eck at Leipzig in June and July of 1519, that Martin Luther broke with the tradition of the church on the question of the OT canon. Luther's colleague at Wittenberg, Andreas Bodenstein of Karlstadt, had argued against Eck in 1518 that the text of the Bible was to be preferred above the authority of the church. At Leipzig, however, Luther was confronted with the text of Scripture; the Roman church had based its doctrine of purgatory largely upon the proof text, *Sancta est et salubris cogitatio pro defunctis exorare* (2 Macc. 12, 46, Vulgate). Luther could not avoid the reading; neither could he deny that the church had accepted this book. When thus pressed, Luther launched into an argument of desperation. He denied the right of the church to decide matters of canonicity; canonicity, he argued, is to be determined by the internal worth of a book. Moreover, while Jerome recognized that the church used this and the other books of the Apocrypha, Jerome denied canonical status to these books. He held the books of the Jewish canon alone to be canonical. Luther recognized the validity of Eck's argument that Augustine and the tradition of the church accepted these books, but he chose Jerome's position. Whether Luther's argument stemmed from expediency in the exigencies of debate or from settled conviction, one cannot say. But the position taken in the debate became a hardened position with Luther so that it was he who for the first time collected the books of the Apocrypha and set them apart from the rest of the OT in his German translation of the Bible (1534) with the heading, "Apocrypha: these books are not held to be equal to the sacred scriptures, and yet are useful and good for reading."[2] Most of the subsequent Protestant translations of the Bible into the languages of Europe followed Luther's lead and relegated the books of the Apocrypha to a segregated section between the testaments.

Already, in 1626, some copies of the King James Verion appeared that omitted the Apocrypha completely, reflecting the influence of Calvinism. Whereas the Apocrypha was placed in an intermediary position in the Reformed churches, an even stronger position against the Apocrypha was taken in the confessional churches. Repeated efforts were made to remove the Apocrypha from the Bible, as at the Synod of Dort (1618–19), until the Westminster Confession (1648) included the following statement against the Apocrypha: "The books commonly called Apocrypha, not being of divine inspiration are no part of the canon of Scripture; and therefore of no authority to the church of God, nor to be otherwise approved, or made use of, than any other human writings" (1, 3).[3]

Continuing agitation against the Apocrypha in Europe finally led to the announcement by the British and Foreign Bible Society, followed by the American Bible Society, in 1827, that they would "exclude in their printed copies of the English Bible the circulation of these books, or parts of books, which are usually termed Apocryphal."[4] The Anglican Church, however, continued the tradition of Jerome in its practice, as summarized in Article 6 of the Thirty-nine Articles: "In the name of Holy Scripture we do understand those canonical books of the Old and New Testament, of whose authority there was never any doubt in the Church. . . . And the other Books (as Jerome saith) the Church doth read for example of life and instruction in manners; but yet doth it not apply them to establish any doctrine."

Thus, the status of the Apocrypha in Protestantism was a closed issue until the evident use of the so-called intertestamental literaure in the NT forced Protestant scholars to deal with this fact. The result was the well-known Alexandrian or Septuagint canon hypothesis, first proposed by John Ernest Grabe (1666–1711)[5] and against independently by John Salomo Semler in his *Abhandlung von freier Untersuchung des Canons* (Halle, 1771). Actually, as I have pointed out elsewhere, an Alexandrian canon hyopthesis is to be found in Augustine, but Augustine's hyopthesis has not informed the modern theory.[6] When Semler's Alexandrian canon hypothesis came into general acceptance, following the work of A. Kuenen, making it no longer possible to defend the closing of the Jewish canon by Ezra and the Great Synagogue,[7] regard for the Apocrypha among Protestant scholars increased greatly during the latter quarter of the nineteenth and early in the twentieth centuries. An International Society of Apocrypha was formed, leading to the publication of the *International Journal of Apocrypha* from 1905 to 1917 in which articles urging that Protestantism should reconsider the claims of the Apocrypha to canonicity were not infrequent. The effort came to naught. In general, while Protestant scholars accepted the Alexandrian canon hypothesis as the explanation of how the early church came to use a wider selection of Jewish religious books than those of the Hebrew canon, the Alexandrian canon of Hellenistic Judaism has been regarded as an abortive, sectarian canon and, therefore, without

authority. The early church had made a mistake in using the canon
of Hellenistic Judaism. As late as 1962 Robert Pfeiffer could still
argue for a *de facto* Hebrew canon in Palestine in the days of
Jesus and the apostles that was ratified at the Council of Jamnia
(A.D. 90).[8]

The publication of the RSV version of the Apocrypha in 1957
renewed attention to the Apocrypha and its relation to the OT
canon in Protestantism. Two other volumes were published at
least in part as a response to this new version of the Apocrypha.
One was Floyd V. Filson's *Which Books Belong in the Bible?*
(1956), the other, Bruce M. Metzger's *An Introduction to the
Apocrypha* (1957). Filson addressed the fourth chapter of his
book specifically to the question, "Should Scripture Include the
Apocrypha?" Of course, his conclusion was negative. But the basis
for this conclusion is important. Filson correctly could find no
evidence for a Septuagint canon. "The Egyptian Jews had no fully
defined and definitely closed canon,"[9] he says. And Philo "held
that divine inspiration still continued in the first century Judaism
in which he shared at Alexandria."[10] However, "Greek-speaking
Jews were hesitant about explicitly widening the limits of the
canon." On the other hand, Josephus should not be regarded as a
Jew of the diaspora. He grew up in Palestine, wrote his first book
in Aramaic or Hebrew, later translating it into Greek; ". . . in general he no doubt favored the Biblical views of Palestine"[11] rather
than Egypt. Since Josephus mentions a twenty-two book canon,
Filson concludes that Josephus' "canon was close to if not identical with the Hebrew Old Testament of Palestine."[12] But even if
there were two competing Jewish canons of scripture, Filson continues, the question is which of them was used by Jesus and the
NT writers? The answer to this question is that, while Jesus may
have spoken some Greek, and while bilingual Christians speaking
Aramaic and Greek were present in the church from the first, still
Jesus and the first Christians lived in Palestine, the setting was
Palestine, the prevailing language Aramaic, and "the overwhelming
probability is that both Jesus and his first disciples accepted the
Palestinian canon of the Hebrew Old Testament."[13] In his treat-
ment of "The Canon of the New Testament Authors," Filson's

arguments parallel the dogmatic Protestant position of John Cosin in his *A Scholastical History of the Canon of the Holy Scripture* (1657).

While Metzger recognized the broad circulation of the inter-testamental literature in Judaism, he nonetheless holds that in the Jamnia decision on canon the Hebrew canon "had been determined by long approved usage of the books, and the Assembly at Jamnia merely ratified what the most spiritually sensitive souls in Judaism had been accustomed to regard as holy Scripture."[14] This is Pfeiffer's pre-Jamnia *de facto* Hebrew canon. As to the process by which the "Writings" were separated from the Apocrypha and Pseudepigrapha, Metzger says, "If one could have interrogated Jewish communities, at worship in the synagogue and at study in the schools, they would doubtless have declared that in certain books they somehow heard the Word of God speaking to them, while in the other books this was not so. The spiritual sensitivity of generations of Jews was finally ratified by the official action of subsequent councils,"[15] i.e., Jamnia, I suppose. "In the nature of the case," he continues, ". . . there can be no human authority outside of and higher than the canonical books themselves which could confer upon them the essential quality of being the Word of God. In some undefined manner, certain books imposed themselves upon the Jewish community as the inspired oracles of God."[16] Thus, Metzger pleads Luther's position that canon is to be determined by the internal worth of a book.

In his chapter on "A Brief History of the Apocrypha in the Christian Church," Metzger notes that Christianity began within Palestinian Judaism and "received her first scriptures (the books of the Old Testament) from the Jewish Synagogue."[17] However, Gentile converts to Christianity, who could not read Hebrew, began to use the Greek translation of the Old Testament called the Septuagint. Antagonism between the Christians and the Jews led to Jewish abandonment of the Septuagint whereas it remained the Scriptures of the Gentile Christians. This Septuagint differed both in order of the books and in the number of books from that which prevailed in Judaism. Additional books were included, most of these being identical with the traditional Apocrypha. There was no indication in the Septuagint that these books were not included in the Hebrew canon. However, the conclusion that the Jews of Alexandria regarded these books as inspired in the same sense as the Law, the Prophets, and the Writings is fallacious, since the number of Apocryphal books is not identical in all the copies of the Septuagint and since the manuscripts of the Septuagint which contain these disputed books were all copied by Christian scribes and, therefore, are not conclusive indication of a Jewish canon. And since Philo knew the existence of the Apocrypha but never once quoted from them, though according to Metzger he habitually used most of the books of the Hebrew canon, Metzger finds it difficult to believe that the Alexandrian Jews received these books as authoritative, similar to the Law and the Prophets. Metzger goes on to explain that the books of the Apocrypha came to be closely associated with the canonical books when early Christians, who changed from scrolls to codices as the format of their sacred books, were able to include a great number of separate books within the same two covers. Thus, the canonical and the Apocryphal books came into close physical juxtaposition. This gave the impression that all the books within such a codex were to be regarded as authoritative. The small number of church fathers who either knew Hebrew or inquired into the limits of the Jewish canon, however, usually did not attribute canonicity to the Apocryphal books, though regarding them suitable for Christian reading. Either through the influence of Origen, or for some other reason, the Greek fathers made fewer references to the Apocrypha as inspired from the fourth century onward, says Metzger. In the Latin church, however, following the example of Tertullian and Cyprian, Augustine treated the books of the Apocrypha as on the same level with the Hebrew OT books. Synodical councils justified and emphasized their use. But Jerome, "standing in this respect almost alone in the West [sic],"[18] favored the Hebrew canon, declaring the Apocrypha outside the canon.

It is evident, therefore, that both Filson and Metzger regarded the Hebrew canon in Palestine to have been settled prior to the days of Jesus and the apostles. Both treat the inclusion of the Apocrypha in Christian OT Scriptures as resulting from mistaken

Christian understanding about the Jewish circumstances of canon. Both favor the OT canon of Jesus and the apostles as the appropriate canon for Christians.

The foregoing has been a description of what may be called the Protestant position with respect to OT canon. There is reason to ask, however, whether this position is any longer tenable. It now appears that the bases upon which Luther and subsequent Protestants separated the books of the Apocrypha from the Christian OT are historically inaccurate and misleading. Not only was the so-called Palestinian or Hebrew canon not closed in Jesus's day, but a *de facto* Hebrew canon paralleling the later Jamnia canon did not exist either. In the days of Jesus and the apostles, the status of Jewish canon (and this prevailed throughout Judaism) was that of a closed collection of Law, a closed collection of Prophets, and a large undifferentiated number of Jewish religious writings consisting of a later defined collection of "Writings," the books later called Apocrypha and Pseudepigrapha, other books known to us only by name, and perhaps other books unknown and lost. And it was this canonical situation[19] that passed from Judaism into Christianity as the Scriptures of the early church.[20] Soon the Jewish categories of Law and Prophets were forgotten and the whole religious literature received from Judaism was treated as one, the Prophets.

It is immediately evident, therefore, that the use of Jesus and the apostles is not an adequate criterion for the OT canon of the church. It is also to be observed that the argument that Jesus and the authors of the NT do not quote the books of the Apocrypha is anachronistic. There was no collection "Apocrypha" in the days of Jesus or the NT authors that could be consciously approved or eschewed. The books of the Apocrypha are those books of Jewish religious literature that were accepted in the OT canon of the Western Church but that were not included in the Jewish canon. And until the status of the Jewish intertestamental literature was clarified in the church, there was no recognizable differentiation in the church between Writings, Apocrypha, and Pseudepigrapha. Moreover, if Professor Filson means direct quotations when referring to the absence of quotation from the Apocrypha in the NT, then presumably Joshua, Judges, Chronicles, Ezra, Nehemiah, Esther, Ecclesiastes, the Song of Solomon, Obadiah, Zephaniah, and Nahum should also not be counted canonical in the church since, as Metzger observes, they are not quoted in the NT. But Metzger is certainly right in saying that this is a poor means of determining canonical status.

Further, it needs to be said that Luther's rubric that "Scripture is its own attester," is a camouflage statement. This rubric seems to place the criteria of canonicity upon the internal self-witness of a writing to its own worth whereas, in fact, the judgment is made by the person arguing this case. Canonicity is thus made to depend entirely upon subjective judgment. And if canonicity is thus to be determined, then, as H. H. Howorth has said, "everybody must in fact either become an infallible pope to himself or else accept Luther as an infallible pope."[21]

In a recent monograph on *The Old Testament of the Early Church*, I have attempted to re-examine the history of the formulation of the OT canon in early Christianity. I assume that my inclusion on this panel on the problem of the OT canon was in part to discuss the implications of that study for the question of OT canon for Christians, including Protestant Christians. In the monograph, it was pointed out that Christianity arose within Judaism and became separated from Judaism during the period from about A.D. 30 to 70. The ancient church, thus, received as its scriptural heritage from Judaism the Jewish canonical practice that obtained in first century Judaism prior to A.D. 70. This was, as I have indicated, a closed collection of Law, a closed collection of Prophets, and an undefined body of writings including those books later identified as "Writings" in the third part of the Jewish canon, the books we now call Apocrypha, the books we now call Pseudepigrapha, and perhaps other books as well. Now it is to be observed that the historical and spiritual heritage of Christianity is thus pre-70 Judaism and not post-Jamnia Judaism with a defined, closed, Pharisaic canon. Since this is the case, I see no reason why Christians, including Protestant Christians, should not own the subsequent struggle of the church to define an OT canon of its own as the legitimate, historical, and spiritual heritage of Christendom. This is in no sense to slight the validity of the so-called Jamnia canon for Judaism; it is only to observe that Judaism and Christianity came to a historical parting of the ways prior to the post-70 activity leading to the closing of the canon about the end of the first Christian century. It is to be noted that those Christians who have argued in favor of the Jewish canon as the appropriate OT for the church, beginning with Jerome, have been misinformed, and have assumed that the Jamnia canon was the canon of Jesus and the apostles and the writers of the NT. Ought one not be able to appeal to Jerome, Luther, and Calvin "better informed," to use the British phrase? That is to say, what validity do the arguments of Jerome, *et al.*, have when they were formed on a misconception? Likewise, the historical and spiritual heritage of Protestant Christianity is the Christianity of the Western Church. What legitimate reason remains for Protestant Christianity, then, to continue to refuse to accept the canonical tradition and decisions of the Western Church? No viable history of canon, whether of Apocrypha or OT or NT, can be written on the doctrine that Scripture is its own attester. The process of canonization is a community process. This is equally true in Judaism and in Christianity. The canonical decisions at Jamnia were community decisions. Likewise, in Christianity it is the church that has selected the canon from among available writings. So far as I know, there is no argument for Christian canon of the OT that is not made ultimately on Christian usage. This was the basis of Jerome's case for the Hebrew canon just as it was the basis of the case of Tertullian or Augustine for the wider inclusion of the church. But now, as has been shown, Jerome's case falls hopelessly to the ground since it was based on the misconception that the Jewish canon was the canon of Jesus and the apostles. Any continuing appeal through the reformers to Jerome and the Hebrew canon comes to this same end. Two different communities were involved in defining canons out of the common material of pre-70 Judaism. And since the church did define her OT canon for herself, what historical claim does the Jewish definition of canon about the end of the first century have for the church? Only that it was the assumed *a priori* claim of the Jewish canon, when it became known in the church following Origen, that pressured the church into defining its OT. But that assumed *a priori* claim of the Jewish canon did not succeed in restricting the OT of the church to the Jewish canon. This is true of the Eastern as well as the Western Church. If Protestant Christianity is to continue its custom of restricting its OT canon to the Jewish canon, then an entirely new rationale and doctrine of canon will have to be described. And any Protestant doctrine of canonization that takes seriously the question of Christian usage and historical and spiritual heritage will lead ultimately to the Christian OT as defined in the Western Church at the end of the fourth and the beginning of the fifth centuries.

Likewise, if it is not possible to argue the validity of the Jewish canon for the Christian OT, since it was not the defined Scriptures of Jesus and the apostles and of the early church, neither is it correct to apply the Jamnia doctrine of inspiration to the Christian doctrine of the canon. So far as I am aware, the Jamnia doctrine of inspiration was first applied to the Christian doctrine of canon by the Calvinists in their proscription of the Apocrypha from the Bible.[22] As you all know, the Jamnia doctrine of inspiration limited inspiration from the time of Moses to the time of Ezra-Nehemiah, that is to say, that the books of the Jewish canon alone were to be regarded as inspired writings. Historically, this doctrine of inspiration first appears in Josephus, *Against Apion,* 1, 8, and appears to be reflected in 4 Esdras. However, not even Jerome in his vigorous championing of the Hebrew canon following his taking up residence in Palestine, attempted to argue against the books of the Apocrypha on the basis that they were not inspired. It is clear that in the proclamation of the gospel and other activities of the early beginnings of the church, the Christians felt themselves possessed by the same spirit that had inspired the prophets. And this sense of inspiration in word and deed carried over into Christian writings. Hence, there was no sharp cleavage between the acknowledged inspiration of the religious literature received from Judaism and the inspiration the early Christians themselves experienced. Moreover, the Christian writings that were themselves to be selected by the church as the NT canon taught the doctrine of the continued inspiration of the Holy Spirit in the Christian community and in individual Christians. Hence, so far as I am aware, the only attempt to define the limits of inspiration in early Christianity are to be found in attacks upon the heretics. Inspiration is denied to the writings of the heretics. But even for the books of the Pseudepigrapha, the Jewish religious literature that was not included either in the Jewish canon or in the Christian OT, the rationalization for the exclusion of these writings from the Christian OT does not attack them on the question of inspiration but rather because it is not possible to attest their authenticity. The doctrine of canon in the church, therefore, was that the canonical writings were the standard of doctrine and inspiration. Thus, the Calvinistic doctrine that the books of the Apocrypha were not inspired was an innovation resulting from the application of the Jewish doctrine of canon to Christian practice, an innovation that has divorced what has been the predominant Protestant doctrine of Scripture from previous doctrine of Scripture in the church. And again the question must be asked, what claim does a doctrine of canon arising in Judaism following A.D. 70 have upon the doctrine of canon in the church? Historically, it is that this Jewish doctrine came to be infused into Christian discussion by the early Calvinists as a further blow against what was then regarded as the Roman Catholic OT canon.

Thus, it is evident that both in content and doctrine, Protestantism, in its view of OT canon, has broken away from its historical heritage. The basis for this rupture has mistakenly been thought to be that the earliest Christian OT usage, that of Jesus, the apostles, and the NT writers, paralleled the Jewish canon. Since that basis no longer obtains, it remains for Protestant Christians either to return to the historical heritage from which Protestantism sprang or to develop a new apologetic for its OT canon.

NOTES

The Old Testament Canon in the Catholic Church.

1. These quotations are taken from the conciliar statements reproduced in *EB* (Rome, 1961), 47.

2. *EB* 57–60.

3. *EB* 61; *cf.* the encyclical *Divino afflante Spiritu* 549.

4. *EB* 77.

5. "L'Ancien Testament a mûri à Alexandrie," *Theologische Zeitschrift* 21 (1965), 358–370.

6. See the summary in P. Grelot, *La Bible Parole de Dieu* (Paris, 1965), 166–178.

7. "Kanon und Text des Alten Testaments," *Theologische Literaturzeitung* 74 1949), 65–74, esp. 73. The position of F. Hesse ("Das Alte Testament als Kanon," *Neue Zeitschrift für Systematische Theologie* 3 [1961], 315–327) can be described as one of calm despair; the extent of the canon cannot be determined, and one cannot say that the word of God is found only in canonical writing to the exclusion of the extra-canonical. It seems almost presumptuous on the part of the Church to define the canon! There is a perceptive essay by E. Flesseman-van Leer, "Principien der Sammlung und Ausscheidung bei der Bildung des Kanons," *Zeitschrift für Theologie und Kirche* 61 (1964), 404–420, which points out, among other things, the association of inspiration with canonicity in the early Church, especially in the East.

8. See the remarks of B. Vawter, *The Bible in the Church* (New York, 1959), 48–73.

9. A. Maichle, *Der Kanon der biblischen Bücher und das Konzil von Trient* (Freiburg i.B., 1929), 19–22, 76.

10. For this and the following quotations *cf.* Rahner, "Inspiration in the Bible," *Inquiries* (New York, 1964), 53, 56, 64.

11. "Inspiration und Kanonizität der Heiligen Schrift in ihrem Verhältnis zur Kirche," *Scholastik* 33 (1958), 208–233.

The Protestant Old Testament Canon: Should It Be Re-examined?

1. See H. H. Howorth's series of twelve articles entitled "The Bible Canon of the Reformation," *The International Journal of Apocrypha* 14 (1908) to 51 (1917). *Id.,* "The Origins of the Authority of the Bible Canon According to the Continental Reformers," *JTS* 8 (1907); 9 (1908); 10 (1909).

2. *Biblia, das ist: die ganze heilige Schrift altes und neues Testaments, übersetzung M. Luthers* (Germantown, 1763).

3. B. B. Warfield, *The Westminster Assembly and its Work* (1931), 172.

4. B. M. Metzger, *An Introduction to the Apocrypha* (1957), 201 f.

5. W. R. Churton, *The Uncanonical and Apocryphal Scriptures* (1884), 12.

6. A. C. Sundberg, Jr., *The Old Testament of the Early Church* (Harvard Theological Studies 20, 1964), 176 f.

7. "Über die Männer der grossen Synagogue," tr. K. Budde, *Gesammelte Abhandlungen zur biblischen Wissenschaft von Dr. Abraham Kuenen* (1894), 125–60.

8. "Canon of the Old Testament," *Interpreter's Dictionary of the Bible* (1962), I, 510–14. I have given the publication date. However, Robert Pfeiffer died on March 16, 1958, and wrote the article cited during 1957–1958.

9. P. 81.

10. *Ibid.*

11. P. 82.

12. *Ibid.*

13. P. 84.

14. P. 8.

15. P. 9.

16. P. 9 f.

17. P. 175.

18. P. 179. However, Jerome did not espouse this position until after he had moved to Palestine and come under the influence of Jewish teachers. *Cf.* Sundberg, *op. cit.*, 148–53.

19. I mean by this the practice of Judaism with respect to the question of canon, not that the Writings, Apocrypha, and Pseudepigrapha were canonical.

20. *Cf.* Sundberg, *op. cit.*, 81–103.

21. *Loc. cit.* 24 (1911), 5.

22. See the statement on the Westminster Confession, 1647: "The books commonly called Apocrypha," not being of divine inspiration, are no part of the Canon of Scripture" (1, 3).